Endorsements for *Ladies, Can We Talk?*

As a Women's Wealth Advisor, I share Debbie's passion for encouraging women to gain more knowledge and confidence so that we all can make better financial and political decisions. I found that, Ladies, Can We Talk, *embraces the traditions of debate and individualism. I was intrigued with her invitation to American women voters to "consider" a conservative view on major issues facing our country today and her encouraging them to embrace the conservative paradigm that supports our American free en-terprise system. Perhaps this book will help us all dodge some of the most unpleasant lessons on the horizon by encouraging critical thought and in-telligent discussion of the issues.*

> —**Pamela P., Financial Advisor, Newport Beach, CA**

Like many successful women, I am comfortable expressing my opinion pro-fessionally and personally, but political discourse has become 'taboo' un-less I am sure everyone in the conversation is 'on the same side'. Ladies, Can We Talk? *will remind you that respectful, thoughtful conversation around political topics is not only possible and safe, but necessary. In her fact-based approach to policies, Debora Georgatos has empowered all her readers to think for themselves and discern the truth on a multitude of is-sues facing voters today.*

> —**Elena H., Sr. Engineering Manager, San Diego, CA**

"Having worked with very strong willed women for years (in law enforce-ment), I found it amazing that our political views remained unspoken. This resonates even more so with our younger generation of women. I never would have thought that a book could connect with every genera-tion of American women, but this one does. I am giving this book to my

daughter and her friends as high school graduation gifts, because you are never too young to learn that your ideas about America matter, and it is ok to share them. "

—Valerie D., Retired United States Probation Officer, Federal Sentencing Guidelines Specialist, Tampa, Florida

"Ladies, Can We Talk? sends an empowering message to women about the important role we play in shaping America's future. It's informative about issues that drive the women's vote, and encourages women to value and to express our views. No matter whether or how you've voted in the past, this book will inspire you to realize how much America needs women to do our part in all elections in the future."

—Lisa R., Entrepreneur, Internationally Acclaimed Interior Designer, Dallas, Texas

Ladies, Can We Talk?

To Barbie —

Speak up

for America!

Debbie G

Ladies, Can We Talk?

America Needs Our Vote!

Debora Georgatos

CWT Publications, LLC
Dallas, Texas

Ladies, Can We Talk?
America Needs Our Vote!

First printing 2012

ISBN: 978-0-9859012-2-6

LCCN: 2012949879

ATTENTION CORPORATIONS, UNIVERSITIES, COLLEGES, AND PROFESSIONAL ORGANIZATIONS: Quantity discounts are available on bulk purchases of this book for educational and gift purposes, or as premiums for increasing magazine subscriptions or renewals. Special books or book excerpts can also be created to fit specific needs. For information, please contact the author at CWT Publications, LLC at www.ladiescanwetalk.org.

Table of Contents

Dedication

This book is one woman's effort to speak out in a momentous time in American history, when so much is at stake. It is dedicated to the women of America, whose natural instincts to nurture and fiercely protect what they love are needed today, to save America. Our dedication to stand with America's values of freedom and equality of opportunity is needed now, and in future generations for centuries to come.

Acknowledgments

I deeply appreciate the help of many people who made this book possible. I wish to thank my "cover models," "video volunteers," and dear friends Cindy, Erin, Betty, Jeni, Lael, Linda, D'Rinda, and Lisa. Your friendship and encouragement are precious to me and invaluable. Both Cecile and Elizabeth provided tremendous logistical and social media expertise and support, as well as great ideas. Thanks so much.

I also sincerely thank the team at CAT Studios in Dallas whose work on the audio and video components of this book's marketing was first rate. From website to videos, their work was stellar, and I thank Trent, BJ, Tess, Michael, Carlos, Meghan, Kristian, David, Benjamin, and Jennifer. The quality editing/publishing support team of Sue, Juanita, and Kate was also excellent, and their expertise sincerely appreciated. This first-rate team was completed with the addition of the publicist and public relations expertise of Virginia and David, whose professionalism and enthusiasm for the book is greatly appreciated.

Most importantly, I thank my husband Eric whose patience, love, encouragement, and steady support took form in a thousand different ways: reading, editing, and commenting on drafts, inspiring me to keep on writing when the task seemed overwhelming, and covering a myriad of responsibilities on the home front while still keeping his entrepreneurial venture running strong.

Preface

I wrote this book to inspire American women to realize their power to profoundly shape America's future through the voting booth. I hope to motivate women to embrace the idea that their wisdom, passion, intellect, and voice are desperately needed today in the American political conversation. I want us to talk to each other more!

After working in and around the political arena, including in campaigns as a volunteer and later as a paid consultant, and countless hours with women's political organizations, I've learned quite a bit about the interaction of politics and women.

Candidates target women with political messaging that is designed to subtly persuade us to abandon our reason and logic and be swept away instead by emotion. The result is that we sometimes vote to support ideas that don't work well and bring about results we never intended.

On top of that, I feel a growing sense of urgency about America that I believe is shared by millions of Americans today:

1. America is at a serious economic and political crossroads, headed in a direction most Americans say is wrong.
2. Politicians are in overdrive in their efforts to emotionally manipulate Americans into voting their way.
3. America is off track and citizens are floundering trying to retain our hold on what it means to be American, and what America's place in the world is supposed to be.
4. Too many women (and American men, too) are convinced that the basic American ideals or views we genuinely hold, the things we actually know in our hearts are true, are not politically correct, so we don't speak up when we should.

You might be wondering why you should read a book by someone you've never heard of. I am not a talking head on any cable TV or talk radio show. I don't work for a political party. I am not a candidate for political office. That said, however, millions of women do know me, because I am a lot like many of you:

★ I'm no heiress or child of privilege; my parents live off Social Security and pension benefits in a retirement home.

★ I am a product of K–12 public schools.

★ I worked hard in school, and earned and borrowed my way through college and law school. My total debt was huge when I finished, but I eventually repaid it.

★ I came of age as the term "feminism" took hold in America; I have supported so-called progressive views on most political issues, from large social spending, to "women's rights," and many other issues.

★ I have voted on both sides of the aisle.

★ I've experienced 60- to 70-hour workweeks in a high-stress professional environment—working as a labor litigator in a major law firm. I know what it means to be a career woman.

★ I've experienced life at home as a full-time mom of three young children so I know what it means to be a stay-at-home mom.

★ Those three young children are now in their twenties. I know quite a bit about their worlds; and my husband and I keep in close touch with them through phone calls and social media and care deeply about their futures.

★ I was raised by parents who taught me by words and example the importance of respect for all people, regardless of background. Consequently, I have throughout my life had close friends of many different backgrounds.

★ I grew up in upstate New York, went to school in New York and Washington, D.C., lived for many years in Southern California, a few years in Maryland, and now reside in the South, in the heart of Texas. I understand the discomfort the perceived Bible-belt mentality engenders in some Californians and New Yorkers, and the puzzlement of some Southerners at the seemingly ultra-secular coasts.

★ I have dear women friends who are single moms, who have had abortions, who have been participants in heart-breaking divorces, and who are happily married to their soul mates. I don't see women's lives through rose-colored glasses; I see and understand the good, the bad, and the ugly.

But here is what I also see, understand, and feel: something is wrong in America. The direction of the country hasn't felt right to me for many years, and recently, the feeling has grown deeply and rapidly worse. And while I'm not a big believer in polls (as you'll see later in this book), the mere suggestion that *women in America* could vote in support of the collectivist style, powerful centralized government policies that some in Washington are supporting, is simply unfathomable to me.

We women desire to live our personal and professional lives, relate to our spouses or significant others, and raise our children with an unmistakable bias in favor of basic American ideals and values that we all can list:

★ Hard work and reward for hard work.

★ Freedom to pursue our dreams with the expectation that we can earn and keep, for the most part, the fruit of our work.

★ Taking responsibility for our own lives.

★ Respect for the idea that we have, as the Declaration of Independence says, rights to life and liberty and the pursuit of happiness that come from our Creator and that government is supposed to protect.

★ The outright rejection of controlling, big government interference in any aspect of our lives.

Most women I know would not voluntarily embrace a controlling, domineering father, boyfriend, or spouse. We love our independence and whether we are career women or stay-at-home moms we have an abiding sense of self-respect and self-reliance. But many of us have sat silently as government becomes more aggressive, intrusive, powerful, controlling, and condescending.

I wrote this book because I think it's time for the women of America to vote in record numbers to push back against a government that is doing to our country what we would never let anyone do to our family and loved ones. Armed with the information and, I hope, thought-provoking arguments and discussions in this book, the women of America will do just that.

Debora Georgatos
Dallas, Texas, 2012

Introduction

Alexis De Tocqueville once said of the United States:

"And if anyone asks me what I think the chief cause of the extraordinary prosperity and growing power of this nation, I should answer that it is due to the superiority of their women."

—Alexis De Tocqueville, French Historian and Political Scientist, author of *Democracy in America* (1805–1859)

Women Have the Power to Lead and Change America

Women vote in higher percentages than men, especially in presidential elections. We make up over half of the U.S. adult population. We literally have the ballot box power to shape America's future for generations to come.

Women are increasingly powerful in America in other ways, too. We now constitute the majority of graduates in many high schools, colleges, and even many law schools, and other graduate schools. Women are emerging as leaders in many segments of American society, more than ever before in our nation's history.

Politicians know this. That is why politicians and political parties tailor messages designed to win the "women's vote."

The Convergence of the Rise of Women's Power with the Profound Turning Point America Faces

Serious Policy Differences Between Political Parties

This growth in women's stature in our country converges with a time when America faces unique and serious challenges in many arenas of our national political and policy life—healthcare, our economic system, unemployment, national debt, energy and environmental issues, growth in size and power of the federal government and public and private unions, growing reliance on financially strained entitlement programs, and racial and economic-class tensions. These are just a few of the public policy arenas where there is a wide gulf between not just the positions but also the *ideals* for which the two major political parties in America stand.

The Deeper Differences
Transformation to Collectivism, or Maintaining Historic American-ness

America's turning point, our fork in the road, is a decision American voters are called upon to make between two very different paths for America's future:

1. One course is to consent to the proposed transformation to collectivism, larger government and a tightly regulated, government-controlled economy and society.

2. The other course is to strive to retain our historic "American-ness" that is based on the freedoms, free enterprise system, and liberties that America embraced from the time of its founding.

"Getting It" on the Uniqueness of America

But the distinctions between the two major schools of political thought in America are deeper than just the economic models of free enterprise versus collectivism. A deeper difference between the parties is whether their leaders comprehend the uniqueness of the United States in all of world history, embrace the idea of its exceptionalism, and recognize the unparalleled importance of retaining the basic values I'll call "American-ness," which are what made America great.

Politicians, activists, and pundits on both sides of the political aisle see this time in American history as a "time of deciding." This fork in the road is a society-altering, future-changing decision. And our children and grandchildren and their children and grandchildren will feel the results of our choice. I love knowing that women are empowered to shape these decisions.

Although this book is filled with examples and details about how these two very different political viewpoints in America play out in terms of policy choices, I want to take a moment to tell you why I think that women, as nurturers, caregivers, and compassionate protectors of our future, must, and I believe will, stand up for these American-based values.

Don't We All Want An America of the Future Where

1. We support individual freedom and the right to achieve. Every generation realistically expects to grow in the prosperity and opportunity that come from the freedom of each individual to choose her path, to work hard, dream, achieve, and then enjoy the fruits of her labor. We reject coerced collectivism, or the equal sharing by all regardless of the effort or contribution made by each.

2. We unite around values. Americans recognize that what unites all of us, and the only thing that *can* truly unite us and bring stability long term, are ideas or values. Those ideas are the basis for our common American culture –timeless values, such as that all men, and women are created equally and endowed by the Creator with unalienable rights. We embrace the other similar and important values in our nation's founding documents.

3. We are judged and judge based on character, not color. Americans live up to Martin Luther King, Jr.'s dream of every American being judged by the content of his character, and not the color of his skin, so we stop dividing ourselves around skin color or where our ancestors came from. Hyphenated America is divided America.

4. We celebrate success. We view those who have experienced success and achievement honestly in building businesses as role models to be emulated, not villains to be demonized. Or, as President Abraham Lincoln said, "That some should be rich, shows that others may become rich, and, hence, is just encouragement to industry and enterprise."

5. We acknowledge American generosity. We continue our unparalleled generosity as a people and our charitable kindness to our American and international brothers and sisters. And we recognize that the best help is a hand up, not a handout.

6. We cultivate independence. We fashion our policies around basic American ideals such as the value and worth of each individual and his capacity and right to independence. We reject the establishment and fostering of a long-term or permanent dependency class of people whose reliance on government deprives them of the satisfaction and sense of self-worth that can only come from self-reliance. We value the potential contribution of each American to our culture and our economy, and affirm the value and merit of encouraging everyone (except those truly unable) to find and pursue a path toward self-sufficiency.

7. We teach children the truth that America was founded on the recognition of rights for everyone from God. We proudly claim and teach children in our schools America's unique place in world history based on the simple yet profound ideas that man has rights from our Creator that include life, liberty and the pursuit of happiness, and that government exists not to define or limit those rights, but to protect them.

8. We honor the greatness of American values. We respect the independence, culture, history, people and choices of other nations, but don't think that requires minimizing or belittling the greatness of the values upon which America was founded. The basic American values of freedom of speech, etc., are values any nation could adopt, and they are also the reason that America continues to be the one country on earth where most people struggling under repression want to come.

A Few Themes You'll Find Repeated

Truth Exists and Facts Matter

We often hear one politician speaking on some subject and throwing out slogans and statistics, and then another on the other side speaking on the same subject and offering totally different statistics. Political manipulation of voters, and endless maneuvering around facts, figures, and truth is both disheartening and common.

Truth is a frequent victim of political battles.

One theme of this book is to affirm that many facts can be looked up. I have included statistics with footnoted references throughout this book so when you hear one politician saying, for example, "The rich don't pay their fair share," and then another saying, "The rich pay almost all the taxes the government collects," you can look up facts and data that give you the straight information. There is data about the national debt; there is truth about whether we spend more on defense or on social programs; and all sorts of other important information. There is even information about the now-famous 99 percent versus 1 percent.

Throughout this book I'll talk facts and figures, big philosophy and individual policy, and refer you to places you can read more about the issues.

I love and agree wholeheartedly with President Lincoln's quote about truth and facts.

> *"I am a firm believer in the people. If given the truth, they can be depended upon to meet any national crisis. The great point is to bring them the real facts."*
> —Abraham Lincoln, Republican 16th President of the United States

Facts and Policy Outcomes Matter.
Good intentions are not good enough

Good intentions for any policy ideas or new proposals are nice but ultimately irrelevant. It matters if the policies make sense and if they prove to be workable and efficacious. We can measure results.

Policies and ideas matter, more than politicians

Political ideas and policies are more important than individual politicians. This book is about ideas and policies, facts and policy outcomes.

This book advocates for policies that work not just to meet an immediate problem, but that also serve the broader goals of empowering women to be independent, and bettering American society. Just as we wouldn't keep using some medication or cleaning product that never worked, we should not keep supporting policies that never bring about the "advertised" results.

Did you ever stop to think about the fact that most Americans want the same things, for the most part?

We all want good schools; safe neighborhoods; personal freedoms to speak and assemble as we choose; personal respect from others; protection from our enemies abroad; freedom to pursue our dreams and to try to make life better for ourselves, our children, and grandchildren; to be treated fairly by society and fairly rewarded for our labors; and to have an equal opportunity for success.

Did you ever stop to think that there is no reason for people of different racial or ethnic backgrounds, or men versus women, to see political issues differently *because* of their gender, race, or ethnicity?

People can differ on issues of all kinds, but if bad economic policies destroy jobs, then women and men of every background are harmed equally. If poor education policy results in graduates who cannot find jobs or contribute to our workforce, then men and women of all backgrounds suffer. The same is true for healthcare policies, environmental issues, entitlement program funding, the national debt and deficit issues, and many other policy decisions America faces.

Not All Ideas or Systems Are Morally Equivalent; There Are NOT Two Equal Sides to Every Story

A close friend from law school commented occasionally, "There really are not two sides to every story. There was the Holocaust. What was the other side?" Sometimes the politically correct pressure to see the "other guy's side," which is noble in many cases, has no place because some things are just wrong, and need to be rejected.

Being able to discern with clarity and speak with confidence about the fact that some values and systems are actually better than others is vital to getting America back on track. As one example, socialism always breeds mediocrity and stagnation, and usually also misery, and free markets inspire invention, economic growth and prosperity for all economic classes. The two systems are not morally equivalent.

Politicians Try to Manipulate Women Voters

We all know and recognize "playing with someone's emotions" as demeaning, demoralizing, and objectionable. While politicians are subtle about it, some, especially those advocating the growing power of collectivist big government, use tactics that are nothing less than manipulative.

Remember the Georgetown law student who testified in Congress that she needed the federal government to force her religious-institution-based insurer to cover birth control that was inconsistent with that religion's belief system?

Regardless of how you view the question in that case, turning a policy issue of whether insurers should be required by the federal government to provide women free birth control, into a supposed "war on women" is an attempt to manipulate women into feeling like victims, and is a prime example of emotional political manipulation.

Other examples abound, and some are mentioned later in this book.

The Default Modes

I will talk quite a bit about the default mode for each of the two political parties in America. What I mean by that is, when faced with any issue the parties fundamentally revert to their respective default modes, which is the way they approach issues. The Republican default mode is very different from the Democrat default mode in America today.

Because I am writing about ideas and policies, I wish I did not have to refer to political parties. So much baggage goes with each label, depending on where you grew up; how your parents, friends, and other relatives voted in the past; and increasingly on where you go for news and commentary. While it's impossible to discuss politics in America without mentioning the parties by name, I will to the extent possible use more descriptive terms about ideas. References to parties are references to parties' ideas and goals as evidenced by party platforms, and leaders' statements and actions. And when Parties drift from the positions they say they stand for, and that made you vote for them, they are not entitled to eternal voter loyalty. There is no law that prevents new political parties from forming if those we support now do not stick with the values they claim to hold.

You Can't Write About Everything

Time constraints and the desire to keep this book a reasonable length prevented me from writing on every important political issue in America. I did not include chapters on immigration, the Second Amendment, social issues, regulation of the Internet and other free speech issues, proper care for our veterans and honoring our military, education policy, the threats of radical Islamic jihadists abroad and at home, or other foreign policy matters, despite the fact that these and other subjects are also important issues in our national political conversation.

Even for those swayed strongly by one or more of these issues I did not write about, I urge you to consider your own default mode: *are you all about increased government control over society, or all about freedom and personal responsibility?*

I won't hold back on sharing with you in this book how strongly and in fact urgently I feel about how the Democrat Party has drifted away from the America we all love. But I will remind you that I used to vote Democrat, and I know that lots of wonderful American women have voted Democrat historically. I want to convince you that the Democrats of today are out of touch with what made America great, and I think it is our job as voters to bring America home again.

America Needs You!

America Needs Newly Energized, Forward-Thinking Women to Help Build and Mold Our Country's Future—to Make It the Best It Can Be for All Americans

Throughout this book you will find examples of American women who dreamed, led, and achieved. I included these women's stories because I want to encourage women to help steer this American ship back on course using their power—our power—at the ballot box.

I am focused on the future, on where America will be next year, in ten years, and beyond. Although I will raise some serious concerns about the state of our nation, I will also tell you that *every challenge we face is completely solvable*. Americans just need to get back in charge of America.

Read, Then Let's Talk...We Are Allowed to Talk to Each Other—Never Give Up on That!

"Political correctness" has overtaken popular thought and the American political conversation to the extent that many people are not comfortable saying what they think. That is not only unfair to American citizens but it also stifles our capacity to solve problems. If we cannot even say out loud what the problem is or what the facts are, we have no chance of solving the challenges we face.

I embrace the idea of the equality of women with men in American society, and respect women leaders throughout American history. American women need to be leaders today and in the decades to come, in the voting booth and the political process, advocating, supporting, and voting for ideas that work. I wrote this book to speak woman to woman about some of the fundamental issues facing America, and to open a conversation about what policies have worked in America, and about those that have not. I also encourage you to recognize the two divergent paths that today's American political leaders are offering, and to consider the idea that the world needs America to retain its uniqueness among nations as a world standard bearer for free markets and free people.

This book is an invitation to American women in the twenty-first century to take a fresh look at how we vote. I invite you, whether you vote Democrat, Republican, a mixture, or not at all, to read this book. Then I encourage you to talk to your friends, coworkers, and families about what makes America great, and about what we want the America of the future to be.

★ ★ Chapter One ★ ★

Let's Talk First About Talking

I've thought quite a bit over the last several years about the importance of talking. Not just aimless chitchat about the weather, the latest movies or sports, but about the things that are important in our lives, the things that are going on in the world. I can engage in meaningless social banter as well as most people, but I have noticed that it has become harder and harder to get below the surface and talk about what matters. And willingness to chatter is not at all the same thing as being comfortable speaking up when we know we should.

Should I Say Something...?

Women Talk More Than Men? Who Knew?

Women are rumored to have a much higher "word count spoken" per day than men. Research from 2006 showed that women outnumber men in average words per day—supposedly 20,000 versus 13,000—but it has been called into serious question. Regardless of research, I'll stand by the observation that most women are pretty experienced talkers. We just need to start speaking up for America!

You've probably all been in the situation where someone in a group is blathering away on some subject in a very *everyone-knows-this-and-no-one-thinks-any-differently* way, but in fact you don't agree with the "soap boxer." And then finally someone speaks up and disagrees, and most of the group joins in that disagreement. You then realize that most of the group had the same reaction as you did to the one who had been speaking so confidently.

A close friend from law school was telling me about a conversation among some parents at her kids' school. One dad in particular was driving home the importance of parental strictness, offering examples of the many behaviors he "would not tolerate for one minute from my kids" and sharing the strict punishments his kids knew would flow from misbehavior. Other parents chimed in to out-do the first dad with their even stricter parental standards.

My friend is a thoughtful mom who has wonderful kids and she found herself debating whether to chime in to offer a comment or two about the importance of talking with your children, understanding what was going on in their lives and thoughts, and addressing some less-than-perfect behaviors more thoughtfully and with less anger. But she wondered what these other parents would think of her and chose to keep quiet (which is rare for her!).

This is a tiny example of the "pressure of the crowd" that can cause smart women to keep quiet, when we actually have a good point to add to the conversation. And in a political discussion, that pressure is greatly magnified. But, ladies, we can learn to speak up, and we should!

Speaking Up On the Big Stuff...

It's one thing to choose to keep quiet in a personal context such as my friend's conversation about parenting, but it's important to look at why we are often timid about speaking up, especially on important subjects. We should also consider the impact our silence has on our families and friends, and yes, even our country, when we don't speak up.

America Was Founded On Talking

America was founded on talking—on the willingness of some early patriots to start to question, to talk to each other, about whether colonists here, who were British, should challenge Mother England about unfair taxes. As we look back today at the Revolutionary War times, we might assume that every colonist got on board with the revolution once the idea was floated, but that is not true. Those who first gave voice to the idea of declaring independence from England were widely viewed as traitors, and they were! They were advocating that English colonists break away from England.

So discussions happened in homes and taverns and public squares and private meeting halls, all over the colonies. Family members disagreed with one another. But the rightness of the idea that people should stand up to tyranny took hold. For years historians taught that colonists were divided roughly into even thirds among Loyalists (or Tories), Patriots, and "Neutrals," and that was based on a misunderstanding about a letter John Adams wrote. It is now viewed as more likely that only about 20 percent of the colonists were Loyalists, and 45 percent were with the Patriots who supported revolution. Whatever the precise numbers, not everyone agreed.

It was the same thing when America rose up to end the evil of slavery in our country. People had to be willing to speak up, to tell their friends, neighbors, and families that slavery was wrong and worth fighting a Civil War to end it. No one speaking up in the pre–Revolutionary War or pre–Civil War time knew what the country would do, how their friends would react, and of course did not know how the wars would come out. But they knew they had to speak up!

Talking about important issues is patriotic. And if we won't talk about them, we are letting others, including the sometimes verbose and overly confident opinion-flingers, shape the American political conversation.

Why Is It That We Sometimes Do Not Speak Up When We Want To?

One big answer is political correctness, meaning the fear that our views do not fit into the template or mold set by others of what is an acceptable opinion in America today. Other reasons to be silent on big issues include fear of being labeled ignorant, intolerant, hateful, or racist; fear of being mocked or ridiculed; fear that we may not be able to back up our views with facts, figures and data; and fear that friends or even family members might take offense.

I wrote this book because I believe American political thought benefits from the input of everyone who cares enough to participate in the American family conversation. I want to support American women in particular and encourage you to know that your views on the important issues of the day matter. If you have a gut level "that-doesn't-seem-right" reaction, probably others do, too, and raising your point of view in conversation just might empower other women to speak up as well.

Talking With Those Who Cross Your Path

I'll share one example of daily life conversation. When we moved to Dallas in 2000, I volunteered to work in the lunchroom at our kids' school that first fall, in part to make some friends in our new city. The very first day I worked that lunchroom cash register, another mom (a strong Democrat) assigned to work with me asked, within 20 minutes of the start of our conversation, "Well, you are pro-choice, aren't you?" in the same tone as though she were asking if I were in favor of keeping poison out of drinking water. To her, no other option was rational. My real answer was that in my younger and professional attorney days, I would have called myself pro-choice. But as time passed and my husband and I had three beautiful children, I had warmed to the pro-life view. I am now pro-life, but then unsure of how to talk about those ideas. That explanation didn't feel like an option at that moment, however, so my answer was, "Oh, yes, sure."

Ladies, that is one of the dangers of not speaking up: strong-willed "opinion flingers" never even know that others do not agree. And listeners to "opinion flingers" assume from the silence of others that they are the only ones who disagree, so maybe they are wrong.

Talk Radio and Mainstream Media Political Talk

You might be thinking that we already have enough political talk today just from conservative talk radio and from liberal newspapers and TV stations. The Internet is filled with political talk on both sides of the aisle. Whether the outlet is liberal or conservative, most of these news sources are "preaching to the choir," meaning talking to people who already agree with them. Your sharing your views and thoughts with someone who knows and respects you, even if she disagrees with you, is more impactful than a "talking head" sitting in a news station far away could ever be.

Especially when you approach the conversations using some of the ideas shared in this book.

Your Voice Is Needed in America

Despite the few chuckles in the background among husbands (I think I heard mine) who think we women don't need any help in talking more, I am here to inspire you to know that your input about the issues facing our country today is needed, and you do not have to be a Rhodes Scholar or Ivy League graduate to have valuable input. There are a host of factors that are shutting down constructive conversation, but if we recognize them and also recognize the stakes for our country, our children, and our grandchildren if we fail to overcome them, I'm confident we women will rise to the occasion.

Keep in mind a few things about talking:

★ Constructive conversation can and should bring light, not heat, to the subject—and women know intuitively what tones and volumes lead to one or the other. Chapter twelve has some good ideas and conversation tips about getting dialogue started.

★ We're living in an era of nearly oppressive political correctness…recognize it when it is operating among your friends and puncture it with a little female spunk and honesty.

★ When your instinct tells you that you don't agree with the rest of the group, it's okay and liberating and satisfying to say so…and you may just find that many in the group actually agree with you.

★ Our moms taught us that in polite social interaction we should never talk about politics, religion, or how to raise kids. Yet the country we love was founded by some of the greatest thinkers and talkers of any era—and their thinking and talking was, ultimately, all about Divine Providence (what they called God) and politics. Stepping up to these topics today is not impolite. It is imperative, and it places us squarely in the line of American patriots of every era.

As for the organization of the book:

★ Until recently I skipped reading the preface or introduction in any book (assuming it was "fluff"), and if you have that same habit, I would encourage you in the case of this book to read those two sections because they "set the table" especially well for this book.

★ I've assumed my women readers will have all levels of appetite for the meat of the issues that confront our country, so each chapter starts with the milk of quotes and personal stories, and moves progressively into more and more substance. You can stop and digest whenever you feel like it. Some may not want to take on the whole meal, but that's okay. The book is designed to let you read into as much depth as you want.

★ There is no reason to read this book through sequentially. If you see a chapter title that covers the topic you're most interested in, go right to it.

★ If you have a group of friends you'd like to start a "Can We Talk?" conversation with, take a special look at the "Did You Know?" sections at the end of almost every chapter.

Talking about what America is all about is actually very patriotic—from the time of our nation's founding until now—and in the future. Your views have value, and your votes will shape America's future.

The Trouble with Words

The trouble with words is that we need them to communicate but sometimes they trip us up. Confusion happens when people use the same words to mean very different things. This is especially true in politics. Sometimes there are just innocent differences of understanding or opinion, and we have to try to explain ourselves to each other.

But more frequently, political correctness takes over a word or phrase and almost overnight it becomes something spoken in a voice filled with scorn, or alternatively, something spoken of with unquestioned adulation.

Take the term *American exceptionalism.* No one "owns" the right to define it, and it has been subject to wide variations in perception of its meaning. For conservatives, it refers to the uniqueness of America's founding based on recognizing God-given rights and freedoms, and to the greatness of the nation that grew out of those ideals, so the term has a positive connotation about the goodness of our country. For liberals, it is seen as an arrogant worldview that we Americans see ourselves as better than others, and it is believed to be a theory that explains what they see as unjustified aggressive military action by the United States to force other countries to create a government and system like ours, so it has a negative connotation. (Just to be clear, I do not agree with the liberal characterization of America's foreign policy history.)

How about socialism?

Most Americans do not associate America with socialism, which in its most strident form means complete government ownership of all of the means of production (stores, businesses, manufacturers, etc.). Yet more and more scholars and writers are speaking about the policies that Democrats advocate today as being socialist.

Specifically, the use of a strictly controlling and sometimes punitive regulatory environment over businesses, use of the tax system to accomplish ongoing wealth redistribution, the seeming intentional expansion of an enormous dependency class, and the government takeover of the healthcare system and numerous other private sector businesses are steps along the road to socialism, and are inconsistent with America's long history based on a free market economy. Compound that with the Democrat-led growing centralization of government at the federal level and their consistent opposition to proposals to pass some issues back to state governments, and it becomes clear why scholars view their policies as trending toward socialism.

Many Democrats still reject the socialism label and some find it offensive, but there is no other honest way to speak about the difference between free markets and what the Democrats support than to call their policies, in some degree at least socialist-leaning. Another term that capture today's Democrat Party leadership's economic and political path is "collectivism," so I'll use that term, too.

How about "Democrat" and "Republican," or "liberal" or "conservative?"

For some Americans, these are loaded words. I know members of each party who have such strongly held negative preconceptions about the other side of the political aisle that it would seem there is no point to a conversation.

And misconceptions abound. We have had conversations with family friends who agreed with the conservative perspective right down the line on every issue we discussed, and then strongly protest that they are not "conservatives." It can be difficult to let go of stereotypes and labels about either party that were held over a lifetime!

Yet discussing policy issues in America and choosing a path forward would be impossible without using the terms Democrat, Republican, liberal, and conservative, misleading or off-putting as they may occasionally seem. I will try to always be clear in tying those words to particular policies or ideals we'll be talking about.

How about "fairness" and "social justice?"

These are frequently used words in today's political world and are among the most prominent words spoken to rally voter support for new spending and/or tax increase proposals. These particular terms have powerful appeal and tend to persuade voters at an emotional level, especially women, into voting for expanding programs, often with little or no analysis of the underlying facts such as cost or basis for believing the program will be successful in addressing the problem. After all, who could be against "social justice," even if we do not know exactly what it means? Same with "fairness." It's a great concept but who gets to say what is fair?

How about a "progressive?"

This word is a recently recycled word adopted by the Democrat Party once the word "liberal" became unpopular with the public because of its association with big government spending. As with "fairness" and "social justice," the term conjures up a positive image, an emotional vision of making progress, and therefore implies that opponents do not wish to make progress. All I'll say for the moment is, not all change is progress, no matter what they call it.

Ever heard of a "constitutionalist," or a "denier?"

One phenomenon I want to talk about repeatedly with you is the use of the tactic of shutting down all discussion on an issue by attaching a scornful label to anyone who speaks out about it. Once this tactic has been deployed, the remaining discussion centers on how ignorant the newly-labeled "constitutionalist" is, and not on whether the Constitution has been followed or ignored or whether following it is important.

A conservative friend of mine was recently called a "constitutionalist" by a liberal woman who did not like that my friend said she thought it was important for the President and Congress to follow the American Constitution. The scornful tone with which that word issued from the liberal's lips (at a dinner table where ten people were seated) cannot be adequately captured in the written word, but the point was clear that anyone who actually thinks that the Constitution has relevance today is a fool.

The entire international discussion of the global warming issue is another example that has brought out the worst in liberals who are determined to shut down anyone who wishes to express a view that opposes the politically correct view held by the Left. Calling someone a "denier" for questioning the global warming prognostications is intended to shame the questioner by equating her with someone who denies the Holocaust, which no sane person does.

This scorn and derision tactic not only silences people who should be allowed to speak, but it also tends to draw the more simple-minded into line, lock step behind the PC "ruling" of what opinions may be shared on key issues.

Political correctness also falsely elevates the value or merit of some ideas.

Examples of this include "bi-partisanship," "reaching across the aisle," and "compromise," which sound virtuous but are not necessarily so. In fact, sometimes they are downright harmful. It depends on what you are being asked to compromise about and where the supposed "middle ground" lies.

Standing uncompromisingly for principle is not automatically "extremist;" it may be the only rational choice. As used in today's political environment, the accusation of being engaged in "partisan politics" is normally an accusation that flows from the Democrats against the Republicans whenever the Republicans will not capitulate to whatever the Democrats want. The media use this "partisan" term that way too. If you were under the impression that the "partisan politics" accusation flows both political ways, tune in to where and when it is used. It is mostly a one-way street.

Note that, as in the case of the "denier" name-calling, the "partisan" accusation is designed to shut down public consideration of the merits of the issues and instead to focus public attention on how supposedly unreasonably the "partisan" is behaving.

My hope is that by exposing these tactics here and throughout this book, you will start to recognize them yourselves and not be drawn in by them. We will be so much better off as a country if we can put a stop to PC tactics and face the issues honestly.

What Kind of Talk Am I Talking About?

I'm talking about sharing with you my political perceptions based on my experience as a lawyer, political activist, policy wonk, and professional political message writer. My immersion in women's political organizations and in the world of politics allows me to offer you some unique and hopefully helpful insights in today's political climate.

Next, I want to empower you to believe that you have valuable opinions and perspectives you can and should share when appropriate. I encourage you to recognize that you do not need to keep quiet while the more opinionated are speaking. Your views have value too and others would benefit from hearing them.

I am urging you to recognize how widespread political correctness is and what a force it has become in American political culture – it can shut down all but the politically correct view on many subjects. While it may seem easiest to comply with liberals' rules about what views may be expressed, unless more Americans stand up, the only opinions your children will ever hear, or be taught in school, are those anointed by the PC monitors.

You will find at the end of some chapters a section called "Did You Know...Stories and Facts to Share," which contains a short list of information you can use as a starting point for your future political talking. Please do read Chapter Twelve, which includes basic tips and techniques for talking about politics that may help to keep conversations calm and focused.

Let's talk....

Chapter Two

PROTECTING AMERICA IS "WOMEN'S WORK" AND IT IS NEVER DONE

Can We Talk…About Women as Protectors

Most of us remember feeling protective about a sibling, a friend, a child, and especially our own children. We know nothing trumps our attention to

the health and well-being of our loved ones. And if we ever sense that a friend or a child or someone else important to us is in danger of making a mess out of his or her life through bad decisions, we won't hesitate to talk (and do a lot more than just talk) to rescue the lives that are so important to us.

We work at nurturing and protecting. Women (and men) across America sense that our country is in major danger as a result of many bad decisions over many years. The need for rescue is acute; the time for rescue is now.

America needs defenders to speak up about the importance of our Constitution-based system and freedoms, the free markets that naturally flourish based on freedom, and the importance of rights from our Creator that government cannot touch. I am urging you to nurture and protect America like you would yourself and your own child.

Let's talk about it.

What We'll Talk About in This Chapter:

Ladies, America Needs Your Vigilance, Now

Why Things Don't Feel Right in America—Things Are Happening That Violate Our Sense of Basic "American-Ness"

A Time of Political Consequence

Why Are So Many People Talking About Socialism in America?

Socialism, American Style: Industry Takeover by Intrusive Regulations, and Wealth Redistribution Through Abusive Tax Policy

The World-Class Uniqueness of America's Founding

A Few of the American Founding Ideas That Really Matter

The Constitutional Line in the Sand

America's Free Market System Grew Out of the Values and Freedoms Woven into America's Founding

Why So Many Americans Are Alarmed by the Democrats' Trend Toward Socialism and Their Disdain for Constitutionally Limited Government

Did You Know…Stories and Facts to Share

> *"… eternal vigilance by the people is the price of liberty, and … you must pay the price if you wish to secure the blessing. It behooves you, therefore, to be watchful in your States as well as in the Federal Government."*
> ——President Andrew Jackson, Farewell Address, March 4, 1837

Ladies, America Needs Your Vigilance, Now

My purpose in writing this book is to make the case to women all over America that our country needs you, in this 2012 election season and for the next 100 years at least, to nurture, protect, and defend our "American-ness."

Americans Are Anxious About America's Future

An October 2011 poll found that more than two-thirds of Americans believe that America, as a nation, is in decline. (http://thehill.com/polls/189273-the-hill-poll-most-voters-say-the-us-is-in-decline; accessed May 17, 2012) A full 83 percent of voters say they are either very worried or somewhat worried about America's future, with 70 percent of men and 68 percent of women saying that America is moving downhill. (Ibid) Many similar polls found the same result.

Why Things Don't Feel Right in America—Things Are Happening That Violate Our Sense of Basic "American-Ness"

Over the past decades, but especially in the last three years, government has taken steps that for most of American history *everyone* knew did not belong in our free market, limited government and rule-of-law-based country. Below is just a partial list, and you will likely be able to add others:

★ Congress forced through the federal takeover of America's healthcare system in 2010 in closed door meetings using a bill that those who voted for it *had not even read*, despite knowing that, by overwhelming numbers, Americans strongly opposed it and still do today. That's not how we do things in America. (See Chapter Five.)

★ Under the power of that legislation, bureaucrats ordered that private companies—healthcare insurers—provide a list of services for free. Government claimed the authority to order certain people, or groups of people, to provide services for free. We don't need to be Abraham Lincoln to sense that something's wrong with that concept. (See Chapter Eleven.)

★ The President and Congressional leaders have repeatedly gone around Congress and, therefore, around the Constitution and the American people, by using unaccountable federal agencies to force into "law" rules and regulations for which the elected Congress did not dare vote. Examples include the NLRB and Card Check (more in Chapter Seven), and the EPA and CO2 regulation (more in Chapter Ten).

★ One federal agency, the Environmental Protection Agency (EPA), engaged in what can genuinely be called tyranny in 2012. It took the position that an Idaho couple could not appeal that agency's decision prohibiting them from building a house on their own land without their paying fines in the amount of $75,000 *per day*. This was too outrageous for every Justice on the U.S. Supreme Court, which ruled 9 to 0 against the EPA. (More on this in Chapter Ten.) (http://www.scotusblog.com/case-files/cases/sackett-et-vir-v-environmental-protection-agency-et-al/; accessed May 17, 2012) Bureaucrats who do this kind of thing have lost touch with the American way of governing.

★ The 1996 welfare reform provisions, which were tremendously successful in helping move millions from dependence to self-sufficiency, were *surreptitiously* reversed almost in their entirety in 2009, without announcement or debate. Again, this is just not how things are supposed to be done in our democracy. States are once again rewarded for increasing the welfare rolls, rather than for helping Americans move off those rolls and into independence and the dignity that comes from self-reliance. (Read more in Chapter Six.)

★ Through executive order, agency actions, and the apparent deliberate stalling of the issuance of permits, government has blocked access to America's massive natural resources including oil reserves that could provide fuel to Americans for centuries. Accessing that oil would create thousands of American jobs, too. Especially because America loans money to Brazil and Mexico for their oil drilling, it makes you wonder what the Democrats are thinking when they oppose drilling here. (More in Chapter Ten.)

★ As American families tighten their belts and live on less, Washington spends more. The debt grows and grows, and some Washington officials just keep thinking of new "free" programs and spending more money. It's like the politicians don't think it's real money they are spending—but it is real, and it is ours.

★ Responsible, thoughtful, and detailed reform proposals intended to protect and preserve federal programs that are otherwise on track for bankruptcy, such as Social Security and Medicare, are mocked by politicians who propose no solutions of their own. You could wonder if they want them to fail.

★ Liberal support for building a mosque at Ground Zero, while at the same time routinely opposing public symbols or expressions of the Judeo-Christian faiths that are at the roots of our country, seems so wrong and inexplicable.

★ The Department of Justice will not allow states to require photo identification when a person shows up to vote. The idea that a voter ID requirement that applies to everyone equally is discriminatory is laughable, but when government officials say that a neutral requirement of a photo ID to vote is racist, most Americans seem to choose silence over speaking up. Everyone can see that opposing voter ID is enabling voter fraud, but we don't want to risk being labeled racist, so we don't say it.

★ Government is too intrusive in our lives in ways that are not right in America. A public high school in Utah has to pay a $15,000 fine for mistakenly leaving a soda machine plugged in during the lunch hour, giving students access to soda with sugar in it. The food police rule! (http://fox13now.com/2012/05/14/davis-high-fined-for-having-unhealthy-vending-food-choices/; accessed May 19, 2012)

★ Americans feel there is a loss of respect for the very concept of truth. That sounds melodramatic, I know, but think how often you and most Americans hear things in the media, and from politicians and wonder what the truth on that subject really is. From reported poll results you know cannot be true, to the over-the-top absurd political slogans, such as Democrats saying that Republicans have declared a "war on women." That mantra arose out of Republican opposition to a Democrat-sponsored mandate that insurance companies give away some services for women for free. There was never any "war;" there was never any truth at all behind that statement. But it was a sound bite slogan that captured the attention of the media and enraged the ignorant. (See Chapter Eleven.)

★ While attacks by politicians on their political rivals are as old as time, Democrats today attack American citizens using scorn and mockery, which seems designed to shut down political dialogue and disagreement.

• Citizens worried about fiscal issues like the massive federal debt and out-of-control spending, and those opposed to socialized medicine or other policy issues, were called by the President of the United States (and other leading Democrats) "tea-baggers," a crass and ugly term designed to humiliate Americans into silence.

- People who question the manmade global warming theory, or whether proposed radical solutions are necessary and appropriate, citing reams of data and many experts raising serious doubts, are labeled by elected leaders "deniers" in an attempt to compare them to malicious Holocaust deniers.

★ The creeping, vague sense that something is wrong has grown into the realization that Washington has developed an attitude of an elite ruling class whose members believe they know more than the ignorant masses and so will force through the policies they know are best, regardless of what the American people or their elected representatives want. They will pass laws and regulations that few Americans support *because they can.*

We all love America. We see so much good in her people, our fellow Americans, yet we know that some things are not right in America. How do we figure out what to do? How do we take charge of the situation? Where are the political parties in all of this?

A Time of Political Consequence

This is an era of political consequence in America. This precious nation needs us to vote to support the basic liberty-based economic and political system that made America the world's standard-bearer in freedom, prosperity, and free markets. We need to re-learn and re-appreciate that the freedom and abundance America historically enjoyed did not come out of thin air: they came about because of the ideas woven through our Founding documents, and that we can lose them if we don't hold to those ideas.

Ladies, we all lose sight of these big ideas in the midst of life's daily challenges and responsibilities. Election season rolls around again too quickly for many of us, and lots of people are tired of the politicians before campaign season even starts. But things are different in this era.

I hope through this book to lay out with clarity and persuasiveness that the two paths ahead offered by our two political parties are very different. Only one can keep America on course to offer future generations the goodness and liberties we have historically enjoyed.

What Two Paths are the Political Parties Offering American Voters?

For many election cycles, most Americans would say that the two parties offer mildly different policies or ideas. In fact, I know people who admit they chose their candidate in past elections based on personal likeability and even on looks. But those who are seriously tuned into the political world today know that the policies and, even more important, the underlying philosophies of the Republican and Democrat Parties are defined and different.

The two paths or choices are:
• *Maintaining the historic American system of free markets, personal freedoms and Constitution-based, limited government that Republicans support, or*
• *Succumbing to the collectivist, socialist-oriented controlled markets and society, the coercive use of government power to tax to redistribute wealth, and disdain for the Constitution's core ideals and limits on government that the Democrats support.*

You cannot have both because they are opposites. Just like you cannot have slavery and freedom at the same time.

Why Are So Many People Talking About Socialism in America?

When I mention to my Republican or conservative friends that I see the Democrat Party of today on the path toward collectivism and socialism, they nod along as though I asked them to agree that the sky is blue. There is no doubt in their worldview that the collectivist mentality and a coercive, unDemocrat, elitist mentality has overtaken the leaders of the Democrat Party.

By contrast, when I used the word "socialist" to describe today's Democrats in conversation with a fairly liberal and very well-educated Democrat, she strongly and actually mockingly rejected that notion. While she acknowledges that she supports a fairly big and centralized government that does lots of things to help people, she sees America as a free market, business-oriented country where socialism would never be welcomed.

And this is one reason for this book: to help make clearer to nonpolitical American women that something very different is happening in America today; that the differences between the Republicans and the Democrats positions today are not the run-of-the-mill political season banter. Just because America did not suffer a military attack with the invaders imposing a new socialistic order through force, does not mean that America's free market system is supported by all in government. Part of why my friend and others don't yet perceive that the Democrat Party of today promotes a kind of socialism is because this shift has been gradually occurring for decades and is at least for now, already the soft socialism I'll describe below.

What Is Socialism All About?

Socialism in its ideal (to a socialist) form is the system whereby the government owns or controls all the means of production, meaning all the businesses, manufacturers, farms, shops, and producers of any product or service. Everybody works for the government and the "from each according to his income, and to each according to his need" Marxist/Leninist standard applies, resulting in a "fairer" society where everyone earns the same amount no matter if or how hard they worked. Private property, and working and saving to achieve your dream of buying your own home, are absent because they are impermissible.

Socialism is the first stage of the path toward the ultimate socialistic goal of communism, according to the architects of this collectivist thinking, Karl Marx and Vladimir Lenin.

Communism is socialism's even-more-evil cousin, and it has all the joys of oppressive socialism plus a one-political-party system that uses coercion, force, and violence to require everyone to keep in line, and stay inside the country's geographic boundaries. Think Cuba.

What's So Bad About Communism?

And for those wondering whether communism might not be such a bad thing, ask yourself why so many thousands were and are willing to risk life and limb to escape from Cuba to America, but not one life has been lost by Americans "fleeing" to Cuba. The answer, of course, is that (1) you don't have to "escape" America, because you are allowed to leave whenever you want, and (2) everyone knows life is so much better under capitalism/free markets in America than under communism in Cuba, so no one wants to make that change.

The East-Germany-versus-West-Germany analogy is equally valid. Communist East Germany made it illegal for its citizens to leave, while free West Germany, on the other side of the Berlin Wall, had no such rule. Between August 13, 1961, and November 9, 1989, 171 people were killed or died attempting to escape at the Berlin Wall. All were headed from Communism to freedom. No one was fighting to get away from freedom and into Communist-ruled East Germany. (http://www.dailysoft.com/berlinwall/history/escape.htm; accessed May 17, 2012)

So why head down that freedom-to-socialism-to-communism path in America? Why even let it get started?

> *"Most people who read ' 'The Communist Manifesto' probably have no idea that it was written by a couple of young men (Friedrich Engels and Karl Marx) who had never worked a day in their lives, and who nevertheless spoke boldly in the name of 'the workers.'*
> *—Thomas Sowell, PhD. Economics, Author and Columnist*

Socialism, American Style: Industry Takeover by Intrusive Regulation, and Wealth Redistribution Through Abusive Tax Policy

Socialism, or the collectivist mindset, has found its way into power in America obviously not via the forced imposition of socialism, but through subtle tactics by collectivist thinkers designed to accomplish those goals under the guise of protecting and caring for the people.

One such less-direct tactic is ever increasing onerous regulation that has the impact of stifling or shutting down business activity (oil drilling and coal manufacturing are two current examples; more on that in Chapter Ten). So government doesn't technically own the business, it just tightly controls it, and sometimes crushes it. Noble motives are always offered, but in many cases are transparently false or involve exaggerated concerns.

Another tactic Democrats use that accomplishes the purposes of socialism without calling it that, involves the use of the income taxing power. Of course, taxes to fund our military and national defense and other Constitutionally mandated purposes are right and necessary. It is the imposition of income and other taxes *for the express purpose of moving wealth around*, away from those who earned it and toward those the government has chosen as worthy recipients, that is collectivist.

Current wealth transfers effectuated by the government's taxing power include massive financial support to avoid bankruptcy for some private companies but not others for companies that could have pursued Chapter 11 reorganization bankruptcy proceedings (auto companies) and thus restructured and reduced their debt in a balanced way supervised by the courts; the staggering increase in government assistance for dependency-creating programs; and the billions of taxpayer dollars invested in "new" or "clean" energy science experiments, or fledgling companies making products very few Americans want to buy.

A scholarly analysis

Dr. Allan Meltzer, a professor of political economy at Carnegie Mellon University, wrote a most informative book recently called *Why Capitalism?* (Capitalism is another and more formal word for free markets, though that word has been so maligned by the Left that a recent poll found that more Americans supported free markets than supported capitalism. Interesting.) Meltzer's book provides a thorough review of the unparalleled prosperity the world has enjoyed as a result of America's embrace of free markets, and also gives a scholarly analysis of the modern trend of socialism via regulation and taxation, which the Democrat Party supports.

One point Meltzer makes that bears repeating a thousand times is:

> *"Capitalism and the market have proved far better than the state at reducing poverty and raising living standards."*
> —*Allan H. Meltzer,* Why Capitalism, *pg. 21*

Examples of the Democrat Party's Embrace of Collectivism...

★ The federal takeover of the healthcare system. The best healthcare system on earth was taken over by the federal government in 2010, despite overwhelming public opposition. The government took over 1/6 of America's free market economy in that one move.

★ The mortgage bailouts. Congress used federal tax dollars (your money) to rescue mortgage holders who bought more house than they could afford: this is nothing other than socialism. Lots of history on how we got to that point, also caused by Democrat policies starting with the Community Reinvestment Act, but that is a whole other story.

★ Washington Democrats actually introduced a bill in 2012 to regulate oil company profits under a "Reasonable Profits Board." No word on why only the oil companies (and not other companies) would have been subject to this (except that they are one of the Democrats favorite villains), or on who would get to set the rules about what profits are reasonable.

  • Also no word on whether *the government that charges more money in taxes on a gallon of gas than the profit the oil companies get,* would impose some new limits on itself.

  • This did not pass, but the introduction of it by six Democrats is a real window on their view of how not-free the free markets should be. Other Democrats have discussed in the past capping salaries of executives and imposing other socialist-style rules on the free markets and individuals. [http://thehill.com/blogs/floor-action/house/205085-dems-propose-reasonable-profits-board-to-regulate-oil-company-profits: accessed May 19, 2012]

★ The Occupy Wall Street protestors have a socialistic tone to their rhetoric—99 percent versus 1 percent—demanding redistribution of wealth, and our Democrat President and the Democrat minority leader praised them. Speeches by the President more commonly take on a strident class warfare tone, and include angry-sounding denouncements that "the rich" and "corporations" do not pay their "fair share." (More on this in Chapter Four.) Those are classic socialist, wealth-redistributing messages. Finding achievement and success scandalous and something to be scorned has no home in the world of America and her free markets. But it has its place in today's Democrat Party.

America Has Never Been Purely Free Market, but...

Congress has historically regulated businesses for a variety of widely accepted reasons: to require honesty in advertising and compliance with labor laws, and for a whole host of other market-based and consumer-protecting reasons. But today's Democrat Party has greatly expanded the scope and onerousness of laws and regulations, often targeting industries that are politically unpopular with Democrats, and the regulations imposed are so draconian that they lead to the wholesale shutting down of businesses and the loss of jobs.

Similarly, Americans have always permitted, and in fact rightfully demanded, that some tax dollars collected go to meet the needs of the poor and to supply funding for needed projects. But the speed at which today's Democrats have rapidly increased spending on direct assistance, that has swollen to unprecedented levels the size of the class of Americans utterly dependent on government, and the Democrats' surreptitious revision of the welfare reform provisions that provided incentives for those receiving assistance to find work, cause consternation.

It can make you wonder what the Democrats real motives are.

Does Socialism Work in the American "Way of Life?"

During the Cold War era, American schoolchildren were taught that Communists would "destroy our way of life," which was a curious expression most kids probably did not understand. I remember wondering, "What, they will outlaw ice cream? I mean, what could be so bad...?"

But I have a better understanding now about that "destroy our way of life" idea, and it is all interwoven with the way that America came into being, which British Prime Minister Margaret Thatcher described well.

> "Europe was created by history. America was created by philosophy."
> —Baroness Margaret Thatcher, British Prime Minister 1979–1990

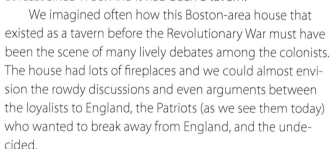

My husband and I spent three months in the Boston area from December, 2010 until February, 2011 for some family-related commitments, and we ended up renting a house in Weston MA for that time. The house was very old; the historical records showed it had been in existence at least since 1730. And it had been a tavern!

We imagined often how this Boston-area house that existed as a tavern before the Revolutionary War must have been the scene of many lively debates among the colonists. The house had lots of fireplaces and we could almost envision the rowdy discussions and even arguments between the loyalists to England, the Patriots (as we see them today) who wanted to break away from England, and the undecided.

Talking about what America is all about is actually very patriotic—then and now!

The World-Class Uniqueness of America's Founding

Ladies, let's talk briefly about America's founding before we return to today's politics because just a few ideas from our nation's founding make the source of America's greatness so much clearer. It's kind of like needing to get the alphabet down before we can sound out the words.

Other nations were formed out of the eviction of colonial powers and the drawing together of various native peoples, or as a matter of military conquest, or the drawing together of people of common ethnic heritage, or the mere passing down of royal power.

But the founding of America was via a deliberate and conscious act of men who sat down together to solemnly deliberate about the ideas would form the best country they could envision. They had no past set of laws or rules of American government to follow, and among them they had a broad knowledge base about the laws and customs of their native England, and about the teachings of philosophers over the centuries.

The point is that they, our Founders, actually set up the structure of the federal government, and the basic rules about the power and limits on the power of the government, and the rights of the people, *based on ideas.* They set out those ideas in the Declaration of Independence, the document formalizing their break with England, and then in the Constitution, which is the core document establishing America's system of government and our rights. (The Founders first tried a system of government with weaker federal power, under a document called the Articles of Confederation, that they quickly found inadequate, and then wrote the Constitution.)

The other great series of founding documents is collected together under the name of the Federalist Papers, which were a series of "letters to the editor" that ran when the colonists were trying to persuade enough of their colonial brethren to get on board with the new Constitution. Alexander Hamilton, James Madison, and John Jay wrote those Federalist Papers, which are widely considered documents to be given great weight in interpreting the Constitution.

A Few of the American Founding Ideas That Really Matter

No Oligarchies: No Small, Elite Group Running Things

The Founders wanted to eliminate the idea of a ruling class such as the royalty was in England. The word "oligarchy" means government by a small group of people. Royalty, dictators, communists, and any other small group that actually holds power to run a nation, are all examples of oligarchies. Our Founders deliberately spread power around. People vote; we have state and national layers of government, and checks and balances between the branches.

We completely choose our government, except, of course, for the bureaucrats who are chosen by the executive branch and the judges chosen by the Senate and the President. We can, for the most part, clean political house every two and four years.

Where Rights Come From

America's formers and shapers, the men who prayed and thought about and discussed the founding of a nation, the rare starting-from-scratch opportunity, relied on their knowledge of philosophers and thinkers to come around to the idea that men, meaning all people, have inherent rights as individuals that come to us from God. They described those rights as including at least the right to "life, liberty, and the pursuit of happiness." Those most famous words of the Declaration are kind of the ground floor of our rights, and later when the Constitution and the Bill of Rights were written, our forefathers spelled out more of what rights from God means.

Ladies, it is really important to recognize that the Founders were not deciding what rights men have from God; they were writing down for all human history the absolute truth that man has always had these rights from God. That's why they called them "self-evident." Whether those rights were recognized by any other nation on earth, the Founders' statements in the Declaration and the Constitution were world altering because they memorialized a "forever truth" that man has some rights that belong to him, naturally, from God.

> *"Our Constitution was made only for a moral and religious people. It is wholly inadequate to the government of any other."*
> —John Adams, Founder, Second President of the United States

What Are Our "Rights"?

This is a good time to make a really important point about the concept of rights. Genuine rights, like the right to pursue happiness (choose our own path etc.), and the right to free speech and to practice religion, are rights that our Founders viewed God to have given men (and women), and they relate to your personal freedom to think and act as you wish, free from governmental interference or control. They are rights you hold as against government power—meaning that the government cannot just arbitrarily decide, for example, to pass a law saying that you cannot talk about foreign policy anymore, or cannot associate with certain people. It does not cost anyone any money to give these genuine rights to you.

That is very different from when people say, for example, "healthcare is a right" or "free healthcare is a right." Good health is in many respects a matter of personal responsibility and also a necessity, like food and shelter. But healthcare services require that other people deliver and provide them (at a cost to them), and products such as medicine, and facilities like hospitals, all cost someone, somewhere money.

★ The liberal who says free healthcare is a right is saying that he has the right to make someone else give him free stuff.

★ When a liberal claims that free healthcare is a right, ask him who has to give him services for free. Does the government have to force the doctor to give you free healthcare? Or, if the answer is the government has to provide free healthcare, he is saying that taxpayers who work and pay taxes have to pay for his "free" healthcare.

★ Once we as a society agree that things that cost money are "rights" that someone is entitled to have for free, then we are agreeing that some group of citizens has the right to force some other group of citizens, to do work for them, for free. There's another word for that, and we fought a war to end it.

> "A right, such as a right to free speech, imposes no obligation on another, except that of non-interference. The so-called right to health care, food, or housing, whether a person can afford it or not, is something entirely different; it does impose an obligation on another.
>
> "If one person has a right to something he didn't produce, simultaneously and of necessity it means that some other person does not have right to something he did produce.
>
> "That's because, since there's no Santa Claus or Tooth Fairy, in order for government to give one American a dollar, it must, through intimidation, threats and coercion, confiscate that dollar from some other American."
> —Walter E. Williams, American Economist, Author, Professor

The Rule of Law, Not of Men (or Women!)

This was among the most revolutionary concepts the Founders embraced: that the laws were the same for everyone. Of equal importance is that the structure of the government they created supported the rule of law and ensured that the people directly elected those who write the laws—the members of Congress. This gave teeth to the concept of "self-government."

The court system added a layer of protection against arbitrary government, and is empowered to determine whether laws are properly followed, and whether they are Constitutional, but the courts are not empowered to make law. The Executive (the President and his or her administration) is empowered to enforce the laws that Congress passes, but not to make his or her own laws. All of this was designed to and had the impact of creating a system where laws were written by the elected officials the people chose, not by the personal edicts of tyrants, kings, or policymakers. This was one way to keep the people safe and free from an arbitrary government.

The Constitutional Line in the Sand

What if California passed a law outlawing churches? Or if Texas passed one mandating weekly church attendance? Or Chicago passed a city ordinance requiring people to carry handguns for self-defense? What could stop them? You may say, "Well, that would never happen," but the reason it really *could* not happen, or to be more precise, the reason laws like that would never stand up in court, is because of the Constitution.

The Constitution is:

★ A line in the sand that says what lines government cannot cross;

★ A contract between the people and the power of government that people can enforce against the government if and when it does attempt to cross the line;

★ A list of the things government cannot do, not a list of things that government can do *to* you or must do *for* you.

What Difference Does the Constitution Really Make Today?

During the "Arab Spring," and in other contexts in the world, countries in this century have been writing constitutions for their new governments. Some of them incorporated sharia law, the law emanating from the teachings of Islam. Although the dangers of sharia law in America are a subject I don't have room to delve into in this book, the contrast between a constitution incorporating sharia and the American Constitution guaranteeing freedom of religion is stark and important.

The American Constitution lays down the structure of law and government and if we disregard it we would enter the chaotic realm where government could pass any law it wanted to. Like maybe a law requiring adherence to sharia law.

> *Many Americans have never given any thought to how much the Constitution protects them, precisely because it always has.*

That same feeling of overall confidence and indeed complacency about America's soundness and stability makes people doubt that any political party could really be as far off track from our basic American-ness as the Democrats are today. We see things we know are not right but we don't speak up or even necessarily feel that worried because of our sense that, for the most part, nothing in America could get too far outside of our normal boundaries.

But consider the reaction of then Speaker of the House Democrat Nancy Pelosi when asked where in the Constitution she thought Congress was authorized to pass a law mandating Americans to buy insurance. Pelosi's scornful, repeated answer was, "Are you serious?" (I included a link to the YouTube audio recording of her answer because the sarcastic derision in her voice is palpable.) She wasn't voicing a studied view of the pros and cons of its constitutionality, she was dismissing the very idea that the Constitution has any limits on the power of government at all. One wonders what is going on with the party she is leading. (http://cnsnews.com/news/article/flashback-when-asked-where-constitution-authorizes-congress-order-americans-buy-health; accessed May 19, 2012; audiotape at http://www.youtube.com/watch?v=08uk99L8oqQ; accessed May 19, 2012)

Have you noticed how everyone is talking about the Declaration of Independence and the Constitution these days?

Why is it that for the first time in my lifetime and probably yours, people are actually reading the Declaration of Independence and the Constitution? Have you noticed how people talk about those two old documents more than we all used to? The reason is that some of the policies coming out of Washington are so far out of line with things that past American Presidents did or said that people are wondering, "Can they do that?" Americans are turning back to remember what our founding documents say, and where the lines can be drawn to stop the growing expansion of federal power.

America's Free Market System Grew Out of the Values and Freedoms Woven into America's Founding

After America gained her independence, the nation developed as one unique in history because she was based on ideas and principles and a structure that left ultimate power in the hands of the people. Unparalleled prosperity followed. The government did not create jobs, but free people chose to build or become employed in businesses that existed to produce a service or product that other Americans either needed or wanted. Individuals chose their own course and were rewarded for hard work ingenuity, determination, and cleverness with abundance. And all over the world, people watched this "New World" country with awe, envy, and respect.

America's economy was the envy of the world, and America has been for at least the last century the one destination above all others that the poor, the political refugees, the persecuted, and the most courageous, adventurous, and self-reliant people in the world longed to come to.

> *"American prosperity and American free enterprise are both highly unusual in the world, and we should not overlook the possibility that the two are connected."*
> *—Thomas Sowell, Ph.D. Economics, Author and Columnist*

For Americans who never lived in a socialist country or an emerging economy country, the bounty of America just seems like the norm, like the only way life can be. Learning to appreciate America's bounty is one thing, but recognizing that her bounty came from *the Constitutional system itself*, and from the free enterprise system, is important.

In America you are free to pursue the happiness of being a starving artist or the best and highest paid baseball player or ballerina or bulldog breeder. Government was not there to slot you into jobs it needed done, which was happening in the Soviet Union and all over the Communist world.

Back to that Cold War era "destroy our way of life" expression

That's what the Cold War era slogan, that Communists wanted to "change our way of life," meant. It meant there is a radical difference between living under the American Constitution, laws and the economic system that flowed from them, and that are formed and shaped by the Constitutional recognition of God-given rights and limits on government's power, as opposed to living under a system where the government does not recognize God-given rights, and that views the role of individuals to be subservient to the State. Americans have, for generations, lived under the protection of the freedoms the Constitution establishes, without necessarily recognizing where their freedoms came from.

Why So Many Americans Are Alarmed by the Democrats' Trend Toward Socialism and Their Disdain for Constitutionally Limited Government

A big challenge for America is to make sure enough voters know these facts and this history—that America's freedom and unparalleled prosperity came from the system the Founders created—the free enterprise, personal-responsibility-driven-individual-rights-and-freedoms-protecting, Constitution-based system. Voters who know this history know that we should not "fundamentally transform" America; we should fight and vote to protect it. Americans who have lived in more socialistic societies observe that America is drifting away from the freedoms and free enterprise system that made America strong and great. Let me introduce you to one of these Americans.

Meet Mei

I want to share a few stories throughout this book that make some of the ideas we are talking about come to life. Sometimes it's easier to understand ideas when they're told through the lens of people's lives.

So I'll tell you the story of one of my new friends in Dallas, Mei, who grew up in Communist China. I'll share different aspects of her life at different points in this book: her story is relevant to several issues we'll talk about.

Mei grew up in the era of Communist Dictator Mao Tse Tung, the First Chairman of the Central Committee of the Communist Party of China who ruled from 1945 to 1976. China was then strictly Communist and because the Communists controlled the entire economy and the lives of all citizens, they (the Communist Party) decided who had to, and who could, go to college.

Mei graduated in the top 10 percent of her class in high school, so she was compelled to go to engineering school for college. Not offered, or encouraged, but required.

Mei's journey from China to Dubai and ultimately to America was one of determination, self-reliance, and spunk. Her perspective on American society, our economic system and freedoms, and our prosperity, abundance, and opportunities, is refreshing and insightful.

I mention Mei in this chapter just to draw the basic contrast between the American economy shaped by people freely pursuing their dreams, borne out of the freedoms our Constitution guarantees, and the economy and life shaped by a controlling centralized communist government, that decides who goes to college for what.

Mei's life experience also includes having her parents sent off to work on a communal farm during the Cultural Revolution, which was a huge contrast from their former lives as a college professor and a dean, respectively. Mei also told me about her high school friend who secretly brought in the signal for and recorded American radio channels and shared them with his friends.

At age 21 he was caught, arrested, tried, convicted, and sentenced to death, a sentence carried out two weeks after his arrest.

Constitutions and freedoms matter. Reading China's Constitution requires patience—it is long and very dogmatic, but breathtakingly short on any assurances of the rights of the people. It refers to the "people's democratic dictatorship"—an oxymoron if there ever was one! You can read it online here: http://www.china.org.cn/english/congress/229722.htm

Compare the U.S. Constitution with that of Communist Russia

Contrast the basic freedoms the Declaration says are "unalienably" ours because they come to us from our Creator, with the rights of the people in former Communist Russia, in their Constitution, which you can read online. (http://www.constitution.org/cons/ussr77.txt; accessed June 16, 2012)

That Communist Russia Constitution is full of things the state must and can do to people and for people. In short, in the name of caring for the people, they could completely control them. And they did. (Another note of interest—Communist Russia's Constitution specifically mentions labor and trade unions in a very respectful and empowering manner: Labor unions were part of the socialist/communist scheme of repressing freedom and the individual.)

Constitutions set limits, basic guideposts—they say what we are all about as a country. Treating our U.S. Constitution cavalierly or with disdain is not just ignorant, it is dangerous to our nation's stability and future.

Did You Know?…Stories and Facts to Share Chapter Two

Why the United States Constitution matters

If you hear people say that the Constitution of the United States is outdated, out of touch with current times, or in any other way irrelevant to modern life,

Speak up and talk about:

★ Freedom to speak your mind without being arrested. The Constitution protects Democrats criticizing Republicans and Republicans criticizing Democrats. It's a beautiful thing.

★ **Freedom to protest.** Or the right of the Occupy Wall Street protestors and of the Tea Party supporters to hold rallies and marches. All of these rights are ours because of the basic guarantees in the Constitution and specifically the First Amendment in the Bill of Rights.

★ **Protection from big government.** The Constitution sprang from the basic rights our Founders recognized in the Declaration of Independence, including that "all men are created equal" and that men are "endowed by their

Creator with certain unalienable Rights, that among these are Life, Liberty and the pursuit of Happiness..". The WHOLE point of the Constitution is to protect people from over-zealous, overbearing, over-controlling big, powerful government.

★ **Religious freedom.** Consider the impact of some of the constitutions created in Middle Eastern countries after the "Arab Spring" that specifically require compliance with sharia law. Sharia is a violence-legitimizing, cruel set of laws and rules growing out of the practice of radical Islam, and they include authorizing violence, maiming, and killing women for such crimes as being the victim of rape.

If freedom of religion seems irrelevant or outdated to your friends, speak up and talk about:

In America, our Constitution provides freedom of religion, which includes the freedom to practice our religion, change religion, and have no religion at all. The Constitution is what protects you from laws demanding or forbidding church attendance. The existence of the Constitution is why we do not have to worry even if, for example, a local community or even a state government became majority (elected) Muslims, they could impose sharia law. The Constitution would not permit that loss of religious freedom—it is the law above all laws. It's our contract of freedom from suppression and repression by government.

Yet today in a striking departure from the respect nearly always accorded churches by government, President Obama's Democrat administration pushed a regulation requiring Catholic institutions to cover in their health insurance policies, procedures and medications (birth control and abortion inducing drugs) that are impermissible under fundamental Catholic church doctrine. If the courts now reviewing the litigation about this regulation decide it is constitutional for government to force a church to act in a manner contrary to its teachings, we will have entered into unprecedented territory in our nation's history.

Meet Virginia

Another new friend of mine in Dallas is Virginia, a lawyer who was exiled from Romania where she lived under the repressive dictatorship of Communist leader Nikolai Ceausescu. Virginia's experiences in Romania included representing Christian churches, which were increasingly under attack as the Ceausescu regime became more repressive, more strictly Communist. One of Virginia's observations about communism and Ceausescu was that Communists require the absolute loyalty of the people, and that is why they repress religion: Communists need to "be" God to the people.

Religious freedom in America—where are the political parties?

The First Amendment to the United States Constitution provides that Congress cannot make any laws (1) "respecting an establishment of religion" (the establishment clause) or (2)"prohibiting the free exercise" of religion (the free exercise clause), which simply means that Congress cannot authorize or establish a particular religion as a matter of law, nor can it prevent people from exercising their religion.

Republicans are more protective of the rights of individuals to practice their religion freely—they protect the free exercise of religion; and Democrats are more determined to eradicate any public symbolism or reference to religion—they are more focused on preventing perceived "establishment" of religion, so they view many public religious activities or symbols as a possible unconstitutional acts that supposedly establish religion.

A Case About Religious Freedom in America Today

One example is the Mojave Desert Veterans Memorial Cross case, which involved a cross erected as a war memorial for World War I veterans in 1934, on what is now federal land. The ACLU (American Civil Liberties Union) took the case representing an American who lived more than a thousand miles away from the cross but who was "offended" by the sight of a religious symbol on public land. More important than the outcome (which was that the cross could remain) was the insider's view of liberal vs. conservative thought as revealed by the United States Supreme Court opinions. To summarize, the liberals wanted the cross removed, and the conservatives voted to allow it to stay. The Democrat-appointed liberal justices opposed the cross, and one in particular went out of his way to make the point that the justices do not need to interpret the Constitution on the basis of original intent of the Founding Fathers, but can instead interpret it as a "living organic Constitution," a view shared by the other liberal justices.

Fortunately for religious freedom, the Court ruled that the cross could stand.

This is a great case to be able to discuss as an example with your friends and others who do not yet understand the difference between how liberals and Democrats, as opposed to conservatives and Republicans, view the importance of religious freedom and the Constitution's protected rights.

Who in America Says the Constitution Doesn't Matter?

Which party is complaining about the United States Constitution? Is anyone seriously criticizing or diminishing it?

These are the words of the current (2012) Democrat President of the United States:

"But, the Supreme Court never ventured (in the civil rights era cases) into the issues of redistribution of wealth, and of more basic issues such as political and economic justice in society.

"To that extent, as radical as I think people try to characterize the Warren Court, it wasn't that radical.

"It didn't break free from the essential constraints that were placed by the Founding Fathers in the Constitution, at least as it's been interpreted, and the Warren Court interpreted in the same way, that generally the Constitution is a charter of negative liberties.

"Says what the states can't do to you. Says what the federal government can't do to you, but doesn't say what the federal government or state government must do on your behalf." (Emphasis added)

Beyond calling the Constitution a "charter of negative liberties," President Obama goes on to label the failure of the civil rights movement to force "redistributive change" as a "tragedy."

This Democrat President is complaining that the Constitution cannot be read to compel wealth redistribution, a central socialist ideal. (http://ohiorepublic.blogspot.com/2009/12/president-obama-constitution-is-charter.html; accessed June 16, 2012)

Here are a few more examples of disrespect for the U.S. Constitution shown by today's Washington Democrats:

★ As described in more detail in Chapter Seven, the Washington Democrats could not get the union-empowering Card Check bill (also known by its absurdly false label Employee Free Choice Act) passed in Congress, where elected officials did not dare pass it due to public outrage over the idea of legalizing union bullying of individuals to join unions. But Democrats, undeterred, are persistently pursuing its passage piece by piece through regulation by the National Labor Relations Board (NLRB). This is a stark rejection of the Constitution's establishment of elective government and of the concept of separation of powers.

★ Similarly, today's Democrat Party could not get the Cap and Trade legislation passed in the duly elected Congress, so they are forcing through regulation of CO2 via draconian EPA regulation that is crippling the energy industry in our country.

★ One last example of the Democrats' rejection of the Constitutional form of government that undergirds America's freedom is the announcement by President Obama that he is, via regulation, putting into place large portions of the Dream Act, an immigration law that Democrats could not get passed in the elected Congress. (http://www.reuters.com/article/2012/06/15/us-usa-immigration-obama-idUSBRE85E17N20120615; accessed June 16, 2012) President Obama announced in June 2012 that the Department of Homeland Security will not deport some younger individuals who are otherwise scheduled for deportation. In short, in an election year Obama decided that he would circumvent Congress and order one of his departments to ignore federal law, with the obvious goal of garnering favor with some voters.

Ladies, I close this chapter with a reminder/plea that we women must step up even more to our places as leaders in American society, to be the nurturers and guardians of our country's precious freedoms. We need to vote to respect and protect the God-given freedoms set out in the Declaration of Independence, and developed and cemented in the Constitution, and the free market system that flows from those freedoms.

America needs us!!

Chapter Three

The "Women's Vote"

Party Identity, and Political and Media Manipulation

Can We Talk…About Our Power In the Voting Booth and About Showing Politicians and the Media That We Are Smarter Than They Think We Are

Ladies, when it comes to women's influence on America, numbers don't lie. Our sheer numbers in the general population, in voter turnout, in the professional ranks, and in graduate and undergraduate universities show an  unmistakable strength—a greater-than-majority status. That means that we have tremendous power to shape America's public policy, her direction as a nation, and the national political conversation concerning what America is all about.

We have a great responsibility—and at this crossroads time in our country's history, an ever more imperative need— to be informed, to test our assumptions, to refuse to indulge in group-think, to decline the politicians' and the media's efforts to manipulate us emotionally, and instead to examine where we are as a country today and what decisions will keep us on the right path for tomorrow.

Girls, what are we waiting for? Let's talk about it…

A little historical humor about the women's vote in America:
"I think I could write a pretty strong argument in favor of female suffrage, but I do not want to do it. I never want to see the women voting, and gabbling about politics, and electioneering. There is something revolting in the thought."
—Mark Twain, Letter to St. Louis Missouri Democrat, March 1867

Mark Twain again, some years later......

"I not only advocate (women's suffrage) now, but have advocated it earnestly for the last fifty years.".....

"I believe in women doing what they deem necessary to secure their rights."
—Mark Twain, interview in Chicago Daily Tribune, Dec. 21, 1909. Pg 5

Topics We'll Talk About in Chapter Three

The Growing Role Women Will Play as Leaders in America – We Rule!

How About the Growing Power of the Women's Vote in America?

Addressing the Issues that Drive the Gender Gap in Voting

Are We Confident Enough to Rethink Our Voting Decisions?

The Truth About Voting for the Individual

Why Should Either Party Think it "Owns" The Women's Vote?

Why Do Politicians Think Women Can Be Swayed By Emotion Without Facts or Logic?

Who Tells You What to Think? The Media?

Do Poll Takers Measure—Or Try to Shape—Public Opinion?

Twelve of the Top Tricks Politicians Use to Fool Voters

How Different REALLY Are Today's Republican and Democrat Parties?
What Are Their Default Modes?

Did You Know?...Stories and Facts to Share

The Growing Role Women Will Play as Leaders in America—We Rule!

Women in America will inevitably emerge as even stronger and more impactful leaders in America's future in the decades to come, because of our academic determination, our growing presence in professional endeavors of all kinds, and our robust participation in the electoral process.

And, to put it simply, there are just more of us!

In America today, women are leading in academic accomplishment including in graduation rates and in the ranks of many professional fields:

★ "Female students graduate high school at a higher rate than male students. Nationally, 72 percent of female students graduated, compared with 65 percent of male students." (http://www.manhattan-institute.org/html/cr_48.htm; accessed May 16, 2012)

★ More women than men go on to college after high school. According to the National Center for Education Statistics, the data for 2009 shows that 73.8 percent of female high school "completers" (which includes graduates and GED recipients) went on to college, as compared with 66 percent of male high school completers. (http://nces.ed.gov/ programs/digest/d10/tables/dt10_208.asp; accessed May 16, 2012)

★ Since 1982, "women have outpaced men in college graduation rates." In 2004, for example, women received 58 percent of all bachelor's degrees awarded that year, and that is
up from 35 percent in 1960.(http://researchnews.osu.edu/
archive/womcolge.htm; accessed May 16, 2012)

College enrollment numbers also signal the increasingly prominent
role women will play as the educated leaders in our communities:

★ Harvard's enrollment in 2010 was 48 percent male and
52 percent female. (http://collegeapps.about.com/od/
collegeprofiles/p/harvard_profile.htm; accessed May 16,
2012)

★ Ole Miss in 2010 had 47 percent male and 53 percent female enrollment. (http://collegeapps.about.com/od/college
profiles/p/mississippi.htm; accessed May 16, 2012)

★ Fayetteville State University, a traditionally black university, reports its student population to include 67.3
percent women and 32.7 percent men. (https://www.
collegedata.com/cs/data/college/college_pg01_tmpl.
jhtml?schoolId=1036; accessed May 16, 2012)

Many more schools, colleges, and graduate schools follow this trend of
majority female classes.

Beyond college attendance and graduation, women are pursuing and
earning advanced degrees in record numbers, and are increasing their
ranks in many professions.

★ In 1950, the percentage of women in graduating classes
of *veterinary schools* was under 10 percent, but in the year
2000, an amazing 70 percent of veterinary school graduates were women.

★ We are approaching the 50 percent measure among *law school graduates.*

★ According to the American Psychological Association, women outnumber men 3:1 among those earning doctoral degrees in psychology. (http://www.apa.org/grad-psych/2011/01/cover-men.aspx; accessed May 16, 2012)

★ Although only 12 percent of America's doctors were women in 1981, today that is up to 31 percent! (http://www.prweb.com/releases/2012/mms-women-physicians/prweb9112174.htm; accessed May 16, 2012)

★ As for women lawyers, as one example, the Florida Bar Association's data show that as of January 1, 2012, women comprised 35 percent of the 93,117-member Florida Bar, whereas 30 years ago women were only 8 percent of the membership. (http://www.miamiherald.com/2012/01/15/2589103/female-lawyers-striking-out-on.html#storylink=cpy; accessed May 16, 2012)

American women already are and will become even more so, in positions of leadership in American society. I cite these figures not to in any way demean the importance of men in education and the professions, but to celebrate the growing ranks of women naturally assuming leadership roles in America.

How About the Growing Power of the Women's Vote in America?

Studies abound about voting trends, and I chose to rely on the data from the Center for American Women and Politics (CAWP), part of the Eagleton Institute of Politics at Rutgers State University of New Jersey. Their data came from the U.S. Bureau of Census *Current Population Reports*, that summarizes self-reporting by individuals. (http://www.cawp.rutgers.edu/fast_facts/voters/documents/genderdiff.pdf; accessed May 16, 2012) Other studies show somewhat different numbers but parallel trends and percentages.

In pure numbers, the women's vote today in America is huge:

★ Since the time we won the right to vote in 1920 and up until the 1980s, women turned out to vote in slightly *lower* levels than men.

★ But starting with the 1980 presidential elections, American *women voted in higher numbers*, and in *higher percentages among the voting age population, than men.*

★ In the 2004 presidential elections, among the voting age population, 60.1 percent of women voted, as compared with only 56.3 percent of men. That translates into the fact that *8.8 million more women than men voted in that election.* (http://womensissues.about.com/od/thepoliticalarena/a/ GenderVoting.htm; accessed June 2, 2012)

★ The winner in that 2004 presidential race, President George W. Bush, won by 3 million votes (actually, by 3,012,166 votes) (http://en.wikipedia.org/wiki/United_States_presidential_election,_2004; accessed May 16, 2012) So, *just the difference* between the men's and women's voter turnout numbers in 2004 would have been more than enough to decide that election. Put more simply, women can sway national elections!

★ In 2008, about 66 percent of women voted compared with 62 percent of men, which is 10 million more women than men who reported having voted in 2008. The raw numbers: 70.4 million women compared with 60.7 million men. (http://blogs.wsj.com/washwire/2009/07/20/census-bureau-heres-who-voted-in-2008/; accessed June 2, 2012)

★ *Women rule! Literally.*

Addressing the Issues that Drive the Gender Gap in Voting

What's the "Gender Gap" in Voting?

The gender gap is the difference between how men and women vote. That gap has fluctuated over the decades. It reached an all-time high point of 11 percentage points in the 1996 presidential race between Clinton and Dole, and another relative low of 4 percentage points in the 1998 Congressional mid-term elections. (IBID, p. 151, 152) In the 2008 presidential election, there was a seven-point gender gap, with women more likely than men to vote Democrat. (http://www.usnews.com/opinion/articles/2008/11/06/data-points-gender-gap-in-the-2008-election; accessed June 2, 2012)

Why the Gender Gap?

As you might imagine, many studies attempt to understand what drives the gender gap in voting. Here is a quick summary of some studies on what drives that gap.

Neither the debt, size of government nor spending drives the women's vote

Women do not report a significant concern for the size of government, the level of spending, the debt, the deficit, or really any fiscal issues as among the top issues that drive their voting decisions.

It's not the social issues.

Despite persistent rumors to the contrary, and probably the best efforts of some liberal groups in our society to make people think so, social issues do not drive the women's vote. "Scholarly analyses of voting and public opinion data have consistently shown that so-called women's issues—those issues most closely associated with the organized women's movement, such as the ERA and abortion—do not appear to be central to the gender gap." (Susan J. Carroll, *Voting Choices, The Politics of the Gender Gap*, p. 135, an article in *Gender and Elections*, Shaping the Future of American Politics, edited by Susan J. Carroll and Richard L. Fox, Cambridge Press, 2010.) This conclusion is repeatedly referenced in other studies about the voting gender gap: the abortion issue does not particularly motivate women voters to support the pro-choice Democrat position, although a small percentage may view it as important.

So What Does Drive the Gender Gap?

Four of the most common reasons offered to explain the gender gap are:

1. Compassion (meaning encouragement of social spending to help people).
2. Feminism (but not the social issues—feminism here is used almost synonymously with compassion, meaning more likely to feel concern for the needy).
3. Economics (heavier reliance by women on direct or indirect government subsidies and funding, thus opposition to reducing the size and scope of government).
4. The role of government (meaning women are more likely to see government spending as helpful, especially as it concerns maintaining a large social safety net, and women are less concerned than men about the size and scope of government).

(*Gender and Elections: Shaping the Future of American Politics*, Edited by Susan J. Carroll and Richard L. Fox, Cambridge University Press, 2010, pp. 133–138)

Other studies suggest additional issues that sway women's votes:

★ Support for environmental protection

★ A desire for racial equality

★ Foreign policy and defense spending

★ Compassion expressed in support for social spending consistently ranks among the top of issues of concern to women

(*Women and American Politics: New Questions, New Directions*, Edited by Susan J. Carroll, Oxford University Press, 2003, pp. 146–158.)

Talking About the Issues that Women Care About

I have dedicated substantive chapters in this book to most of the core issues that concern women. Specifically, I've focused on the compassion-related issues of the healthcare system, social spending and social justice, race relations, along with the environment and energy supplies.

Another overriding motivator of the women's vote is the basic concept of fairness. Women, and really everyone, want life to be fair, and we most certainly want our elected officials to do everything to set the rules and systems to support fairness.

Fairness issues arise in our economic system, our taxes, our budget priorities, and even our national debt. Fairness is integrally related to the economic system, jobs, and opportunities. So I'll talk about all of that, too. The foreign policy piece was just too big to dive into in this book, but I'll touch on defense spending as a portion of the national budget.

It is my contention that on every one of those issues, the parties offer very different solutions, and those solutions are based on contrasting views of what kind of country America is and should be in the future.

The answers the parties offer need to be viewed in the larger context of whether we are a collectivist-based, socialist-leaning country, or whether we are going to retain our historic and unparalleled commitment to freedom. I am unabashedly making the case for continued freedom.

Are We Confident Enough to Rethink Our Voting Decisions?

For those of you who have historically voted Democrat, or see yourself as an Independent who likes to assess the issues and candidates each election cycle, I understand that rethinking political party affiliation may seem uncomfortable. It may be risky to your social standing with family and friends, and sticking with past voting patterns might seem simplest.

Reexamining support for or commitment to a political party can seem a bit like being asked to consider whether you voted the wrong way in the past. But that is not it at all. Parties change, countries change, issues change, and current events change our priorities. I am all about thinking forward, and encourage you to do the same.

A lot of us are turned off entirely by the whole concept of political parties and labels; we just want government to work better and don't want to have to think in terms of political parties and philosophies. But wherever we've been in the past, we're on a new threshold in this early part of the twenty-first century, and there is no escaping the call and the duty to engage in fresh thinking about how we will vote going forward.

Peer Pressure

There is a kind of peer pressure among some groups, whether it is your work colleagues, your high school or college friends, neighbors, and of course your own family. Well-meaning friends who are ardent supporters of one political party can often hardly believe that friends they know and love actually vote with the other party.

But there is a reason that parents warn their children not to give in to peer pressure, but instead to always and carefully think for themselves, to use their own good judgment and values to reach decisions. Parents want kids to think through their actions and to have good reasons for doing the things they do.

The same holds true for adults and voting. Pressure from anyone to vote against what you believe to be right, is wrong.

Here are a few examples of how this peer pressure works when Democrats pressure Republicans in America in 2012:

★ "But don't you care about the poor like I do?" is the argument of Democrats who are proud of ever-increasing government assistance and other social spending. In this case, the facts that should matter to responsible adults are whether these programs have a track record of actually lifting people out of poverty, or driving them deeper into dependency and helplessness. (The latter is the answer; more on that in Chapter Six.)

A relevant fact you may not know: One common trait that the poorest large cities in America have in common is long- term Democrat mayors and government. No kidding. It is not that the poor prefer Democrat government; it is that Democrat policies perpetuate poverty. (More on that in Chapter Six.)

★ "What about racial equality?" is another (sometimes unspoken) Democrat peer pressure/talking point. The facts? It was the Republicans, not the Democrats, who passed the 1866 (post-Civil War) Civil Rights Act after President Andrew Johnson (a racist southern Democrat) vetoed it. And the 1964 Civil Rights Act? It was Democrats who tried to *stop* the Civil Rights bill from passing (Senators Strom Thurmond and Robert Byrd in particular) and the *Republicans who forced it through to passage.* Eighty percent of Republicans voted *for* the Civil Rights Acts 1964, and only 61 percent of Democrats supported it. (More on this in Chapter Thirteen.)

★ "Why aren't you for the party of the 'little guy?'" is another common Democrat theme. Democrats tried to grab that identity in part through their support of unions, which leads to another main point of this book. Democrats back big unions and big union control, which is exactly the opposite of supporting the "little guy." (More on this in Chapter Seven.)

★ "But don't you want unity?" was the response by one of my friends who was stunned to learn that I was going to vote

Republican in a recent presidential election. This poor guy heard on the evening news that the Democrat candidate urged unity, and that was enough for him. Just because a party claims it will bring unity, or makes any other broad claim, does not make it true. The parties stand for different ideas and those ideas will shape America's future. (More on this, all through the book.)

The Truth About Voting for the Individual

For voters who say "I vote for the individual, not the party," it is vital to know that no matter what any candidate says while running, he or she will vote overwhelmingly with his or her party upon arrival in Washington.

Votes virtually always fall along party lines, especially on the important matters. So knowing the views of the party you are choosing is more important than knowing the candidate you are supporting. For some amazing data on how nearly absolute the commitment is by elected officials to vote with their party (called voting "along party lines") check out a website maintained by the *Washington Post*, at (http://projects.washingtonpost.com/congress/112/house/members/; accessed June 2, 2012)

You can read more about party line voting in the Study of the Presidency and Congress. [FN=http://thecenterforthestudyofthepresidencyandcongress.wordpress.com/2010/07/02/politics-by-the-numbers-proving-the-partisan-divide/ Accessed June 2, 2012]

Why Should Either Party Think it "Owns" the "Women's Vote"?

Did you know that the head of the Democrat National Committee claimed in an interview in January, 2012 that the Democrat Party is the "natural home" for all "minorities," including women? She said that this is because "minorities" feel "comfortable" in that party, and she proceeded to list all the minorities she apparently sees as thinking exactly alike: "Hispanics...women ...Jews...Asian-Americans..African Americans..." (http://www.realclearpolitics.com/video/2012/01/13/wasserman_schultz_natural_home_for_minorities_is_the_democratic_party.html; accessed June 2, 2012)

Ladies, the political parties should have to *earn* your vote by standing for policies that work. And by treating each of us women, as though we possess intelligence, reason, and individuality.

When Did Women Agree to Be a Mindless Voting Block?

Women, do you think just like every other woman you know?

Who really believes all women think alike? Or for that matter, that all members of any racial or ethnic group think alike because of the color of their skin or where their ancestors were born? Why let politicians and political parties get away with treating women (or any group) as a unified voting block?

Down With Stereotypes...Ours and Theirs

Reject the efforts of the political parties to stereotype women, and reject the stereotypes about Democrats and Republicans created by the media. Stereotypes are just not good enough. We all need to think past those stereotypes, and *look instead at the real life results of the policies each party stands for.*

Why Do Some Politicians Think Women Can Be Swayed By Emotion Without Facts or Logic?

One goal of this book is to illustrate how politicians present their policy positions in a manner designed to obscure or hide facts by making emotion-based pitches that lure voters, especially women, into supporting things they would never support if they were relying on just the facts.

In an extreme but common example, take the complex problem of dealing with reforming the Medicare program, which is nearly insolvent and cannot continue to meet expenses on its present path. Republicans have introduced various proposals to protect and preserve the program by restructuring it so it doesn't run out of money, to protect seniors. (More on this in Chapter Seven.)

The Agenda Project, a Democrat Party support group, put out a You-Tube video showing a wheelchair-bound grandma being thrown over a cliff, and in the video accuses Republicans who are trying to protect Medicare from insolvency of trying to kill off Medicare recipients. Politicians who share the goal of that Democrat Party support group—which is to create fear among seniors and ignorant voters—say or imply that if Republicans win elections they will let seniors starve.

Everyone has senior relatives. Most of us will be senior citizens some day. No one has advocated leaving seniors vulnerable and impoverished, or advocated for policies that will have that result. This is especially egregious because at least as of the time this book is going to print, Democrats have not put forth any proposal to save Medicare from insolvency. They just fling false accusations at people who are actually trying to solve the problem.

When the Democrats and their followers make wild accusations like this, intelligent discussion of how to reform Medicare is shut off. Responsible elected officials who are trying to solve the problems these programs face are maligned, and voters who pay little attention are manipulated.

Who Tells You What to Think? The Media?

Let me cut right to the chase: if you try to stay informed by reading and tuning into what passes for mainstream journalism in America (the *New York Times*, the *Washington Post*, CBS, ABC, NBC Evening News, the *Los Angeles Times*, etc.), you are being manipulated.

Media Bias in America?

The fact that the media overwhelmingly lean to the left (meaning biased in favor of Democrats and liberal policies, and against Republicans and conservative ideas) has been shown in a multitude of ways over the last four decades.

The University of California at Los Angeles—UCLA—in a very extensive study reported in the Quarterly Journal of Economics, confirmed what news-watchers already know: the vast majority of what is considered "the mainstream media" leans sharply to the left. (http://newsroom.ucla.edu/portal/ucla/Media-Bias-Is-Real-Finds-UCLA-6664.aspx)

One specific and measurable example is the data about media and their voting in presidential elections.

A Media Bias Bonanza

Do you know what the following groups of "journalists" all have in common?

"Reporters, journalists, the White House Press Corps, major newspaper reporters, U.S. newspaper journalists, White House bureau chiefs and correspondents, newspaper editors, campaign journalists, TV and newspaper journalists"

All, repeat all, of the above categories of journalists vote Democrat far more than Republican, and they vote Democrat far more than the rest of America, and/or hold liberal views on policies that are much more liberal than America is.

(Media Research Center compilation of a multitude of studies and surveys http://www.med..iaresearch.org/biasbasics/printer/biasbasics3.asp; accessed June 2, 2012)

So...when you read the newspaper or tune into the evening news, know that what you read or hear is a highly partisan, unbalanced, nonobjective view of the so-called "news."

Democrats mock Fox News as biased. But at the very least, balancing the "news" you get from ABC, NBC, CBS, CNN, MSNBC, the *Washington Post*, the *New York Times*, the *Los Angeles Times*, and all of the other alleged "mainstream news sources" with a little Fox, might get you slightly back toward center from the far left view of the world.

And use the Internet to broaden your news sources. Try the Lucianne.com and American Thinker websites. In the future we may all have to be our own editors in order to get to the most complete and balanced information about the issues of the day. But whatever you do, stop trusting the mainstream media!

One Astoundingly Brazen Example of Media Manipulation

As I write this book, the Trayvon Martin case is ongoing in Florida. Trayvon Martin was a 17-year-old African American teenager who was killed in Sanford, Florida on February 26, 2012. The alleged shooter is a 28-year-old Hispanic man, a neighborhood watch coordinator, named George Zimmerman, who claims he acted in self-defense in response to being beaten by Martin. A great deal of national anguish and turmoil surrounds this case, including protests by black Americans claiming that the failure of police to arrest and charge Zimmerman immediately was a racially motivated decision.

Enter NBC News, reporting on the call to 911 Zimmerman made the night of the shooting. Here is the full transcript of the relevant part of that call between Zimmerman and the 911 dispatcher:

Zimmerman: "We've had some break-ins in my neighborhood and there's a real suspicious guy. It's Retreat View Circle. The best address I can give you is 111 Retreat View Circle. This guy looks like he's up to no good, or he's on drugs or something. It's raining and he's just walking around, looking about."

911 Dispatcher: "Okay. And this guy, is he white, black or Hispanic?"

Zimmerman: "He looks black."

Here is the edited version of that conversation that NBC played on *The Today Show*:

Zimmerman says the following about Martin: *"This guy looks like he's up to no good. He looks black."*

Ladies, the bias you see here is worse than the usual anti-Republican, anti-conservative bias. The NBC-edited excerpt is designed to make Zimmerman sound racist, when he was in fact answering a question. The editing gymnastics follow along with and support the left-wing Democrat/media view of America as a country full of bias, prejudice, and evil—a view that bolsters the Democrat role in America as the party swooping in to save helpless victims in this mean-spirited country.

Another bit of media bias? Zimmerman is reported (but not in the mainstream media) to be a registered Democrat who volunteers tutoring black children, and he is Hispanic. But those three facts do not appear in the narrative that NBC or most of the other supposed mainstream media present. The lack of integrity in our media is almost staggering.

Trayvon Martin's death is, of course, a tragedy, whether or not self-defense was involved. Everyone's hearts rightly go out to Trayvon's family and loved ones because losing a young life is deeply painful and tragic.

Protests about the alleged racist motivation behind the shooting and behind the initial decision not to charge the shooter consumed the news for weeks after the event, and yearning for the unbiased administration of justice was at the core of those marches and protests. It makes the NBC editing decision that much more egregious since it appears to have been a decision designed to fan the flames of racial suspicions and to steer the wheels of justice toward a predetermined "verdict" that racism must have been involved. Although NBC did ultimately terminate the employment of at least one individual involved, we'll never know if that action was due more to public outcry about the editing than a commitment to integrity.

Do Poll Takers Measure— Or Try to Shape—Public Opinion?

When UCLA and many other credible sources tell us that newspapers and other media are biased, what does that tell you about how we should read the polling data those media sources create?

Politicians and candidates, political parties, the media, and interest groups do polling in many cases not to test public opinion but to shape it. Be wary—and stay alert.

There are numerous ways pollsters manipulate poll results, and two of them are (1) by manipulating the list of people they decide to poll, and (2) by asking the question in a way that allows them to get the answer they want.

On Manipulating the List

At the simplest level, just think if you were to poll a group of friends that you know already agree with you on the best vacation spot or their favorite candidate. You could find that "100 percent of Americans surveyed said that New York is the best place for a vacation" or that "100 percent of Americans surveyed like Candidate X better than Candidate Y."

The results wouldn't be a lie, because you really did get 100 percent of those polled to give the answer you wanted. However, the results would also not be truthful, because you didn't ask a "representative sample." You chose people who already agreed with you.

The key is to look behind the data and find out who was polled. If pollsters ask a significant majority of Democrats and few Republicans which candidate they favor, and the Democrats wins the poll, that survey is simply not truthful. Most polls offer the background information on who was surveyed, if you dig deeply enough into the poll.

This tactic of manipulating the list shapes public opinion, because if polls say most people prefer Candidate X, there are many voters who will go for "X" either because they want to vote with the winner (and now they think they know the winner), or because they just assume others who answered the polls probably know more than they do. So those who shape poll results can impact election results.

Many polls ask direct questions such as "which is your favorite candidate," or "who do you support?" But others ask more convoluted questions.

About the "Push" Poll...

Candidates hire experts to do polling, to determine name recognition, or to test how strong support is for their campaigns.

Push polls add a feature. They will ask for example, "Do you support Candidate Joe or Candidate Susan?" If the person being polled says "Candidate Joe," the pollster asks, "Would your opinion change if you knew that Candidate Joe was investigated for failure to pay income taxes?" Or, "Would your opinion be different if you knew that Candidate Joe supports tax increases?" Or, "would your opinion change if you knew that Candidate Susan opposes tax increases but Candidate Joe supports those increases?" You get the point. By the end of the call, the person being polled no longer supports Candidate Joe! And this is a simplified version.

I am not suggesting that all polls are unreliable, but I am suggesting that poll results are often a political tool to shape public opinion, rather than to report it. Savvy voters should not accept reported poll results at face value.

Twelve of the Top Tricks Politicians Use to Fool Voters

An entire book could be dedicated to just this subject: politicians use psychology and tricks to manipulate voters into supporting them. They confuse voters so they don't have to discuss the real issues. They sidetrack voters so they lose sight of the real facts and issues, and they redirect voter attention away from their critics. They use emotion, contorted logic, and tricky "logic-less" leaps.

Here are a few examples of how politicians trick voters.

1. The "My motive is good, therefore no questions can be asked" tactic

Politician Joe tells voters that his policy idea—like extending unemployment insurance benefits for as long as it takes someone to find a job —is offered out of compassion. He rallies support for the idea by making voters and elected officials think they will be seen as selfish unless they agree to support his idea. By focusing the discussion on his good motive of concern for the unemployed, Politician Joe avoids having to prove that his idea represents sound policy. Will extending unemployment benefits in this manner actually help the unemployment problem, or perpetuate it?

The *motive* of compassion is all that Joe has had to offer.

A real life example of this in 2010 was the passage of the Obamacare healthcare reform bill, when supporters (Democrats and the media) focused on concern for the allegedly large number of uninsured. Almost no media focused on the failures and weaknesses of similar socialized medicine programs in Canada and England, nor did supporters have to answer why the American proposal would result in any better system than Canada and England have.

Given the legal and fiscal problems the bill has already created, not to mention the fact that estimates for its costs have skyrocketed, it would have been a great thing for America if the media had pursued facts and data instead of being drawn into the emotion of the supposed good motives behind this bill, and the historic drama of creating socialized medicine in America. A good motive is not a policy analysis!

2. The "just listen to my story (and not the facts)" trick

Most politicians and the media tell "real-life" anecdotal stories to make their points. Speechwriters and advisors encourage this because stories, instead of just plain facts, are memorable. But the emotion of the story often overrides the facts.

One example during the 1996 congressional debate on reform of government assistance programs was a news story by an obviously sympathetic reporter. The bill, the 1996 Personal Responsibility and Work Opportunity Reconciliation Act (PRWORA), included limits on how long mentally and physically healthy individuals could receive government assistance. There were lifetime limits as well as work requirements.

One reporter interviewed a young single teenage mother who lived with her child and her own mother, and the three were featured in a story designed to create opposition to PRWORA. The essence of the story was that if the reform passed, this young mother would be required to look for a job, but she felt strongly that she wanted to stay home full-time with her baby.

The conclusion that viewers were being not-so-subtly urged to make is that reform was bad for families, "mean" in fact.

Nowhere did the reporter remind viewers that many mothers and fathers are forced to work outside the home when they have babies or small children, because they need the income to pay their bills. And those who work are paying taxes to the government, that in turn was giving that money to recipients of government assistance so they (the government-assisted mothers) would not have to work.

3. The impossible choices method

This is a popular tactic used by politicians on the left that is very effective in silencing discussion and shutting down opposition. Here are some examples:

"You must support my affirmative action proposal, or else you are a racist." Or "If you don't support this bi-lingual education plan, you are intolerant." Giving the reasonable thinker no way out of the trap leaves the American Left the victor too often, because most folks do not wish to have unpleasant confrontations. So people are silenced, and they wonder if they are the only ones who don't see those as the only two choices.

One response tactic is to just say: "I don't agree with your two choices; you don't get to decide what the two choices are."

4. The "don't listen to my opponent...she is an idiot" tactic

Although many may have used this tactic over decades and centuries, it seems rampant now. The basic tactic is to respond to serious questions or criticisms of policy proposals by attacking the person raising the criticism.

So when a political opponent points out that some policy is not financially sound or has some specific flaw, the response is "don't listen to her, she is an idiot."

Once the "she is an idiot" concept has been launched, many voters will never consider what "the idiot" said, which is exactly why this method can be effective. In fact, when you recognize this tactic being used, tune into the "idiot" because he or she is probably making a good point!

5. The "dishonest labeling to hide an unpopular idea" trick

This involves choosing a label for an unjustifiable new law or new policy that is exactly the opposite of what the new item will actually do, so maybe the people will not notice.

This ploy was on full display when in 2009 many Democrats in Washington supported the Employee Free Choice Act, also known as Card Check. Employee Free Choice was the Democrat-sponsored and union-supported proposed law that would have destroyed an employee's "free choice" to vote "no" on unionizing his work place.

In place of the time-honored and legally-required voting procedure where workers vote in secrecy (like we all do every election day), the bill would have authorized union bosses and officials to approach employees at any time or place (say a dark alley or parking lot), "ask" them if they wanted to join the union, and secure the employee's signature on a card to confirm they wanted to join. Once a majority of employees had "voluntarily" signed, the union had "won" the election.

The Employee Free Choice Act was union-empowering legislation designed to eliminate employees' free choice to decline to support a union. But the Democrats who backed the proposal explained their support by claiming they were standing for "basic workers' rights" and "ending discrimination and harassment in the workplace," *although the bill would have done exactly the opposite.* (A federal agency, at the behest of the Democrats, is still trying to force it through using regulations because Congress would not pass it.)

6. Falsely threatening a bad consequence to avoid dealing with the real issue

During the 2011 debt ceiling debate, some Democrats claimed that we had to raise the debt ceiling, or else we would have to cut military pay or withhold Social Security checks. They knew most Americans don't want to cut military pay or withhold Social Security checks. But neither of those was required if the debt ceiling was not raised; they were just a few of the many options Congress could have chosen to deal with a short term cash flow problem.

Raising the fear of cutting military pay distracted public attention from the serious issue of endlessly spiraling debt and allowed the Democrats who were advocating for unrestrained increase in the debt limit to falsely appear to be taking the moral high road.

Don't be duped. It is hard to speak in broad terms about this phenomenon, but it is real and quite common. Don't accept at face value that whatever is being asked for must be done instantly or else our seniors and/or other sympathetic groups in society will suffer.

7. Stirring up anger, then appealing to the anger you just stirred up

Anger tends to generate a feeling of righteous indignation, and then people think they must be right because they are so angry about some issue. When Democrats expressed and still express support for the Occupy Wall Street protesters of 2011 and 2012, whose message is largely "give us other people's money and give us everything we want for free," and when Democrats vilify the achievers, the wealthy individuals, and businesses as "not paying their fair share," they are engaged in an overt class warfare attack. They want to make the average American angry with successful individuals and businesses.

Once liberals have succeeded in enraging the ignorant, they pile on by depicting themselves as the rescuers of America who stand up to these "villains" (they created) and then they enlist voter support for whatever it is the Democrats wanted to do all along.

8. The slogan slingers

Slogans can be grossly misleading, and often do not mean anything. They are intentionally that way. Slogans are memorable, easily repeatable, and tend to invoke emotion, not thinking. "Yes We Can" is a perfect example. It is fun to say (for some people), it has a feeling of empowerment and standing up for (or against?) some (vague, unspoken) enemy. But "Yes We Can" do what?

Democrats in America are currently onto the slogan "Stop the GOP's War on Women," that is simultaneously the most idiotic and yet malicious slogan they have come up with recently. The slogan came out of the debate over the policy question of whether the federal government should force religious institutions such as Catholic colleges to offer birth control as a benefit under their insurance policies when birth control violates the teachings of that religious institution. This is at least a serious question. Thoughtful, intelligent people can differ. But this is an example of *how* slogans can be used to avoid tough questions, to avoid discussing ideas, to avoid defending the substance of what a party or candidate stands for.

It's interesting to note that historically Socialists and Communists were especially likely to embrace slogans that similarly had no broadly understood meaning but served the purpose of simultaneously engaging the populace on an emotional basis, increasing support for the slogan-creators, and utterly eliminating rational conversation over the merits of the ideas they were proposing. Lenin called for "peace, land, bread" as he crushed the freedom of individuals and forced them into working on collectivist farms he had seized from landowners.

9. *False before-and-after, cause-and-effect claims*

The textbook example is that the rooster crows every morning, then the sun rises shortly thereafter, but the rooster did not make the sun rise. But in the far more serious political context, claims that a policy went into place and later something in the economy or the world improved, are made to suggest that the policy caused the improvement. Before and after claims should make sense—logically.

10. *The hurling absurdities such as "the other side wants to starve your grandmother" tactic*

I believe that most Americans are good, honest, and moral people. When anyone (and it is usually the far left Democrats who do this) starts saying that the motive for some policy idea is to starve someone's grand-mother or make senior citizens eat cat food (and yes, Democrat leaders have said these things), it is time for Americans to call time-out, to demand more honest and intelligent discussion of issues and policies.

This tactic is especially on parade and absurd in the area of environmental issues. Environmentalists (and some elected Democrats) agitating for some new regulation or limitation will assert "Republicans just do not care about clean air or clean water." As if there were some other secret stash of air and water the Republicans and their children and grandchildren can turn to in the future.

Usually this absurdities tactic is used when the accuser has no genuine answer for the points some opponent is making. So when you hear someone doing this, recognize that they probably are at their wits' end because they are wrong!

11. The bullying by mockery tool, or "you just can't say that!"

No one likes to be mocked or to have others think they are ignorant, which is why mockery is such a successful bullying tool. Have you noticed how some subjects just cannot be discussed because the media and the Democrats have mocked those who raise those subjects as ignorant?

One great example is the global warming debate, in which Democrats and the media label anyone who dares question the "global warming is real and manmade and dangerous" liberal orthodoxy as a "denier." This is meant to signal that people who question the Al Gore–based global warming theory are as ignorant, or worse, as evil as the truly idiotic and malicious who deny the Holocaust. The mockery is designed to make intelligent and thoughtful people afraid to speak—you just can't say that you challenge the global warming liberal orthodoxy.

Climatologists and other genuine experts, in growing numbers, are expressing doubts about the Al Gore global warming theory. The world now knows about the repeated attempts by scientists who are global warming supporters to mislead the public by hiding and misrepresenting and making up data. Yet the mockers' reaction is to increase their venom, instead of trying to figure out the facts. (More on the global warming news in Chapter Ten.)

12. And the granddaddy of them all—the political correctness "silencer"

Political correctness (the noun), or politically correct (the adjective) or "PC," have had an enormous impact on American culture. Some of that impact is positive, to the extent we speak more thoughtfully about sensitive subjects. As one example, a good friend of mine is the mother of a young man who is autistic and this friend welcomed the use of the word "typical" in reference to her son's nonautistic or healthy peers, rather than "normal." While sometimes it can be hard to keep up with the latest "PC" language changes, the overall effort to have Americans speak respectfully toward one another is positive.

But another kind of political correctness has had an extremely detrimental impact on the ability of Americans to speak about important subjects. This PC-ness is the kind whereby we are supposed to show extreme deference to certain viewpoints or sensitivities at the expense of being able to talk about facts and truth. And politicians use political correctness to avoid discussing facts they cannot deal with, and to bully voters into supporting their views. One example (among thousands) is in the arena of education.

Liberal politicians point to poorly performing public schools—places where the dropout rate is tragically high, and the students perform badly on standardized testing. The usual liberal position is to argue "we need to spend more money—raise taxes—look at all of those wonderful schools in suburbia that have more money and the kids do better." Blaming insufficient funding is politically comfortable, politically correct.

But did you know that the public schools in Washington, D.C. (as one example) are among the most poorly performing schools in the country and that in recent years they spent the most per pupil in the entire country? And that we Americans have doubled our per-pupil spending over the last 30 years (even adjusted for inflation), yet student performance fell? And that more and more studies show that parental involvement, influence, pressure, or the lack of it, is among the top factors impacting student performance? That teachers' unions, that have a stranglehold control over the Democrat Party, significantly influence how wisely and effectively your academic tax dollars are spent and incessantly try to block the development of alternative education plans such as charter schools and especially voucher programs that often bring provably better academic results?

It is not politically correct to bring up these points in the discussion of the future of academics and public schools in America. But if we cannot talk truth, how will we solve anything? Refusing to be bullied by the political correctness police is vital.

How Different REALLY Are Today's Republican and Democrat Parties? What Are Their Default Modes?

Because our gender gap data says that women are slightly more likely to vote Democrat than Republican, I want to take some time to talk with you about where the two parties stand today, in terms of their broad stated policy goals, their default modes when facing challenges, and some of the tactics and approaches they choose.

Some people claim that the Republicans and Democrats in America today are similar, and only offer mildly varying approaches for how to deal with America's issues. They could not be more wrong.

A few disclaimers before we get started: not every elected official of either party always stands up for or votes for every position his or her respective party holds; not every new law or bill completely aligns with the party views of the sponsor; neither party has always held true in every circumstance to its party's platform.

The Democrat and the Republican Parties are far apart today in America, not just in policy proposals, but in their views of what America and government are all about. They have totally opposite default modes.

The Democrat Default Mode

For Democrats, the answer to America's every problem is to grow government—in size, scope, and power—to raise taxes, and to create more and farther-reaching government programs. Whether the issues are unemployment, Americans falling behind on their mortgages, an imperfect (though best on earth) healthcare system, or any other economic or societal condition, their knee-jerk view is always that government can and should take charge of more and more of what used to be the private sector and the free enterprise system. Their policies inherently (and I would argue, intentionally) grow economic and social *dependence* on government, by more and more Americans.

They are cultivating future Democrat voters.

> *"I predict future happiness for Americans if they can prevent the government from wasting the labors of the people under the pretense of taking care of them."*
> —Thomas Jefferson, Third American President (1801–1809), author of the Declaration of Independence

Democrats ultimately prefer big government control despite the resulting diminishment of individual liberty. The result of their views is not only the creation of vast and expensive federal programs to meet our every need. The other and very sad outcome is a whole class of Americans who live, in the words of black author and activist Star Parker, on "Uncle Sam's Plantation." In utter economic dependence. (More on this in Chapter Six.)

Today's Democrat Party default mode is to trust government, not the people, to solve our problems, and to trust the federal government over the governments of the 50 states.

> *"The natural progress of things is for liberty to yield and government to gain ground."*
> —Thomas Jefferson, Third American President (1801–1809), author of the Declaration of Independence

The Republican Default Mode

For Republicans, the answer to many of the same issues is to trust the greatness, ingenuity, and goodness of the American people to solve many of our challenges through the vehicle of the free enterprise system. They support and prefer smaller government to bigger government, and they support respect for the idea set out in the Constitution that the federal government is a one of limited powers.

They respect the Americans who serve their country as governors and state legislators as much as those who happen to serve in Washington. Republicans tend to believe that growing dependence on government tends to erode the spirit of and commitment to mutual and societal responsibilities that would otherwise be carried out by individuals, families, and charities.

The difference between the Republican and Democrat default modes was on full display in the summer of 2010, when Democrats passed the healthcare system takeover in secret meetings and in defiance of overwhelming polling that showed that Americans strongly opposed the Democrats' socialized medicine prescription.

Democrats are determined to take care of us—whether we want them to or not.

In Chapter Five I discuss healthcare and include in that discussion the numerous ways in which the healthcare takeover was both unwise and unwelcome.

The Republicans' default mode is to trust the people through their resourcefulness and native abilities to solve most of their problems through the freedoms offered in the free enterprise system, to trust state governments to handle many issues, to recognize that big-government federal programs that are inherently one-size-fits-all often fail to resolve the problems they are intended to address, or are ridiculously inefficient. Republicans try to keep the massive power of the federal government under control by limiting it to the powers spelled out for it in the Constitution.

> *"I believe there are more instances of the abridgement of freedom of the people by gradual and silent encroachments by those in power than by violent and sudden usurpations."*
> *—James Madison, Fourth American President (1809–1817), father of the Constitution, co-author of the Federalist Papers*

The Fish-Givers Versus the Teachers

Most of us know the ancient adage "if you give a man a fish, he will eat for a day. Teach him to fish and he will eat for life." That adage summarizes succinctly one of the big differences between *today's* Democrat (the fish-givers) and Republican (the teachers) Parties' approaches to the problems America faces.

Another great modern example of the difference between the default modes of the Democrat versus the Republican Party is in the area of federal entitlement spending.

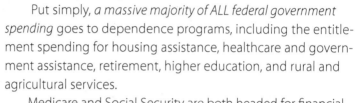

Put simply, *a massive majority of ALL federal government spending* goes to dependence programs, including the entitlement spending for housing assistance, healthcare and government assistance, retirement, higher education, and rural and agricultural services.

Medicare and Social Security are both headed for financial insolvency. Republicans offer solutions. Democrats reply by flinging slogans and absurd accusations. And promising more spending. (Read more about this in Chapter Six.)

Democrats are known as the party that will always expand eligibility for federal entitlement programs, always raise spending for food stamps, and unemployment insurance, and always think of new programs and entitlements that will soon become "rights." They will give out fish. This fish-giving brings the Democrats enormous control, because what does the poor guy who did not learn how to fish do the day after he got the free fish handed to him? He goes back for another one. This fish-giving creates a class of helpless and weak citizens who have no recourse but to go back to the government for more. And then to vote to keep the fish-givers in power so he can get a fish again for many more tomorrows.

On the other hand, the party of those who teach the man to fish (the Republicans) will be accused of cruelty. "Why make him work—why not just give him the fish?" or "the rich already have so many fish—they should just give some to the poorer guy who doesn't have enough fish." The self-sufficiency that will result from learning to fish will give the recipient the dignity of independence, and the prospect of prosperity for his whole life, but that does not have the emotional appeal of the falsely-generous sounding liberal "just give it to him."

Ashamed of Versus Grateful for America's Greatness, Abundance, and Strength

I'll talk more about this idea in Chapter Ten on energy and the environment, but you can start to recognize this theme easily as you listen to politicians speak. Think how frequently you hear Democrats speaking of Americans and/or America as "unfair," "greedy," or "using more than our fair share of the resources." There has been a great deal of talk in the last three years demonizing the successful achievers in our society that has led even long term Democrat donors to criticize the Democrats' conduct in villainizing them. Democrat leaders frequently elevate new groups of citizens as the latest "victims" of some perceived unfairness—engendering resentment about American society. And they criticize oil and gas consumption as greedy or selfish and block access to the wildly abundant resources right here in the U.S. that would eliminate our need to depend on imported oil.

Republicans have a more grateful sentiment and tone about America's abundance, an unapologetic stance about our nation's prosperity, strength, and historic greatness. You hear it in their words and see it in their policies.

Dividing Americans Around Race and Ethnicity Versus Uniting Americans Around Founding Ideals

Democrat National Chairwoman Debbie Wasserman-Schultz staked a claim for her party as the one that should be made up of all voters she labels as minorities, including women. Even President Obama's re-election campaign website lists supporters in groups of hyphenated Americans, made up of people whose only commonality is where their ancestors were from or the color of their skin. Hyphenated America is divided America, an America made up of competing groups. It creates a perpetual "what's in it for my group" attitude.

Republicans unite around basic ideas like limited government, support for the Constitution, personal responsibility, inspiring the free enterprise system to grow and prosper, individual liberty, and so on. The beauty of a good idea, a right idea, is that it is good for everyone, regardless of background. It offers a way to unite and not divide.

The Democrats' CVVR Mode (No Republican Equivalent or Opposite Exists)

Have you noticed an abundance of crises recently? Democrats have mastered a technique I call CVVR mode: Crisis, Villain, Victim, Rescuer.

Democrats use this to get other politicians and the American public to support what they want them to do. The most recent example, which I discuss in greater detail in Chapter Five on the healthcare takeover, was the creation of a healthcare crisis or insurance crisis (neither one existed), that they embellished by making villains out of insurance companies, doctors, hospitals, and anyone else they could locate. The victims part was easy—all of those (greatly exaggerated in number) Americans were made to feel victimized and downtrodden. The rescuer is always the same—the Democrats swoop in to play rescuer to the crisis they have created.

There are a couple of telling surveys that show how effective the Democrats have been in turning thought and in duping people into thinking a crisis is occurring. A June, 2008 ABC News/*USA Today*/Kaiser Family Foundation poll found that 89 percent of Americans were satisfied with their healthcare. Other polls found similar results.(http://www.weeklystandard.com/Content/Public/Articles/000/000/016/943pfdxe.aspnn).

Yet a year later almost the same percentage of Americans said they thought the U.S. healthcare needed to be fundamentally changed or completely rebuilt. (http://www.republicanassemblies.org/klein-the-matter-with-myths/; both accessed June 2, 2012)

All that happened during that one year between those two polls was a drumbeat by Democrats telling Americans we had a crisis in the healthcare system. And they created one!

Ladies, the remaining chapters will tell you about challenges America faces and how the parties propose to handle them. All of us envision a world where our children and theirs, and everyone's children's children, are prosperous, participating, productive members of a robust society filled with opportunity. You just cannot get there under the "fish-giver, " crisis creator, division-producing model that today's Democrat Party embraces and pushes. As you examine the facts for yourself and then talk to your friends and family, I think you'll agree.

Did You Know?...Stories and Facts to Share Chapter Three

Ladies, in this Chapter's DYK's, I am offering some tips you can take with you into discussions on many subjects related to politics and voting.

If your friends say "It doesn't matter how I vote, one vote won't matter," you can say:

"Actually, the women's vote runs the country! We vote in higher numbers than men and we need to be on top of the issues—all the issues. We must understand the impact of economic policies, tax-and-spend decisions, and all sorts of things, to really vote to protect America's future—for ourselves and our kids."

If your friends say "But I vote to support women's issues ... so I vote Democrat."

Ladies, I want to tell you about my friend, Julie. She told me she votes Democrat because of "women's issues," and when I asked her what she meant by that, she said, "well, you know, choice." So I said "So you are strongly pro-choice?," to which she replied "well, not totally...I'm not sure...". She was voting out of a perverse sense of duty to "women" when she didn't even agree on the supposed "women's issue!"

My point is that some women choose to vote Democrat in a kind of lock-step, style of thinking, and are not even sure why. So, question your friends (nicely) who say they always vote Democrat, about the reasons they do that. Question yourself—be sure you are voting based on facts, and not hype or emotional manipulation!

Facts to share—Here are just a few

Democrats think they own the women's vote—that's offensive! The head of the Democrat National Committee is actually on record lumping all women and all racial and ethnic minorities together politically and claiming in essence that her party owns your vote. Make her and them earn your vote!

Is there really a media bias?

Ladies, whole books have been written on just this subject, and I encourage you, if you have any lingering doubt, to just read one study on the subject---the study conducted by the very liberal UCLA, which found unquestionable media bias against Republicans and in favor of Democrats. [http://newsroom.ucla.edu/portal/ucla/Media-Bias-Is-Real-Finds-UCLA-6664.aspx] Hopefully the next time you hear a story of the "evils" of some conservative policy or candidate, you'll decide to do some research to find out what is really true.

Recognize the political manipulation the politicians try— and don't get fooled again!

Don't get bullied by the impossible choices trick—you don't have to support raising the national debt ceiling to protect our soldiers receiving their paychecks.

Tune into the critics that politicians are calling "idiots!"

If politicians are stirring up anger at the latest villain they've identified—the pharmaceutical companies, the doctors who will supposedly unnecessarily remove kids' tonsils, insurance companies, or whoever the latest Democrat-created villain is, refuse to join in the fray. Make politicians justify their policies with facts.

Recognize when federal spending is the fish-giving kind

Our current social spending is largely the "fish-giving" kind, in which we are giving free things to people, such as food and food stamps, housing assistance, straight-out cash using the EBT system, and a whole host of other items, with little or no expectation of moving these precious Americans off dependence and into a life of self-reliance and dignity. Stand up for the idea of a hand-up and not a handout, and consider what kinds of programs the two political parties are offering.

Decline to be divided!

Don't agree with the liberal mindset that says "because you are a woman you stand for 'this' and you believe in 'that.' " Agree with yourself to be a strong and independent thinker who needs to be convinced of the virtues of any new policy ideas, and don't let politicians treat you as a member of a group. Make them respect your individuality and your unique worldview.

Although I won't hold back on sharing with you how strongly and in fact urgently I feel about how far left the Democrat Party has drifted away from the America we all love, I will remind you of my own Democrat-voting background in my younger days. I know that lots of wonderful American women have voted Democrat historically. I just want to convince you that the Democrats *of today* are out of touch with what made America great, and I think it is our job as voters to bring America home again.

★ ★ Chapter Four ★ ★

She Works Hard for Her Money

Taxing, Spending, and Jobs
Rewriting the Laws of Economics

**Can We Talk…About the national budget, taxes, spending, jobs—
the economic stuff. In plain English, please. (Because even if these are
not issues that drive the women's vote—they directly impact our lives.)**

What's the big deal about free market economics that Republicans support anyway?

How different is that from the controlled economy/collectivist ideas that
the Democrats are pushing?

Politicians throw out so many statistics that it's hard to
figure out what's true and what's a bunch of baloney! Democrats are always claiming "The rich don't pay their fair share!"
Republicans say, "Government doesn't tax too little, it spends
too much!"

What are the facts, the real numbers, about our taxes?
And about how we spend our national family budget?

And what about jobs? We need jobs, and our daughters,
sons, parents, and grandchildren need jobs. Can't the government do something about that?

Let's talk about this!

Ladies, many of you have likely read about the financial disaster that has befallen Greece. One Greek "woman on the street" interview I read reported that when asked what she thought could be done to salvage Greece from economic ruin, her answer was, "If they would just tax the rich, it would solve everything." That's the sound-bite world of economic policy. So simple sounding, but no actual connection to reality.

"Economics is boring... I care about people."
(So said a Democrat-voting friend of mine.)
America needs women to use their compassion and our wisdom, to think economically.
Because if we don't have some basic understanding about economics, politicians fool us into accepting ideas that hurt our children, America's future, and ourselves.

Topics We'll Talk About in Chapter Four
Where Are We Economically as a Country—and What Should We Do About It?

Just What Are the "Laws" of Economics in a Free Market System?

Twelve of the "Universal Truths" in Free Market Systems

So Where Is America Today on Free Markets Versus Controlled Markets?

The Moral Case for Capitalism and Free Markets

Where Should Jobs Come From?

The Federal Government Spending Bonanza—What Could Go Wrong?

Vote for Free Markets!

Did You Know?...Stories and Facts to Share

★ ★ ★

> *"One of the wonderful things about free markets is that the path to greater wealth comes not from looting, plundering, and enslaving one's fellow man, as it has throughout most of human history, but by serving and pleasing him."*
> *—Walter E. Williams, Economist, Author, Professor*

Dealing With Today's Economic Realities

Americans are out of work: The official unemployment rate early in 2012 is 8.3%, but the "real" unemployment rate is almost twice that.

(The "real rate" includes those who have given up looking for a job. That's right, when people just give up looking because they cannot find a job, the government no longer counts them in the unemployment figures. How handy is that little trick to make the economy look better than it is?)

Your federal government spends money it doesn't have: The federal government debt (which is your debt, *our* debt, everyone's *children's* debt) is nearly sixteen trillion dollars, that's $16,000,000,000,000. And rising daily.

Half of all Americans pay no taxes, while the top 1 percent pay up to 40 percent of the taxes, and one-quarter of Americans—that's 25 percent—bear *almost the entire country's tax burden.*

Seventy percent of America's budget is spent on dependency programs, meaning programs that pay out to some citizens money the government took in taxes, for programs that make people more dependent on government.

Where Are We Economically as a Country—and What Should We Do About It?

How each political party deals with these economic realities reveals a lot about at least two things:

1. The parties' default modes.

2. What party leaders think our country's economic system
    is supposed to be: free market or collectivist/socialist.

These are the parties' default modes, the two very different directions
they head when America faces troubles.

The Democrat default mode (DDM) is to use the federal government's
power to raise taxes, to pull more money out of the hands of the people and
businesses, to increase government assistance payments of many kinds,
and to orchestrate or attempt to facilitate job creation by putting the money
just removed from the economy via taxes back into the economy via stimulus and other targeted, incentivizing maneuvers.

In essence, the DDM relies on government power and control over
the economic system to orchestrate job creation. This approach has failed
miserably, as we'll see in how poorly the stimulus performed in creating
jobs. This Democrat approach, along with viewing income redistribution
as a legitimate goal of the tax system, and other proposals I'll describe later,
is at the least a mild form of socialism. This is also referred to as Keynesian
economics, after John Maynard Keynes.

The Republican default mode (RDM) to deal with economic challenges
is to lower tax levels and reduce the regulatory burden on businesses, so
that businesses are naturally incentivized to retain their employees, and to
make plans to grow, and so individuals are confident enough in the economic and tax future that they move forward building and investing in
businesses. Businesses built by American people create jobs.

The RDM trusts in and relies on the industrious spirit of the American people, their basic work ethic, and their desire for economic wellbeing. Real private sector jobs are not "created" by government in the free
market system. The RDM approach leaves freedom and the free markets
that brought America's historic prosperity and abundance, for the most
part, intact. Milton Friedman is the modern father of free market economics.

Free Markets or Controlled Markets?

The free market/Friedman/Republican/conservative line of thinking in economics is often contrasted with the controlled economy/Keynesian/Democrat/liberal ideology. While not all economic policy issues fall neatly into one camp or the other, and no country has ever pursued an entirely pure free market approach, the two schools of thought offer one way to think about policy proposals.

America has historically embraced the free market approach, and the recent Democrat move toward increasing government control over the economy represents a significant philosophical and practical departure from America's historic free market economic policy.

Just What Are the "Laws" of Economics in a Free Market System?

I do not attempt in this book to delve into high-level economic analysis. I won't even review the law of supply and demand basic economic rules. Instead I'll just present some basic economic concepts, basic truths that are also common sense but that need to be talked about in this era when political speeches include relentless repetition of "tax-cuts-for-the-rich" hysteria, which is really just economic baby-talk.

Economics based on free markets are in part just observations about natural human behavior, government, and society, all based on the realities that there are never unlimited resources, and that we all make choices because we cannot afford to have everything we want.

Are There Really "Laws" of Economics?

Think of the laws of economics as laws like the "law" that water will freeze below 32 degrees, or the laws of aerodynamics that describe how and why birds and planes can fly. They are just facts.

People cannot and do not make these laws of economics, nor can governments or people change them. Governments can attempt to manipulate around them, to shape people's behavior, but even coercion does not really change these laws—it just forces unwelcome results contrary to these laws.

Twelve of the "Universal Truths" in a Free Market System

Universal Truth Number One: The Government Has No Money

No, I am not talking about the fact that the United States is in serious debt. I am talking about the fact that government, all by itself, has no money. It only has any money at all when it takes money from people or businesses that worked to earn it.

The Reality Island Story. Consider the idea of an island with thousands of people living on it, including you, with no government or societal structure. The islanders discover at some point that chaos is not as much fun as they had hoped and decide to form a government, meaning a group of people they select to be in charge.

Whatever kind of government the Reality Island residents form, it will have no money until one of two things happens:

1. The people agree to a tax system, or
2. The government uses sheer power and seizes money, things, or land from people (like socialist and communist governments do).

Next, the islanders and the new government will face the questions of how much of people's money government should get, and for what purposes. Residents should be telling the government what things government needs to be doing for the people, what things it shouldn't be doing, what things the people can do for themselves and should not have to be paying the government to do.

Use Reality Island as an imaginary basis for re-evaluating our American government.

The Reality Island story offers us a fresh perspective, a new way to think about any proposal a politician makes for a new government program or new project. When you hear a new idea that requires government spending, consider:

Is this new benefit or program a legitimate use of the money government collects in taxes? Or is it something that…

★ Each individual should provide for himself or herself, or

★ Some people should provide through the private sector business, or

★ We should turn to private, voluntarily funded charities to address?

Universal Truth Number Two: Whatever Government Spends is Your Money. It is *Always* Your Money, Ladies

You and your parents, friends, neighbors, and relatives pay for everything the government pays for, gives away, or provides for free.

This should be obvious, and flows necessarily from Universal Truth Number One, but remember one thing—every time someone says "the government should pay for _____," they are asking you and your friends and family to pay for it.

So when the Democrat-supported Occupy Wall Street protesters demanded that the government should pay off their student loans, they are talking about spending your money and your family's money to pay back the student loans they chose to take out and for which they received the value of a college education.

Envision government spending as similar to going house to house, knocking on doors, and asking your neighbors to contribute some money so you can pool it together. Asking for money to help provide for mutual defense against invaders might seem rational, but asking everyone to kick in to pay off a college loan debt you chose to incur is a whole different story.

Universal Truth Number Three: The Economy is Interconnected—There is an Inevitable Law of the Ripple Effect

You will often hear politicians urging that the "rich" or "the corporations" should pay higher taxes or more of their fair share. Normally this is done in a manner that suggests successful individuals and corporations are somehow bad guys and the politicians are swooping in to save Americans from these rich, mean villains.

What would your family do if you knew you were suddenly facing higher taxes than you planned for?

Consider for a moment what you and most Americans would do if you had a big, unexpected and unavoidable expense arise, such as a much higher tax bill than you budgeted for. Unless you had a big pile of cash on hand, you would look at your budget and decide what to cut out. It might be a vacation, or a newer car, or a series of smaller things, such as deciding not to eat out as often as you used to. You would adjust your spending behavior to deal with the big upcoming tax bill.

New taxes would have a ripple effect in your world.

The Ripple Effect is the same everywhere
For businesses…

Because of the Law of the Ripple Effect, when the government increases taxes on big corporations and small businesses, those corporations and small businesses react the same way you would to an impending tax increase. They make financial adjustments. Corporations lay off employees, cancel plans to expand that included hiring new workers, cut hours of the existing employees, or make other adjustments.

Suppose, for example, a corporation decides as a result of a large impending tax increase to cut costs by laying off 50 employees. Each of those 50 people goes home to his or her family, and those families make adjustments to their family budget because they will now have less income. They decide they cannot afford their kids' piano lessons, or new soccer uniforms, or to take the family out to dinner, or a thousand other possible economic choices. Each of those 50 families whose breadwinner was laid off makes these kinds of decisions.

Then the local family-owned restaurant, where the families of those 50 laid off workers normally ate on Friday nights, suffers a great drop-off in business, and lays off 12 of its wait staff. So those 12 people who formerly made their living at the restaurant go back to their homes and take a look at their budgets and start planning their budget cuts.

All of these families now shop less at the local grocery store, buy fewer clothes, and purchase fewer items in the stores, so the stores start to lose money, so they in turn lay off workers.

And on and on and on.

For the rich....

The same ripple effect is true for raising taxes on "the rich." Everyone has a budget, and even very wealthy people make adjustments that have an inevitable ripple effect. The budget cuts the wealthy make may be not hiring that new person as an assistant (who was counting on the job), or not making a planned donation to the local charity that helps the poor or the sick, or not providing the seed money (loan) for a new business that would have provided employment for the business founder and her staff.

No one lives in an economic vacuum

Natural market fluctuations regularly occur, based on forces outside of the political realm, and cause their own ripple effects.

But when politicians urge that successful individuals and corporations should pay more in taxes, remember that if they succeed in getting that tax increase, there will always be a harmful negative effect on all of the families and businesses hit by that ripple. And when some politicians' (Democrats) relentless "default mode" is to urge raising taxes on business to meet every problem, uncertainty settles in and businesses hold on tight to their cash. They do not expand, they do not hire. And high unemployment rates remain the same or get worse.

Universal Truth Number Four: The Zero Sum Fallacy the "Limited Pie Myth" about the American Economy.

It is so important to understand this truth, because liberal politicians frequently try to sell the idea that if someone becomes wealthy, that means someone else lost some wealth. This is completely false.

A prime example of uninformed Americans believing the limited pie myth is the Democrat party supported Occupy Wall Street movement of 2011 and 2012, in which small numbers of people literally camped out for months in parks and other locations in major cities, demanding the forced redistribution of America's wealth, and protesting the unfair concentration of wealth in a small group of Americans (their "99 percent versus 1 percent" mantra). The protestors demanded to be given some share of the wealth other Americans have. (We'll save discussion of the unequal distribution of wealth in America for later in this chapter.)

The Occupiers seem to believe that the U.S. economy is something like a pie chart, with a firmly set and unchangeable size and limit, and taking away someone else's share of the pie is the only way to improve their own plight in life. They do not know they can grow the pie themselves. (Or they'd prefer to avoid the hard work growing the pie requires.) The reality is that the U.S. economy grows and shrinks regularly. People choose to create new products, offer new services, and others want these products and services, and the "American Pie" grows bigger.

Here is just one great "America is not a limited pie" story:

An Irish friend in Dallas, Texas baked shortbread cookies, using her family's original Irish recipe, for a neighborhood party a few years ago. Many of her friends loved and devoured them. So when the next gathering came along, and the next, people kept asking her to make them. Then one wise friend suggested that she go into a catering business selling those cookies, and she did. This led to many more months of developing a business plan (and working all the time), and then her Original Irish Shortbread Cookies became a new American small business.

This friend, who is from Ireland and still speaks with an engaging Irish brogue, had always felt disappointed that most Americans associated only leprechauns, St. Patrick's Day, and beer with her homeland and began to consider expanding her wildly-successful business beyond just the shortbread cookies. She now sells Irish linens and tea towels, and all sorts of Irish original products and foods.

So, the Original Irish Shortbread Cookie Company helped to grow the American Pie. And people all over America do this every day with their own hard work and ingenuity.

Most of us move around within America's income brackets

On top of that, people's economic "place" in the upper, middle, and lower income brackets shifts at various points in their lives based on new and changing jobs, education, family circumstances, and an infinite number other life issues. I have been in all three brackets, more than once in my life. Many Americans have. It comes with the package of freedom and free markets.

Universal Truth Number Five: Businesses, Even Big Corporations, are Just Made Up of People. Attacking "Business" is Attacking People.

Studies show that many women choose careers outside of the business world, and if that's true for you it may be that you end up thinking like my good friend who told me she always "votes to help people, not businesses." She even wondered aloud why politicians seem to talk so much about businesses instead of people.

What's so great about businesses?

Did you ever stop to think about what a business really is? It is just made up of people. An empty building or a closed down factory is not a business—it is just a pile of bricks.

Businesses are just ways people organize themselves so they can make a product or service that friends, neighbors, communities, and the world either needs or at least really wants. From a small corner bakery to a large pharmaceutical company, they all exist to provide something for society, and usually it is something we could not make or do for ourselves.

Businesses, Jobs for our Neighbors, and the Ripple Effect

Major businesses in America, like the big oil companies, employ literally hundreds of thousands of people. So what some critic may attack as big business is for many Americans the source of a paycheck that puts food on the family table.

All of this is, of course, very basic, but it ties into the universal truth that the economy has an unavoidable ripple effect. Every attack, or raised tax, or fine on a business will have consequences not just for the employees of that company, but on the individuals around the country who are company shareholders, and on everyone who is touched by the economic ripple that follows.

Private Ownership and the Stock Market

In our American economy, businesses were historically, and still mostly are, owned by private individuals and/or shareholders, who buy stock so they own some percentage of a company. Many Americans have pension funds from their years of hard work and those pension funds invest money in the stock market, including in big companies. So when a business fails, the value of every pension fund that owned shares in that failed business is impacted, meaning that a failed business could hurt your retirement—or your grandmother's.

But Big Businesses make Big Profits—Isn't that a Greedy Thing? Doesn't That hurt people? Shouldn't the Government Control That?

Profit in business just means the amount of money the business owner has left over after taking in income from selling the good or service her company makes, and paying all the bills and expenses she incurred in building or creating the goods and services she sells.

Profit equals income minus expenses. Profit is what motivates people in business to work because if there is no profit there is no point in working, no point in having a business.

Yet profit is one concept that the liberal thought in America has attempted to demonize by trying to take advantage of some Americans' economic ignorance. The small business owner has no trouble understanding the idea of profit: it is what she would have left over in her account after counting up what she earned from her paying customers, and subtracting out all her expenses (like rent, employees' salaries, and bills for supplies she buys for her business, etc.). If her expenses were constantly higher than her income—she would have no profit, and she would have to close her business.

Closing any business necessarily hurts people; it leaves all of the former employees without a job. The bigger the company that closes, the more people—your family, friends, and neighbors—are put out of work.

> *"Profit is a payment to entrepreneurs just as wages are payments to labor, interest to capital, and rent to land. In order to earn profits in free markets, entrepreneurs must identify and satisfy human wants in a way that economizes on society's scarce resources."*
> *—Walter E. Williams, Economist, Author, Professor*

Universal Truth Number Six: The Human Self-Defense Instinct Applies as Much in the World of Taxes as it Does in World of Nature

The self-defense instinct in humans and animals is well known and a wonderful and healthy thing. The mother's instinct to protect her children from harm is the stuff of legend and also the reality of our everyday lives. We would do anything to protect our children.

That same human self-defense instinct extends to protection of our homes and our property. We naturally do not just willingly and happily surrender when someone attempts to steal our wallets or our property.

That same instinct kicks in when people sense that the government is taking too much of what we have worked to earn.

People know we need to pay taxes to have a peaceful, orderly, and safe society. However, they also know there is a point at which the pure amount of taxation, and/or the uses of tax money, is just wrong.

And individuals and businesses will resist.

Even Big Moves Happen!

One example is my friend Danny, a Dallas resident who, along with his wife, moved to America from his native England. He obtained permanent residency in 1983 and American citizenship in 1988.

His reasons for coming to America? In 1979 the highest marginal rate of income tax in England was 98 percent, and the Labor Party (England's version of the Democrat Party) candidate for re-election as Prime Minister, James Callaghan, was running on a platform of introducing a Wealth Tax in the amount of 3% every year on all of the taxpayer's assets.

So, in addition to forking over 98 percent of his income, Danny would have been forced to assess his total net worth and send in an amount equal to 3 percent of that valuation.

Unsurprisingly, the self-defense instinct kicked in, and the English did not support the proposed excessive tax. And, fortunately for America, Danny and his family moved here.

People will act to avoid higher taxes

From small matters such as driving over state lines to purchase cigarettes because the sales tax is lower in a neighboring state, to moving an entire company to a more tax-friendly state, life in America is filled with examples of the predictable notion that people will act in a way so as to avoid letting the government have any more of their hard-earned money than they must.

Why move to Texas? (It is not for the mild summers, believe me!)

Many of you likely know that Texas, where I live, does not have an income tax, and strives to minimize regulations on businesses. That is why Texas is repeatedly ranked at or near the top of national surveys on business-friendly states. (http://chiefexecutive.net/best-worst-states-for-business; accessed June 3, 2012)

Businesses move to Texas in record numbers every year, and they move away from states with better weather (California) but a higher tax and regulatory burden.

Taxpayers, corporate and individual, will adjust behavior to stop government from extracting excessive amounts of their hard earned money. This self-preservation is as instinctual as defending yourself from danger in the wild.

France will also be finding this out shortly, it appears. The winning candidate in the May 2012 French presidential elections, an avowed Socialist named Francois Hollande, ran on a "soak the rich" campaign, urging a 75 percent tax on income. Unsurprisingly, wealthy French citizens are already calculating whether to move across the Channel to England, as London-based property agents, wealth-managers, and lawyers report a great increase in the number of calls from French citizens seeking refuge. One London wealth manager said such calls had increased by around 40% since a Hollande speech condemning "the world of finance." (http://www.ft.com/intl/cms/s/0/278412e6-9538-11e1-8faf-00144feab49a.html?ftcamp=published_links%2Frss%2Fworld_uk%2Ffeed%2F%2Fproduct#axzz1uCadn9fH; accessed June 2, 2012)

Billionaire Facebook cofounder Eduardo Saverin renounced his U.S. citizenship in May 2012 just prior to an IPO (initial public offering) for Facebook. His move to Singapore may help him cut his tax bill and avoid or reduce capital gains taxes on investments in the future. Even a guy who can clearly afford to pay exorbitant taxes, just will not voluntarily do it. (http://www.bloomberg.com/news/2012-05-11/facebook-co-founder-saverin-gives-up-u-s-citizenship-before-ipo.html; accessed May 16, 2012)

Ladies, I am not commending people for renouncing their precious American citizenship over taxes, but I want to be clear that the notion that America can solve her financial woes by just raising taxes on the rich has no grounding in reality. Saying that it does just makes for good headlines and the creation of class-envy.

Universal Truth Number Seven: Financial Rewards Inspire Hard Work. Conversely, the System that Rewards Everyone the Same No Matter How Hard You Work, "Dis-Inspires" Work

(This explains why socialism never brings the prosperity that free markets bring.)

Truth Number Seven cuts two ways:

1. People will work hard to bring themselves and their families the reward of more income (to provide a better life for themselves), and

2. If you remove the incentive of reward so that no matter whether you work hard or not at all you get the same reward, most people will not work, or at least won't work very hard.

The Group Project Parable

Discovering you can get the same reward whether or not you work hard destroys incentive. Just ask any parent of a diligent student who has been assigned a "group project." Once four of the five students in the group figure out that Ms. Diligence will do all the work because she really cares about her grade, and the project only gets a group grade anyway, they will sit back and play video games as Ms. Diligence labors away. Students learn at a young age that these academic experiments into socialism (group effort for group grade) result in few workers and many loafers. The loafers have figured they'll get the same grade whether they work or don't work— so why help out?

High taxes and income limits, like socialism, destroy the incentive to achieve or to work hard.

The basic truth of Universal Truth Number Seven is self-evident to all hard-working people. Even in a relatively free, free-market system, when government removes the incentive to work hard, achieve, and succeed by limiting income potential, or by taxing at such high rates that there isn't

The Pilgrims' Failed Socialist Experiment

America learned that lesson shortly after the Pilgrims landed in Cape Cod in 1620, when their first farming season involved an experiment in communal property, or what we today call socialism. A historical side note I just learned is that the Pilgrims did not choose this socialistic plan. Instead, the "deal" the Pilgrims had struck with the London investors who supplied them the loans for their venture to the new world required these early pioneers to establish communal farming. So instead of each family owning a piece of property, which they were responsible to farm, the entire population owned the land and was expected to work the land and divide up the harvest.

Governor William Bradford wrote his history of that era, *Of Plymouth Plantation*, and in that book he described that common ownership demoralized the settlers, and that the hard working Pilgrims were forced to subsidize the slackers. He wrote "the strong had no more in division of victuals and clothes than the weak, and the older men felt it disrespectful to be equalized in labours with the younger men."

Bradford reported "under communal land stewardship, the community was afflicted by an unwillingness to work, by confusion and discontent, by a loss of mutual respect, and by a prevailing sense of slavery and injustice."

So Governor Bradford decided after this brief experiment into socialism, with its miserable, insufficient crop production and discontent among the people, and after consulting with leaders in his group, to turn for the next farming season to a system where each family had its own plot of land for which the family was responsible, and which provided that family's food.

Hard work flourished.

(http://www.hoover.org/publications/hoover-digest/article/6580; accessed June 3, 2012)

much net benefit left over from working, people will adjust their behavior and stop working so hard. It ain't rocket science.

Socialism in Today's Healthcare System

One great example of this is in the healthcare reform bill that Democrats pushed through in 2010. It is an example, in more ways than one, of

American socialism (which is why it is called "socialized medicine"). The plan does not connect the incentive to work hard with the potential for financial gain for doctors, our most vital healthcare providers.

So, doctors are talking about leaving the practice of medicine.

To put it simply, doctors' pay will no longer be decided by the free markets, but by a complicated system of government controls, regulations, and mandates.

For a very detailed study and report on doctors' reactions to America's new socialized medicine system, look up online "The Physicians Foundation, Helping Doctors Help, Health Reform and the Decline of Physician Private Practice, which you can find here: http://www.physiciansfoundation.org/uploadedFiles/Health%20Reform%20and%20the%20Decline%20of%20Physician%20Private%20Practice.pdf; accessed June 2, 2012.

Only 26 percent of doctors surveyed intend to continue in their practice as they were. All the rest plan to cut back on hours, cut back on patients, switch to a nonclinical job, seek a different job unrelated to healthcare, close their practices to new patients, or some other choice. (Ibid p. 94)

We will talk more again later about what is so detrimental to society about socialism as an economic (and political) system. For now, it is enough to note that socialism inherently and necessarily slashes the vital connection between hard work and financial reward. So good workers (including doctors) will not just keep on working when the economic system destroys their financial rewards.

Universal Truth Number Eight: There Still is No Such Thing as a "Free Lunch" (and there never will be).

Many people around the world have repeated the phrase "there's no such thing as a free lunch," and for those of us who have thought about it much, it is as unquestionably true as 2+2=4.

The basic point is, of course, that even when something is given away for free, someone pays for it; someone worked to create or build it. When things are given away by the government, whether it is free cell phones for the poor (yep, we do that, too!), free clean needles for drug abusers, food stamps, housing assistance, free healthcare screenings, free money in the form of unemployment checks or any other transfers of money, any program offering "free" anything—is only free to the person who received the product or service.

Someone paid for it, and that someone is the taxpayers: you, your friends, and your neighbors.

One Occupy protestor's four-word sign spoke a thousand words:
"Free Everything for Everyone."
Now there's a realistic economic proposal! Let's all sign up!

Probably no two people could agree entirely on what should be provided free by the government. But reverting to our Reality Island mindset, we should think of all the things government provides for free, from the perspective of our question:

"Is this benefit or program a legitimate use of the money government collects in taxes? Or is it something that …

★ Each individual should provide for himself or herself, or

★ Some people should provide through a private sector for-profit business, or

★ We should turn to private, voluntarily-funded charities to address?"

Universal Truth Number Nine: "The Rich" and "the Corporations" are Not a Bottomless Pit of Potential Tax Revenue

A frequently repeated argument by Democrat politicians is that the rich and the corporations should "pay their fair share." Pretty safe argument, because, after all, who could be against fairness? This "if only the rich would pay more" is usually in the context of a speech about some serious problem facing the country, with the obvious implication that the problem exists because the rich and the businesses just will not pony up enough money. OK, we're all intelligent women here, so let's talk about the facts.

Who pays taxes now …. and how much do they pay?

What individuals pay…

According to Internal Revenue Service (IRS) data, for income taxes paid by individuals for the 11 years between and including 1999–2009, here is who paid and how much:

★ **The top 1 percent** of American income earners paid between 33.71 percent and 40.42 percent of all the income taxes paid. (That is 1 percent of Americans covering 40 percent of the tax burden.)

★ **The top 5 percent** of Americans in that time paid OVER HALF—between 53.25% and 60.63 percent —of all the income taxes paid.

★ **The top 10 percent** of Americans paid between 64.89 percent and 71.22 percent of the income taxes paid.

★ **The top 25 percent** of Americans paid between 82.9 percent and 87.30 percent of the U.S. tax burden.

★ **The top 50 percent** of Americans – the top half—paid almost the whole US tax burden: between 96.00 percent and 97.74 percent of the income tax burden.

★ **The bottom 50 percent** of Americans—that's the bottom half—have paid in their highest year only 4 percent of all income taxes paid, and at the lowest, 2.25 percent.

WHAT are those numbers? In plain English?

★ *Half of the entire population basically pays nothing. NOTHING.*

★ *Five out of every one hundred Americans, that is 5 out of 100, pay well over half of all taxes paid. (That's 5 percent paying 60 percent of the taxes.)*

★ *The top 10 percent, meaning only 10 out of every 100 people, pay nearly three-fourths, or 75 percent, of the entire tax burden.*

★ *The top 25 percent pay nearly all tax money collected.*

And by way of comparison, did you note that the top 1 percent pay up to 40 percent of the tax burden? That is that same 1 percent the Occupiers are calling selfish!

(To read all the details about who pays how much, you can find a great chart online at the website for the National Taxpayers Union, at http://www.ntu.org/tax-basics/who-pays-income-taxes.html?print=t#; accessed June 2, 2012).

What corporations pay—and shouldn't they pay more?

Liberals love to conjure up images of rich corporations who are greedily failing to pay their fair share in taxes, and before discussing briefly the corporate tax rates, consider the following:

★ Corporations are just groups of individuals who make things or provide services, and they employ people. They are a source of people's jobs.

★ Much of America, liberal and conservative, politicians to unions to job-seekers, has bemoaned the fact that many American businesses have moved out of the U.S. over the last decades and relocated overseas. When the companies leave, the jobs leave. And the reason they go? Friendlier tax laws, fewer regulations.

★ When American corporations move abroad, we just plain lose that tax revenue, as well as the jobs.

The corporate income tax rate in America is among the highest in the world. With a federal corporate income tax rate of 35% for 2010, plus the imposition of income tax by the respective states, the U.S. corporate income tax rate was recently second only to Japan. And Japan is about to reduce its rates, so the U.S. will become the highest. (http://www.nytimes.com/2011/05/03/business/economy/03rates.html?_r=1&adxnnl=1&adxnnlx=1338697848-suTRZN/eswpt7YIpbV+SkA; accessed June 2, 2012)

Remember Universal Truth Number Six?

People adjust behavior to avoid taxes, with the same self-defensive mechanism that instinctively compels them to defend their children, their property, and their homes. The fact that corporations move abroad is another example of this concept; they will not just sit still and be taxed relentlessly and unnecessarily. They will adjust their behavior, too. The following story about "Hauser's Law" is another validation of this same idea—it's an outcome of Universal Truth Number Six.

Consider the Truly Amazing "Hauser's Law"

One of the most amazing and important economic facts that shows that taxing the rich more will not change anything, is something called Hauser's Law. If you are unfamiliar with the economics terms used here, check out the box below called "Definitions so we can follow Hauser's Law." This is a law like the law that water freezes below 32 degrees. It is an observation of fact, not a decision someone made.

W. Kurt Hauser, an economist, author, and chairman of a San Francisco investment management firm, studied the total amount of tax money our federal government took in each year (revenue), over a 60-year period, and compared it with the activity or health of the economy, as measured by the gross domestic product. (The GDP is one popular calculation that the government does as a way to determine how active our economy is. It measures the value of the total goods and services produced each year.)

Hauser discovered that no matter what tax policy was in place, at the end of the day, the government never collects more than 20 percent of the GDP in total tax revenues. Roughly, the discovery means that the amount

What is Hauser's Law?

Federal government tax collections as a percentage of GDP have stayed the same-- just under 20 percent of the GDP—over the last 60 years, despite over 30 major changes in the tax code, including changes in income tax rates, capital gains taxes, corporate tax rates, and a long list of tax law changes. Whether the top marginal income tax rate was 92 percent as it was in 1952, and 1953, or as low as 28 percent as in 1988 to 1990, total revenues to the government stayed just below the 20 percent of the GDP rate.

The moral of the story—to grow actual revenue to the government, you have to grow the GDP, meaning you have to free up resources to let the job creators create jobs.

the government can successfully collect in taxes is always about one-fifth of the amount of work, goods, and services Americans produce.

Hauser wrote an editorial called "There's No Escaping Hauser's Law" in which he explains the reasons why the law is true. Quite simply, people will adjust their behavior to avoid tax consequences; high taxes discourage entrepreneurship and business development and money hidden in tax shelters to avoid high tax rates is not busy in the economy supplying funds to build businesses and create jobs. Lower tax rates, conversely, inspire people to work, build businesses, save, and invest.(http://online.wsj.com/article/SB10001424052748703514904575602943209741952.html; accessed June 2, 2012)

Conclusions from Hauser's Law?

★ If the goal of tax policy is to increase revenues to the government, (and not merely to punish those nasty rich) then we need to encourage the growth in the GDP—encourage businesses to make products, produce services, and sell them.

★ You cannot grow the GDP—you can't encourage businesses to act—by raising taxes.

★ Raising taxes reduces production, because (as we saw in Universal Truth Number Three), businesses will respond to tax increases by cutting expenses, so they won't hire people or grow their businesses.

Definitions so we can follow Hauser's Law:

For those of us who have never studied economics, let's define a few terms so we can follow this:

Revenue = the income government takes in from collecting taxes.

GDP= Gross Domestic Product. This is the total market value of all the goods and services produced within the borders of a nation (usually measured within a year). In plain English, it is the total of the market value of everything built or made (cars to computers to clothing plus the fair market value of all of the services provided (from gutter cleaning to tax preparation). It's one measure of how active and healthy our economy is.

OK, so we cannot collect more and more money from the rich by taxing them more, but what if the government just confiscated "stuff" from the rich—took their homes and cars and everything—and sold it all. Wouldn't that fix our economic woes?

Well, no. The famous and widely respected economist, Dr. Walter Williams, explained in an article called "Eat the Rich" that our federal government is currently spending so much money that if Congress did all the following:

★ Imposed a 100 percent tax on all income above $250,000

★ Seized all the nearly $400 billion in profit earned by all the Fortune 500 companies

★ Confiscated all the stocks, bonds, jewelry, businesses, yachts, airplanes, and mansions belonging to all 400 billionaires in America and sold it all to get cash

If they did all of that, Congress could not even pay the federal government's bills for even eight months of one year. (http://www.creators.com/opinion/walter-williams/eat-the-rich.html; accessed June 2, 2012)

Stop and think about that. Even if Congress chose to act like a dictator and just seized (stole), the assets of the country's most successful businesses and individuals, there would not be enough money to pay the bills. Even for a year. And if they did do such a thing, started taking money and assets away from people, those are one-time seizures, so once that money was spent, they could not go back and take it again. It would be gone. Forever.

But Warren Buffet said...

Warren Buffet, a Democrat billionaire who heads up Berkshire Hathaway, announced that he thinks that the super-wealthy should pay more in taxes. While another short book could be written on this subject, and on the political nature of his proposed tax generosity, it is important to know at least a few points:

★ The "Buffet Rule" would not, according to the non-partisan Joint Committee on Taxation, produce more than $47.6 billion in annual revenue, which is *less than 1 percent of the deficits the current Democrat budget would produce*, so is financially insignificant.

★ The Buffet Tax would need to produce 18 times that amount to replace the revenue the government gets from the AMT tax, which is the tax Democrats proposed to eliminate and replace with the Buffet Tax. So the Democrats' continued pursuit of the new tax is to make political points, not to bring more revenue to government.

★ Berkshire Hathaway is embroiled in long-term battle with the IRS over taxes, dating back to 2002, and reportedly owes in the range of $1 billion in back taxes. Wonder why Mr. Buffet doesn't just pay up? Could it be Universal Truth Number Six?

Universal Truth Number Ten: The Power to Tax is the Power to Control

Government needs to collect money in taxes to provide for legitimate governmental purposes such as national defense. We all agree on that.

Just as you know that wealthy people are more powerful than the poor, a government that collects more and more of the people's wealth is much more powerful than a government that has limited funds. Government growth through taking more and more of the people's money results in less freedom and wealth held by the people.

> *"With various people complaining about price gouging...economist Walter Williams has coined a new term: Tax gouging. But government is never accused of either greed or gouging — not even when it bulldozes people's homes in order to turn the land over to businesses that will pay more taxes."*
> —Thomas Sowell, Ph.D. Economics, Author, Commentator

Universal Truth Number Eleven: Risk and Competition are Required in the Free Market System

Risk and competition are basic elements of the free market economy, and government interference skews both.

Risk makes businesses and individuals plan carefully and wisely

Taking risk in the economic sense just means making your own decisions about your money, your work, and your investments, and accepting the consequences, good or bad. It can be as simple an idea as whether someone decides to go to work for an established business and receive a paycheck, or takes some of his or her own money and tries to start his or her own business. Americans are free to pursue their dreams, to build businesses, try new ideas, to invest in their businesses or someone else's, and to succeed or fail in these pursuits. You are free to risk your money, but not to force other people to share in the risks you choose.

Government investment in private companies is government using your tax dollars—your money—to make investments you might not have made, such as Solyndra, General Motors, and AIG. It is putting your money at risk in an investment you did not choose.

Also, when Government deprives businesses of the element of risk by bailing out failing businesses, it interferes with the basic free market idea of letting businesses take risks using their own good judgment and then deal with the consequences. Businesses will tend to be less cautious in their decision making if the "big-government-will-rescue-us" approach is in place. And it is grossly unfair to the competitors of AIG and other government-funded private companies who have to live (and die!) by the rules of the free market economy.

Competition—another free market virtue

Competition among manufacturers and suppliers and service providers is a hallmark feature of free markets. Competition keeps prices down, quality up, and customer service an important priority. But when the government is meddling in the natural competitive process by investing in some businesses and not others, imposing stringent regulations and various tax-incentivizing schemes, the whole natural competition arena falls apart. Businesses that would otherwise make plans based on their view of customer preferences make plans instead tailored around government regulation and tax avoidance.

Universal Truth Number Twelve: Uneven Wealth Distribution will Always Be with us—Under the Free Market System, and Under Socialism, and Under Communism.

No one and no system can make life perfectly fair

Lots of things in life are not fair. My sister is a much better musician than I am. Some kids are born with stunning natural athletic ability and some who dream of playing professional sports have no athletic ability. Protesting that life is not fair is protesting the very nature of life.

Some children born with disabilities or in disadvantaged homes strive and succeed and melt us with their courage, and others born to privilege struggle, flounder, and fail. Success in life is about the tenacity and energy and passion you bring to your life's journey.

In the realm of careers and life, people pursue and achieve different dreams. No one can guarantee that everyone comes out with the same degree of success, financial or otherwise. Coerced economic equality not only severs the vital link between hard work, risk, and financial reward, but it de-motivates; it dis-incentivizes the achievers from achieving, the workers from working, the dreamers from pursuing their dreams, leaving all of society worse off.

Unequal redistribution of wealth exists in every society

Yet every few years, news stories re-emerge about the inequitable distribution of wealth among Americans. The Democrat-backed Occupy Wall Street movement has made that point a centerpiece of their protest.

Because free markets produce the most prosperity, they can produce wide ranges of wealth between the wealthiest and poorest individuals.

But you must know that socialism and communism—the supposedly more equitable wealth distribution systems—produce similar and worse disparities of wealth in society, with the poorest of the poor in America living better than the middle class in countries burdened by those economically repressive, inspiration-crushing, incentive-destroying "fairer" systems.

Free markets strive to offer equality of opportunity, not outcome

The American free market system offers equal opportunity to participate, but not equal outcome. Instead, outcome is determined by hard work, the kind of career you choose, and a whole host of factors such as native talent and skill, educational achievement, some under the individual's control and some not. And while the outcome for each individual is not equal, our American system has given our nation unprecedented prosperity, and economic stability, across the board, for all citizens. The American system is unparalleled in the world's history in its creation of sustained economic wellbeing.

So Where Is America Today on Free Markets Versus Controlled Markets?

One of the most important reasons I am urging American women to step up and take political and economic note of what the Democrats are doing today, is that they are taking steps toward a soft socialism at least, a controlled market approach that is a major deviation away from the system that brought America its unparalleled success in history.

Most Americans still know that strict socialism, actual government ownership or control of all part of a country's economy, breeds poverty, misery, and mediocrity, and destroys freedom.

But many Americans do not know that there is not some clear, bright, and shiny line between socialism and free markets. Leaders who favor socialist style economic and political systems are not likely to announce that in countries whose citizens are accustomed to free markets.

That's why countries slide into socialism, because the people don't see it coming. Bad ideas are wrapped in good and noble-sounding packages and people are dragged down before they recognize the path their leaders have taken.

America Embraces Some Mutually-Agreed "Common Funding" Already

We are not purely a free market country, and have in some areas agreed to a pooling of monies to pay for each other's needs (a socialistic idea), such as commonly taxpayer-funded programs like Medicare and Social Security. Taxpayers pay into these and then receive benefits when eligible, often in amounts in excess of what they paid in. These were commonly agreed upon programs voted in by the elected representatives we chose. But even these programs are facing tremendous financial pressure and are on track for bankruptcy unless some changes are made.

Similarly, for decades in America public government assistance programs and private charities worked to meet the needs of the poor, and our widely accepted American societal goal has been to help people in need by giving them a temporary hand up, back into the free market system. (Read more in Chapter Six.)

But the track today's Democrats are on is way outside these long-standing programs.

Democrats Have Moved Further Left Today Than Ever— Away From Free Markets and Toward a Soft Socialism

There is a fundamental change on the part of Democrats today away from the goal of helping the poor by giving them a hand up, and toward the seemingly intentional creation of a larger dependency class. Democrats push now more than ever for stronger government control of the economy, and taxation of personal and business income for the purpose of redistribution.

In the Democrat Party leadership there is a general undercurrent of disdain for free market ideas and for the economic freedoms and prosperity that flow from free markets.

For example, using the tax system to redistribute income was once a clearly and overwhelmingly recognized evil in America, a fundamentally anti-free market and anti-freedom approach. But within the last decade voices in the Democrat Party have gradually begun inserting the idea into discussions on tax policy and in our national political conversation. They do it subtly, speaking in undefined terms of "fairness," and "social justice," that they equate with taxing some people more because they have been successful in the free market system, and using those tax monies to further fund dependency inducing government assistance programs. (More examples of the leanings of today's Democrat Party are below, after a brief excursion into defining our terms...)

Defining our Terms: Free Markets, and Socialism and its Nastier Cousin, Communism

While many Republicans readily recognize why today's Democrat Party policies are being described as "socialist," many Democrat voters do not yet, so I wanted to take just a moment to speak to that. I talked about socialism in Chapter Two also, briefly, and recognize there is some repetition.

But because I encourage readers to skip around and read the chapters you are most interested in, and because this is such a significant and dangerous trend in the American political scene, I concluded that discussing these ideas again, here, is the wiser course.

Our schools do not teach the virtues of free markets any longer, or the realities of socialism and communism, so I'll offer a series of one-paragraph history lessons.

★ Under free markets, the private sector, meaning different individuals and groups of individuals own businesses, and hire people to work for them. The free market determines salaries, wages and prices. People pay taxes to the government for the limited purposes of things like providing for the common defense.

★ Under strict socialism, the government (the state) owns or completely controls the businesses, manufacturing, service-providers, (the means of production), and everyone works for the state and is dependent on the state. The state sets prices, wages and salaries. The government owns or effectively controls everything. The main mantra is "from each according to his income, to each according to his need." Redistribution of wealth is a core goal of government. No point in working hard or exceling—you can't keep the fruits of your work—you need to share with the guy who did nothing.

★ Under Communism, you get all the misery of socialism (with essentially no private ownership of anything) plus a one-party totalitarian rule of the government, which exists to control nearly every aspect of life, and which historically has only been able to maintain its stranglehold on power by making "trying to leave the country" a crime, punishable by death.

The answer to the question that is the title of this section, "So Where is America today on Free Markets vs. Controlled Markets" is "it depends." The Democrats are down the controlled market path, and the Republicans are fighting to turn the helm back toward free markets.

Some of the Democrats' Socialist-leaning Steps so far

There are many ways that today's Washington Democrats have crossed the line and now advocate for socialist-style policies and solutions to America's challenges. Some of them (the healthcare takeover, the mortgage bailouts, the proposal to punish oil companies for making profits, the support of the Occupy movement) were described in Chapter Two. Add to those the bailout of some U.S. automakers, the support for taxpayers to cover student loan debts, and the Democrat effort to grow the size of the "dependency class" in America.

This last item, the unmistakable determination to grow helpless dependence on government by the masses is a hallmark of socialism and a hallmark of the Fish-Giver mentality (see Chapter Two) that Democrats support. More detail on this in Chapter Six, but the combination of the facts that the sheer number of those helplessly dependent on government has grown, and that laws written under this Washington Democrat leadership reward adding people to welfare rolls, leave no doubt as to motive. They are cultivating future, helpless Democrat voters.

Sometimes the unfairness of collectivism and the virtues of self-reliance are easier to grasp through examples and stories, so here are two. The first is true-to-life, and the second is my family's story.

A true-to-life story

A young woman was about to finish her first year of college. She considered herself to be very liberal, and was very much in favor of higher taxes to support more government programs, in other words redistribution of wealth. She was deeply ashamed that her father was a conservative. She felt that her father had for years harbored a selfish desire to keep what he thought should be his.

One day she was challenging her father on his opposition to higher taxes on the rich and the need for more government programs. He responded by asking how she was doing in school. She answered that she had a 4.0 GPA, and let him know that it was tough to maintain, that she was taking a very difficult course load and was constantly studying, which left her no time to go out and party. Her father listened and then asked, "How is your friend Audrey doing?" She replied, "Audrey is barely getting by. All she takes are easy classes, she never studies and she barely has a 2.0 GPA. She parties all the time, and lots of times she doesn't even show up for classes because she's too hung over."

Her wise father asked his daughter, "Why don't you go to the Dean's office and ask him to deduct 1.0 off your GPA and give it to your friend who only has a 2.0. That way you will both have a 3.0 GPA, a fair and equal distribution of GPA."

The daughter angrily fired back, "That's a crazy idea, how would that be fair! I've worked really hard for my grades! I've invested a lot of time, and a lot of hard work! Audrey played while I worked my tail off!" The father replied, "Welcome to the conservative side of the fence."

We all know people in need…my family's story

One false argument liberals make to defend their redistributionist goals is that Republicans or conservatives are the party of the rich, and that because of that wealth, they cannot relate to the needs of the poor. The truth is, almost everyone knows of a family member or friend who has in the past been struggling, or who is struggling now. The difference is not whether we are rich or poor, or know people who are poor, it is what ideas we bring to the table to solve that poverty. (And, FYI, the Democrats are the party of the rich today, if you count Hollywood, and lots of other famous liberals. The working people, small business owners and job creators I know vote Republican.)

My family's story includes an era when my grandmother was left alone to raise seven kids by herself, after her husband abandoned her. Her five boys and two girls were all relatively close in age, and they lived on the outskirts of a big city. My dad told me that his mom did turn for assistance temporarily to some type of welfare funding (this was long before the 1960's Great Society). But she did not wish to live her life relying on that welfare, and she spent no time blaming society or the "rich" for her plight. She took a job washing dishes overnight in a nearby sanatorium, and she walked back and forth to that job every day. She lived in Minnesota where that walk happened throughout cold and snowy winters and muggy summers. Her family attended church and likely was the recipient of some voluntary benevolence from that church.

She taught her kids that at Christmastime they had to find ways to help "the poor," even though those kids were poor by anyone's standards. They would receive very limited Christmas gifts themselves. My dad said a common gift was a pair of warm socks, or a new pair of mittens. And that was it—one gift.

Those seven kids all graduated from college, and one became a doctor. The entire difference between her family and some families today that struggle in poverty is their respective views on personal responsibility and the role of government. My grandma did not think government or society owed her a living. She raised kids who grew up understanding the importance of hard work and self-reliance. Poverty and struggles are not unique to any generation. Many, many Americans have similar stories in their family backgrounds, as do families around the world. The question has always been—do we create a system that "helps" by inflicting dependence and helplessness, or a system that offers help along the way toward independence and self-reliance?

The Moral Case for Capitalism and Free Markets

Capitalism, the free markets, and freedom, are more moral and more fair than any other system of economics or government known to humankind. This is such an important idea, yet it is rarely adequately expressed in the American political conversation.

Free markets motivate hard work, inspire people to dream and to become successful at their chosen endeavors, and reward success. And success is not limited to the wildly financially successful endeavors: it is true of any accomplishment that we work hard to achieve, in any niche of labor or employment.

A basic tenet of fairness must be that people are rewarded for hard work and achievement, that inspires them to continue working and achieving. Whether the incentive to work hard is destroyed at the front end by an overtly socialistic equal-pay-for-all system, or at the back end by an oppressive tax structure designed to punish success and redistribute wealth, destroying the incentive to work and achieve has a negative impact on our economy.

Free markets are fair to people who work and strive to achieve, because they allow reward for success. And big government liberalism/collectivism that extracts high taxes from the achievers and passes that money along to people ensconced in a long-term dependency lifestyle, is not "fair" to the achievers.

But supporters of dependency-cultivating government assistance programs are unfair both to the over-taxed achievers who pay for the programs and to the recipients whose worldview and life aspirations get dumbed down from the American dream to the American dependent status. Some most eye-opening research was recently reported in a great book by Arthur C. Brooks, *The Road to Freedom: How to Win the Fight for Free Enterprise.* (2012, Basic Books, a division of Perseus)

Mr. Brooks reports on in-depth studies that produced intuitively true findings: people who earn their success are the most content, the happiest people, and this is referred to as "earned success;" while those who are the recurring recipients of donations and handouts they did not in any way work to earn, develop what the research refers to as "learned helplessness." (Ibid. pp. 24–25 and 30–31)

Liberals argue that Republicans care about businesses while Democrats care about people, and that is a really important argument to refute. First, helping businesses is helping people—businesses are just made up of people who live off the paychecks and profits the business generates. Second, the meanest thing of all a system could do is to create an entire class of dependent Americans who are excluded from the potential for success and the dignity of self-reliance, which is the inevitable outcome of the learned helplessness the Democrats' policies cause.

Democrats would lose elections if they ran campaigns openly touting their plans to redistribute wealth, so instead they devise an alternative and false picture of America. They paint successful Americans as greedy, recipients of the government spending as victims of society's unfairness, and plant and cultivate the seeds of class envy by persistent characterizations of life in America as unfair. They encourage groups within society to see themselves as likely victims of some unfairness and then volunteer to step up and fight for them by getting them "free stuff."

Socialism Is Not the Same Thing as Coming Together to Help Your Neighbor

I'll guess everyone reading this book has jumped in to help when a friend was in need, or when a family member or neighbor was having a hard time. We drive each other's kids around, bring dinner over, and in a thousand other ways, help each other. Many of us do volunteer work through churches and neighborhood organizations. We give of our time and resources for causes and people we know and we choose.

Too often people think that voting to support big government assistance programs such as the collectivists advocate is just doing the come-together-to-help-our-neighbor thing on a national level. But it is not. I discuss these same ideas in Chapter Six in more detail, but here is a quick summary.

Those who vote to have government engage in big social spending are not giving of themselves, they are voting to impersonally give away other people's money. That is not charity. Once any program for the poor in Washington gets started, it will inevitably attract the unending growth and expansion inherent in having government bureaucrats run it and the eligible pursue benefits from it. Our fiscal systems in Washington using baseline budgeting never, never reduce funding to these programs, and they almost instantly morph into overgrown, government-dependency-creating programs.

All of the opposite dynamics are in play in private charity. You know the recipients, you choose out of love and friendship to help, you gauge actual help needed, and you and the recipient have the advantage of the personal connection that naturally serves as the buffer against abuse.

Defending free markets is actually easy: they work. The concepts of personal responsibility and inspiring each individual to pursue his or her life dream are actually invigorating. Attempting to instill undeserved guilt among hard working Americans by labeling them as greedy, and treating whole segments of citizens as incompetent to care for themselves is not at all inspiring. Turn the liberal lie ("liberals care about people") on its head! If liberals really cared, they would stop assuming that one in seven Americans needs food stamps, and that people who have lost their way in life can never find it again and must be relegated to the stupor of dependence.

Ladies, no one is advocating ending all social spending—beware of this Democrat tactic ("the Republicans will starve your grandmother!"). Government assistance under welfare reform was a great example. It provided temporary assistance and incentivized states to help recipients on the road back to self-sufficiency by requiring responsibility. It's the way we women would help a friend.

Where Should *Jobs Come From*?

The unemployment numbers in America have been dismal since 2009, and this is another arena where the default modes of the Democrats as opposed to the Republicans, are very different in terms of what they would do to respond.

"Businesses in our free market system!" is the short answer and the Republican answer to where jobs should come from in a free market economy. Americans form businesses, large and small, and hire people to work in those businesses, and that is how we create jobs in free market countries. Republicans trust the people and the free markets. In times of high unemployment, the conservative approach is to free up more money in the private sector so people will build businesses and create jobs.

Democrats must meddle. The Democrat answer is, of course, in some part to hold out vague hope that the free enterprise system might create some jobs, but their default mode requires them to meddle and manipulate. And their meddling is (1) ineffective if not harmful, (2) way too close to the way socialist governments intervene in their countries' economies and try to orchestrate everything, and (3) far too wasteful of the people's money.

This Democrat determination to meddle in the economy led them in 2009 to deal with high unemployment and a stagnant economy by concocting a convoluted plan to spend more money. They spent it via handouts and bailouts, in the hope that a demand for goods and services would be created with all of that money floating around out there, and that would, in turn, inspire investment and job creation.

The summary of this Democrat-led fiasco:

★ Democrats in Washington passed the American Recovery and Reinvestment Act of 2009 (ARRA) that provided $637 billion dollars in increased spending, the purpose of which was to create jobs to "fix" the unemployment problem. (And again, because the government has no money of its own—Universal Truth Number One—that $637 billion came from borrowing more money and from taxes, so it was money out of your pockets, your neighbors' pockets, the pockets of businesses, which then did not have it available for use to develop and sell new products and services, and hire people to make that happen.)

★ In February 2009, when ARRA became law, 12.5 million Americans—8.1 percent of our work force—were out of work.

★ In December 2011, and with 80 percent of the ARRA's government stimulus money had been spent, 13.1 mil-

---

On the Moral Superiority of Capitalism

"Popular capitalism is on the march ... Of course, there will always be people who, in the name of morality, sneer at this and call it materialism. But isn't it moral that people should want to improve the material standard of living of their families by their own effort? Isn't it moral that families should work for the means to look after their old folk? Isn't it moral that people should save, so as to be responsible for themselves?

"And it is for government to work with that grain in human nature to strengthen the strand of responsibility and independence: it benefits the family; it benefits the children; it is the essence of freedom."
—Baroness Margaret Thatcher, Prime Minister of England, 1979–1990

---

lion people—8.5 percent of Americans—were out of work. More jobless than before, and the money is all gone.

★ In addition, scores of stories floated around about inappropriate recipients and misuse of (your tax dollar) funds, which is another reason all by itself to greatly limit the power and authority of government to use your money to "fix" the economy.

Some Democrats may have had good intentions when they chose this big tax-and-spend approach. *But it matters that it failed miserably.* We need to learn from this and stop voting for people who support these debacles.

The lure of appearing to be "doing something"

Part of the reason that Democrats get some support for these multi-billion-dollar boondoggle programs is because they have the appearance of "doing something" drastic, when the economic situation seems drastic. But swooping into save the economy has never worked.

The Bottom Line on Job Creation

America's free markets, borne out of America's freedom, created the most prosperous, abundant, and successful economy in world history.

For everyone. Our poorest live better than the middle class in socialist and communist countries around the world. That prosperity was powered by the energies of a free people who worked in a system that rewards hard work, and creates businesses, products, services, and jobs as a natural outcome of letting the free markets be free. It never created perfection, but it created sustained prosperity and million and millions of jobs. As you'll see below, the competing socialist models never come close.

Don't let the Democrats mess up America's greatness!

> *America has created, over the last four or five decades,*
> *an upward trend in government spending.*
> *and*
> *a corresponding trend in increased voter/citizen/corporate expectation of*
> *government-provided services, programs, and assistance.*

The Federal Government Spending Bonanza What Could Go Wrong?

When we are nearly $16 trillion dollars in debt, there should be no reason to need to argue that we have a national spending problem. From what you read in this chapter, you can surely see that all of the Democrat economic mantras about "tax the rich more" and "make the rich pay their fair share" that are flung out there in the national political conversation should be dismissed as the economic baby talk that it is.

Another reason I urge you to vote for conservatives (and they only exist in the Republican Party) is that they are the only ones making any serious effort to bring federal spending under control. The response of the current batch of elected Democrats, the party's leaders, in Washington, to our current economic crises, has been to encourage more government spending. And borrowing.

The spending bonanza has resulted in the highest national debt ever, and an enormous and ever-increasing dependency class in our nation that relies for their very being on more and more government spending.

Top signs that the American government spends too much:

★ We are nearly $16,000,000,000,000 in debt, (that's $16 trillion) and the only votes Congress ever takes on the debt
   are to raise the debt ceiling (to increase how much we can
   borrow).

★ We spend money on absurd and crazy stuff, both in our
   regular budgets as well as with stimulus money. Check out
   the list of "doozies" in expenditures below.

★ One in seven Americans receives food stamps, and the
   number of food stamp recipients have increased dramatically in the last three years.

★ More than 70 percent of federal spending goes to dependence programs, meaning programs that provide
   assistance to individuals in areas where society used to
   take responsibility—housing, healthcare, welfare, retirement, higher education, rural, and agricultural services.
   (More in Chapter Six on this.) (http://www.heritage.org/
   research/reports/2012/02/2012-index-of-dependence-on-
   government; accessed June 2, 2012)

Some of the doozies expenditures include:

★ The federal government sent an average of $120 million
   in retirement and disability payments to deceased former
   federal employees every year for at least the past five years.

★ Hocus pocus! Nearly $150,000 in federal funds went to the
   American Museum of Magic in Marshall, Michigan which
   celebrates magicians and their magic.

★ Back in the USSR! Documentary about how rock and roll contributed to the collapse of the Soviet Union – (CA) $550,000.

★ Federal funding in the amount of $593,000 went to a primate research center to study where in chimpanzees' brains they get the idea to throw their feces.

★ A new grant of $176,000 joined $350,000 already spent to study how cocaine hurts or helps the sex drive of Japanese quail.

There are literally millions of other ways government could spend your money. Check out how our U.S. government already does spend your money in Senator Tom Coburn's December 2011 report called "2011 Wastebook." (http://www.coburn.senate.gov/public/6946d43b-bccf-4579-990e-15a763532b40.html ; accessed June 2, 2012)

This should at least prove that the federal government can, should, and must cut spending!

Republicans are the only ones proposing solutions to the oncoming fiscal train wreck.

U.S Representative Ryan, a Republican from Wisconsin, has developed several plans designed to help rein in spending, and bring the federal entitlement programs under control. He proposes solutions that protect our seniors and our most vulnerable, but require that wealthy receive less of the handouts they do not need, and offer Americans more choices in terms of controlling their own healthcare and spending.

Representative Ryan and the Republicans are doing the heavy lifting, the serious work, required today to make adjustments, to save the economy from collapse, to save these programs so they will be there for future generations. You can read more in Chapter Seven about Representative Ryan's Roadmap to America's Future.

Democrat opponents revert to name-calling and fear mongering, increasing spending and hurling a few slogans. No hope in that at all.

Freedom and free markets "made" America's greatness and prosperity

America was, of course, founded on the idea of freedom and rights from our Creator. Free markets were one of the logical outgrowths of at precious ideas. Freedom was woven into our national fabric as a given, from the start.

Our culture has a deeply rooted assumption and expectation of freedom that includes freedom to pursue your dreams, education, path, and economic wellbeing through hard work, and freedom to achieve as much as you can with your talents, inspiration and determination. And we expect to have the freedom to keep most of the fruits of our labors.

Vote for Free Markets!

America has some challenging days ahead of her, and two very different paths. One is the path of free markets, hard work, and continued prosperity, and the other is the dark path toward ever-growing government control, limitations on freedom, and the dismal mediocrity of a softly socialistic society.

I hope you will follow the politicians' speeches and remarks with a renewed commitment to look beyond the class warfare language ("the rich don't pay their fair share"), and keep your well-informed ears tuned into what they are asking you to believe. Keep in mind those 12 universal truths of a free market system! Recognize that when politicians or parties claim that government can fix all our problems with a new program and new expenditure, or make promises of compassionate sounding programs, you know how much better and long-lasting free market based solutions are for America's future.

A Story Told to Me that Conveys More than Many Long Speeches:
Recently, while I was working in the flower beds in the front yard, my neighbors stopped to chat as they returned home from walking their dog. During our friendly conversation, I asked their little girl what she wanted to be when she grew up.

She said she wanted to be President of the United States some day.

Both of her parents, liberals I should add, were standing there, so I asked her, "If you were President, what would be the first thing you would do?"

She replied, "I'd give food and houses to all the homeless people."

Her parents beamed with pride!

"Wow...what a worthy goal!" I said. "But you don't have to wait until you're President to do that!" I told her.

"What do you mean?" she replied.

So I told her, "You can come over to my house and mow the lawn, pull weeds, and trim my hedge, and I'll pay you $50. Then you can go over to the grocery store where the homeless guy hangs out, and you can give him the $50 to use toward food and a new house."

She thought that over for a few seconds, and then she looked me straight in the eye and asked, "Why doesn't the homeless guy come over and do the work, and you can just pay him the $50?"

I said, "Welcome to the Republican Party."

Did You Know?...Stories and Facts to Share Chapter Four

How Has the Democrat Big Government, Big Taxes, Big Spending Approach worked out?

Question: What do the top ten largest American cities—population over 250,000—with the highest poverty rate—all have in common?
Answer: Democrat leadership. Democrat mayors.

Based on the U.S. Census Bureau, 2006 American Community Survey, August 2007, the top ten cities with the highest poverty rate, ranging from the highest poverty rate found in Detroit, Michigan, of 32.5 percent, down to the lowest (within this top ten list) of Newark, New Jersey, at 24.2 percent, all have in common not just current Democrat Mayors and Democrat leadership, but very long-term Democrat control of those cities. (http://www.city-data.com/forum/politics-other-controversies/728564-what-cities-below-poverty-level-have.html; accessed June 3, 2012)

The long-term impact of Democrat ideas and leadership in these cities is poverty. It is not that poor inner-city families choose poverty, it is that they vote Democrat because Democrats claim to be the ones who "care," and Democrat policies inflict poverty.

Democrat, big government, big spending ideas have poverty as their outcome.

Further proof that Democrat fiscal policy brings human misery and Republican fiscal policy brings hope and jobs?

There were 17 states that elected Republican governors in the 2010 elections. Guess what those states have in common today? The unemployment rate *dropped* in every single one of them. The job market in those Republican-run states improved 50 percent faster than the national rate.

By comparison, the unemployment rate in states that elected Democrat governors in 2010 actually grew larger, or dropped on average only the same as the national rate. (http://www.breitbart.com/Big-Government/2012/07/07/Unemployment-Rate-Dropped-In-Every-State-That-Elected-A-Republican-Gov-In-2010; accessed July 9, 2012)

★ ★ Chapter Five ★ ★

Healthcare
(If it Ain't Broke, Don't Fix It!)
Crisis, Quality, Cost, and Access

Can We Talk…About What's Really the Best Way to Provide Good Healthcare in America?

Getting healthcare policy right in America is a challenge, partly because it is an emotion-evoking issue, and partly because it seems so overwhelming and complex. Too many healthcare policy discussions start with confusing and sometimes bullying political rhetoric like "Don't you care about sick people?" "Healthcare is a right!" "What are you going to do about the (fill-in-the-blank) millions of uninsured?"

Of course we all care, but it is a gargantuan leap to go from agreement that we care about sick people to agreement that the best way to care is to go along with the national takeover of the healthcare system by Washington bureaucrats, especially when the healthcare takeover passed in a 2,700-page piece of legislation that not a single lawmaker had read. When you combine that with the fact that America had the best healthcare system on earth before the government takeover, it makes most people convinced that Congress made a big mistake.

Our American healthcare system is one-sixth of our economy, which makes the government seizure of the healthcare industry pretty radical. We just don't do that in America. Well, we didn't used to anyway… So let's talk!

> *"It is amazing that people who think we cannot afford to pay for doctors, hospitals, and medication somehow think that we can afford to pay for doctors, hospitals, medication, and a government bureaucracy to administer it."*
> —Thomas Sowell, Ph.D Economics, Author, Columnist

Ladies, this book is about urging women to vote conservative, not about substantive healthcare policy. I will talk here about how and why the national healthcare takeover came about, why American women should stand up against socialized medicine and the political power grab represented by its passage.

Topics We'll Talk About in Chapter Five

If You Wondered if There's a Difference Between the Republicans and the Democrats in Washington Today.

America—Best Healthcare System on Earth?

So HOW and WHY Did Obamacare Pass?

Why Review All of the Ugly Passage of the Healthcare Takeover Again?

Even if Obamacare Is a Bad Law, Healthcare is a Right, Isn't It? People are Entitled to Free Healthcare!

Did You Know?...Stories and Facts to Share

★ ★ ★

If You Wondered if There's a Difference Between the Republicans and the Democrats in Washington Today

The differences between the Republican and Democrat parties were on overwhelmingly clear display in 2010, when the U.S. Congress passed, and President Obama signed, the law implementing the takeover of the American healthcare system by the federal government. Even if you think that the nationalizing of our American healthcare system was the best idea since abolition or women's suffrage, I urge you to read and consider the ideas in this chapter.

Democrats and Republicans agreed that some aspects of the healthcare system needed reform, and both parties have worked on and presented different ideas over the years, including the time leading up to the passage of Obamacare. But the Obamacare vote was almost completely along party lines, with no Republicans in the House or Senate voting for it, and almost no Democrats voting against it.

Adopting socialized medicine in America was the decades-long dream of many far Leftists in America, and was a huge stepping-stone down the path of socialism. If you think the label "socialism" doesn't belong in this discussion, read on. I have taken several different approaches in this book to explain the concept of socialism in our American political and economic system (in Chapters Two and Four). With each explanation I hope it is easier to understand and clearer to see that the changes Democrats are foisting on America have their philosophical roots in socialist/collectivist thinking that does not belong here.

How good or bad was our American healthcare system that the Democrats nationalized? What did the Democrats pass in its place?

America—The Best Healthcare System on Earth?

America had (and perhaps still has) the best healthcare system on earth. Regardless of whether other nations agree, citizens around the world "vote" on that question with their healthcare decisions every year.

★ Newfoundland Premier Danny Williams came to the United States in February 2010 to have heart surgery. This senior elected official left Canada with its long-standing national health insurance program to get surgery in Miami, and his statement to the press speaks volumes: "This is my heart, my choice and my health. I did not sign away my right to the best possible healthcare for myself when I entered politics." (http://sayanythingblog.com/entry/canadian_premier_unapologetic_about_coming_to_america_for_health_care/ Other Canadian leaders have done the same; accessed June 3, 2012)

★ British superstar singer Adele chose in November 2011 to come to America for her vocal cord/throat surgery, which occurred at Massachusetts General Hospital. Adele made the decision to use America's healthcare system over England's socialized medicine system, "...on the advice of her doctor and voice therapist in the United Kingdom..". (http://www.billboard.com/news/adele-undergoes-vocal-cord-surgery-in-boston-1005484652.story#/news/adele-undergoes-vocal-cord-surgery-in-boston-1005484652.story; accessed June 3, 2012)

★ A mere six months before Obamacare passed, a news article pointed out that 400,000 non–U.S. citizens come to America every year for medical care. (http://www.weeklystandard.com/Content/Public/Articles/000/000/016/943pfdxe.asp; accessed June 3, 2012)

★ Remember when we talked about the fact that no one ever tried to escape from West Germany to East Germany? And no one jumped on a ramshackle raft in Florida to try to get into Cuba? (The refugees all go in only one direction)? Well, Dr. Stanley Goldfarb of University of Pennsylvania School of Medicine, an expert on world-wide healthcare systems, pointed out "Not too many people get on a plane and fly to Cuba or to France" to see a doctor. (That would be, of course, with the exception of Venezuelan President Chavez who does travel to Cuba for cancer treatments, apparently concluding that the care he might receive in his socialist home country is even worse than in Cuba.) (http://www.weeklystandard. com/Content/Public/Articles/000/000/016/943pfdxe. asp; accessed June 3, 2012)

★   America has more and better healthcare equipment, as a result of the free market economy under which our healthcare system evolved. Dr. Scott Atlas of Stanford University's Medical School pointed out that the United States has 27 MRI machines per million Americans, as contrasted with the socialized medicine systems in Canada and Britain which have a mere six per million. CT scanners are also more available in the US than in our socialist cousin nations: the U.S. has 34 per million, Canada has 12 per million and Britain has 6. Our cancer survival rates are far, far better than those of the Europeans. (http://www.weeklystandard.com/Content/Public/Articles/000/000/016/943pfdxe.asp; accessed June 3, 2012)

So HOW and WHY Did Obamacare Pass?

Obamacare passed the Congress in 2010 and was by far the most controversial piece of legislation passed by the U.S. Congress and signed into law by a President in the last 100 years. This national takeover of the healthcare system constituted the seizing by regulation and law of about one-sixth of the overall American economy. The government's takeover of it was the most dramatic and major shift away from free markets, and into socialism, that ever happened in America, even for an industry that was already heavily regulated.

How Obamacare Passed Congress

To state the obvious and true, Obamacare passed Congress because a majority of elected Representatives and Senators voted for it, and the President signed it. But the story of its passage warrants close attention because it is a quintessential case study of how the modern Democrat party operates in America. We need to study this enough to learn their abuses, so we recognize them in the future.

The Crisis Generation Phase

While living in the same America that most people know has the best healthcare system on earth, Democrats set out to demonize it. They relied on one of their most commonly used ploys—the generation or creation of a false or exaggerated crisis which they then propose to solve with some new law or policy.

In this case, many Democrats spoke repeatedly of the "crisis" of a supposedly large number of uninsured Americans who were just one illness away from bankruptcy and financial ruin. An often-repeated Democrat statement was that America had *46 million Americans "without healthcare."* Just so we have the facts straight, this was based on a U.S. Census Bureau report, that in 2007, there were 46 million people who answered "yes" to the question of whether they were ever without health insurance "at any time in the past year."

Ladies, I know you are smarter than the Democrats think you are, and we are not going to let this slide without arming ourselves with the facts!

★ Lack of insurance is not lack of care! For someone to say that he or she was without health insurance at any point during a year is an entirely different thing than saying that he or she is without healthcare generally in life.

★ That Census Bureau data showed that 9.7 of that 46 million were not U.S. citizens—which at the least changes the nature of the issue being discussed.

★ A 2003 study by Blue Cross showed that about 14 million "uninsured" Americans who were eligible for Medicaid or SCHIP had not signed up, but could and likely would have signed up had they arrived at the emergency room with some problem.

★ Lots of folks, especially young healthy people just starting out in the working world, choose not to purchase insurance they could afford, as a basic budgetary priorities decision.

So this vision the Democrats created of 46 million folks wandering the streets of America without healthcare was a brazen and obnoxious exaggeration designed to generate fear and anger among the people. But it worked.

Another stunt among many the Democrats used to build hype, hysteria, and fear was to hold a White House "conference" in March of 2009 on the healthcare "crisis" at which President Obama announced, "The cost of healthcare now causes a bankruptcy in America every 30 seconds...by the end of the year it could cause 1.5 million Americans to lose their homes." (emphasis added). (http://money.cnn.com/2009/03/05/news/healthcare_summit/index.htm; accessed June 3, 2012)

That kind of phony number flinging and "could cause" unsubstantiated fear mongering has no place in the American political dialogue. There are at least a thousand other crises that "could cause" home losses and bankruptcies. This is pure emotional manipulation!

Politicians make these melodramatic statements because they think they will manipulate voters—especially women, who will respond with our innate compassion to these imaginary crises and leap to our feet and demand that Congress *do* something. Ladies, I am as compassionate as the next gal; we must be smarter than to be manipulated by this stuff!

A Few More "It Wasn't a Crisis" Insights

Whether you like or don't like the Obamacare bill, the Democrats did not decide based on any economic crisis in 2008, 2009, or 2010, or any calculation of the alleged number of uninsured Americans, to pursue universal healthcare. This was a long-standing goal of the far left wing of the Democrat party. Congressman John Dingell, a Democrat from Michigan, has been in office since 1955 and his father served before him from 1933 to 1955. In the Democrat jubilation that followed the House's passage of Obamacare, reporters made note that the current Representative Dingell and his father before him had both introduced universal healthcare legislation throughout their careers.

Long before this 2010 law was passed, the Socialist Party of America had lobbied and pushed for universal healthcare. This bill was the result of decades-long work by the far left wing of the Democrat party, which has now become the mainstream of the Democrat party.

The infamous words of Rahm Emanuel, former Chief of Staff for President Obama, sum up how the Democrats view crises: "You never want to let a good crisis go to waste...."

And if there isn't one, pretend there is.

The Democrats' Thought Manipulation Phase

Among the clearest examples of depth of manipulation the Washington Democrat leaders succeeded in carrying out to get American support for their impending healthcare takeover, is revealed by the contrast between these two polls:

★   A June 2008 ABC News/*USA Today*/Kaiser Family Foundation poll found that 89 percent of Americans were satisfied with their healthcare. Other polls found similar results.(http://www.weeklystandard.com/Content/Public/Articles/000/000/016/943pfdxe.asp; accessed June 3, 2012).

★ An April 2009 CBS News/New York Times poll found that
    87 percent of Americans believed that the U.S. healthcare
    system needed to be fundamentally changed or completely
    rebuilt. (http://www.republicanassemblies.org/klein-the-
    matter-with-myths/; accessed June 3, 2012)

Translation: The Democrats were so successful in demonizing the
healthcare system, exaggerating the problems, and emotionally parading
the relatively few problems or cases the system did not handle well, that
they convinced (if these polls are to be believed) a vast majority of Americans that some major reform was needed, while nearly exactly that number
of Americans were perfectly happy with their own healthcare.

The Back-Room Deals in the Dark of the Night, Find-Out-When-We-Pass-It, Who Needs to Read It Phase of Democrat Law-Making

Then Speaker of the House and Democrat, Nancy Pelosi, famously announced just days before Congress passed Obamacare that we would have
to wait for the Democrats to pass the bill to find out what was in it. (http://
www.unitedliberty.org/articles/5233-pelosi-we-have-to-pass-the-bill-so-
that-you-can-find-out-what-is-in-it; accessed June 3, 2012)

That, combined with admissions by many elected officials that they
voted for it without reading it, and the contrast between the Democrat's
earlier pledge of openness in the legislative process with the deals made in
back rooms, left Americans simultaneously sickened, frustrated, outraged
and stunned. The American government isn't supposed to act this way, and
ladies, we should not stand for it. We pay their salaries, after all!

The Democrats in Congress succeeded in passing the most transfor-
mative, big-government takeover of a major segment of the American
economy in American history. They did this through a combination of
generating a false crisis, lathering up unsuspecting Americans into a hysteria of concern through blatant emotional manipulation, hiding the process
and the bill's content from public scrutiny until after its passage, creating

a bill so long and convoluted and complex that even those who voted on it wouldn't and couldn't read it, and then shoved it through via last minute deals and horse-trading. And they were proud and unapologetic.

Why Obamacare passed Congress

America did NOT want Obamacare.

Obamacare, socialized medicine, was not the will of the people. It is vitally important that we American women understand and absorb that fact because one of the core ideas underlying our unique American system of government is that we have representative government. We hire our elected officials by voting for them, and they are supposed to represent us.

Rasmussen Polling, among the most reputable polling organization in America, has tracked public opinion about the healthcare reform bill since the time the Democrats began discussing it in 2009. A September 2009 poll showed that 53 percent of Americans opposed the Democrats' proposed healthcare reform, and only 44 percent supported it. Those numbers remained constant even after President Obama made a major speech strongly pitching it. (http://www.rasmussenreports.com/public_content/politics/current_events/healthcare/september_2009/support_for_health_care_reform_hasn_t_budged_since_july; accessed June 3, 2012)

By November 2009, only 38 percent of voters supported the bill. (http://www.rasmussenreports.com/public_content/politics/current_events/healthcare/november_2009/support_for_health_care_plan_falls_to_new_low; accessed June 3, 2012)

And for those few of you who may have missed it, the national protest in the streets of Washington against the passage of Obamacare, in September 2009 was among the largest marches ever in American history.

Americans, even many Democrats, want Obamacare repealed.

Three weeks after it passed, support for repeal was at 58 percent. (http://www.rasmussenreports.com/public_content/politics/current_events/healthcare/april_2010/support_for_repeal_of_health_care_plan_up_to_58; accessed June 3, 2012)

In December 2010, support for repeal was at 60 percent.(http://www.rasmussenreports.com/public_content/politics/current_events/healthcare/december_2010/support_for_health_care_repeal_at_60; accessed June 3, 2012)

As of May 2012, 26 percent of Democrats supported repeal of Obamacare. (http://www.weeklystandard.com/blogs/new-poll-one-four-democrats-favors-obamacare-s-repeal_642263.html; accessed June 3, 2012)

Independents support repeal by a margin of 52 to 31 percent, and among likely voters, there is overwhelming support for repeal of Obamacare, 55 percent to 36 percent.(http://www.weeklystandard.com/blogs/new-poll-one-four-democrats-favors-obamacare-s-repeal_642263.html; accessed June 3, 2012)

So why did they pass it?

The answer to why the Democrats resorted to the depths of manipulation they did to force Obamacare through over widespread public objection is both complex and yet simple. The simple part is just that they seized the first opportunity they found to force through one of their most deeply cherished left-wing goals, because they could. They had the numbers in Congress and they had the White House.

The more complex part and the part that so many American women have a hard time grasping, is that the Obamacare bill was not, for the Democrats, about healthcare. It was about seizing the chance while they had it to take control of a huge part of the American free market economy. With the healthcare system thoroughly under their fiscal and legal thumb, Democrats have consolidated federal power over much of the commerce in America, and with it, the control of the people.

If you wonder if that is true, consider this. If the real goal was just to ensure that more Americans have access to good healthcare, they could have built and staffed more clinics around the country, offered healthcare for free or at a reduced rate, *and spent much less money*, and left the 89 percent of Americans who are happy with their healthcare, free to remain happily insured using private insurance. There was no reason to nationalize the healthcare system.

Why Review All the Ugly Passage of the Healthcare Takeover Again?

It would be easy to say "passing Obamacare is water under the bridge—move along—we need to fight today's battles." That is exactly what the Democrats hope all of America will say.

Ladies, the reason it is so important not to forget the Democrat party's actions during the healthcare passage episode is because it reveals so much about their motives and agenda, which we need to understand going forward.

Washington Democrats Knew America Did Not Want Socialized Medicine, but They Forced it Through Anyway

One of the most troubling aspects of the passage of the national healthcare takeover was that we saw an ugly example of the exercise of raw political power, taking action to do something the Democrats knew the people did not want. The Democrats were fully aware that America did not want socialized medicine; we had a relatively long—several months at least—national conversation about it; but the Democrats just decided they wanted this more than they wanted to listen to the people.

There's an "eliteness" there that does not belong in America. It's a "we-know-better-than-you-ignorant-masses-about-what-is-good-for-you-and-for-America's-future-and-you-are-just-not-smart-enough-to-see-it-so-we'll-just-do-it-for-you" attitude.

That's what dictators do.

I remember when I was in junior high school or high school and watching the evening news with my dad on the kitchen TV, and we saw a story about a South American government nationalizing some large industry, including American-owned companies. I actually recall saying to my father, "They can't do that; it belongs to the company." He replied, "But they can—and they just did."

I had enough intuitive sense as a young student to know that nationalizing a business is just stealing. Somebody, in fact many somebodies, built that business, invested their money in it, and those somebodies are just plain being cheated. It's that same feeling now, about the healthcare take-over. The government didn't take ownership of the hospitals or doctors' practices, but under the scope and breadth of regulation now in place, they have effectively taken complete control. It's the Democrats' American version of socialism.

But "the Republicans wouldn't do anything about the crisis; they were just being the party of no"

The number of bold-faced lies the Democrats told to get the American public to go along with the healthcare takeover is astonishing. Among the biggest whoppers, one that you likely heard, was that the Democrats "had to act" because the "do nothing" Republicans had not stepped up to do anything about the healthcare crisis. The depth of deception to which the Democrats sunk to force through socialized medicine is another telltale sign of how desperate they were to pass it while they could.

Contrary to the Democrat lies, the Republicans had brought up numerous bills in Congress. They could find no Democrat support for them. Democrats were only interested in the "take complete control of the entire system" type laws they were proposing.

Even if Obamacare Is a Bad Law, Healthcare Is a Right, Isn't It? People Are Entitled to Free Healthcare!

One of the promises of Obamacare was to give more people more free healthcare services, to require that insurance companies cover certain procedures without charging any co-pay or deductibles. But as we all know, there is no such thing as free. Someone will always pay for something that is a good or service, even if the recipient does not pay. And when Democrats arrange for free things (just like the free food that food stamp recipients receive), Democrats have just bought themselves another lifetime Democrat voter.

Republicans DID propose healthcare legislation before the take-over—but Democrats would not settle for less than complete control.

Here are just a few of the Republican proposals, ideas which far more comport with life in a free market economy.

• Republican Senator Jim DeMint proposed the Allowing Americans the Opportunity to Purchase Insurance Across State amendment Lines, rejected by the Democrat-controlled Senate in August 2007.

• Republican Senator Jim DeMint introduced the Allowing Americans to Deduct Their Health Care Costs amendment, rejected by Senate Democrats in March 2008.

• Allowing Americans to use funds in their health savings account funds to pay for health insurance, was proposed by Senator Ensign and rejected by the Democrats in 2007.

• Republicans introduced three proposals in 2009 containing substantive provisions, including low-income family coverage, tax credits, and protections for pre-existing conditions. All were rejected by the Democrats.

The president's website boasts:
"...54 million Americans have coverage for preventive services, free of cost."
It goes on to say:
"Insurers are now required to cover a number of recommended preventive services, such as cancer, diabetes, and blood pressure screenings, without additional cost sharing such as copays or deductibles."

We all learned in Universal Truth Number Eight in Chapter Four that there never has been, and never will be, a free lunch. If these insurers provide free coverage for certain services—meaning they pay for the cost of the services and the payment to the service providers, doctors, nurses, and other aides who provide, set up, and administer these tests or procedures, or read or interpret the test results—the insurer is actually out money. So they will, in turn, charge some policyholders higher premiums, or they will raise deductibles or co-pays, or lay off some employees, or take some other economic action to make up for the money they pay out. And Universal Truth Number Three also kicks in—there is always a ripple effect.

Much of this discussion parallels ideas we talked about in Chapter Three about socialism versus free markets, so I'll not repeat all of those points in detail here. Collectivism is not patriotic in America, so Democrats avoided acknowledging the economic reality that the healthcare reform bill was a socialized medicine bill, by steering thought down the path of "don't you care about the uninsured, or the poor, or women?"

Elected officials who voted in favor of the healthcare reform bill knew perfectly well that they were bringing in the era of socialized medicine in America, and that the control over the healthcare system would mean a much larger and more powerful centralized government. Calling the bill what it was (socialized medicine) would have deepened the already widespread opposition to it, so emotional stories and often false and grossly exaggerated statistics were marched out into the public discussion so the vote appeared to be over whether we have compassion.

The national takeover of the healthcare system was at the core the outcome of the raw desire to accumulate political power. Nothing noble, nothing helpful. At a time when the national debt was already staggering, when there was no crisis, when the American people took every conceivable legal step available to send the signal that we do not want socialized medicine, the Democrats response was to do it because they could. For some low level Democrat Congressmen, the vote did not necessarily represent anything sinister. But for the leaders of the Democrat Party, it represented the seizure of power and control over the people and their healthcare that simply does not belong in America.

Ladies, if no other issue in this book captures your concern, the passage of this bill alone and the way it was passed should be enough to motivate you to vote the modern Democrat Party out of power as soon as you can, for a long time.

The U.S. Supreme Court Upholds Obamacare

Just as the book you are reading was going to print, the U.S. Supreme Court announced its ruling in the case that challenged the constitutionality of the federal takeover of the healthcare system. The Court ruled that the healthcare takeover law is constitutional—which is not a stamp of approval of the law by the Court, just a ruling that the law as interpreted does not violate the Constitution. Specifically, (and ladies, this is important!) the Court decided that government does not have the power under the Commerce Clause of the Constitution to require that Americans buy health insurance (something that the government had argued that it could do), but that the government does have the power to impose taxes to fine or punish Americans who do not buy insurance. So the Court upheld Obamacare as constitutional under Congress' taxing power, but ruled that a mandate to buy insurance is not constitutional.

But please never forget—even if the Court had struck down the healthcare takeover law, the leftists in Washington would have been back again next time around working to pass another similar law. And if conservatives ever manage to get this healthcare takeover repealed, the leftists will bring it back again. And, even if Obamacare stands, the liberal Democrats will continue to pass new laws and new regulations that will further strangle the healthcare system, ultimately and inevitably making it more bureaucratic, inefficient, ineffective and expensive.

What about the IPABs—the Death Panels?

Ladies, there is one last very important fact to understand about Obamacare. Some of the most sinister provisions in this bill passed in secrecy and ignorance, and by brute legislative force, are just now coming to light. The healthcare takeover law includes the creation of the IPAB, the Independent Payment Advisory Board, also referred to as the "death panels." The purpose of the IPAB is to restrain Medicare spending, and the panel is required to issue legislative proposals to reduce future spending, if projected spending exceeds targets. Those proposals will almost certainly include drastic cuts that jeopardize seniors' access to care in some manner.

But it is not the existence of the IPABs that is the most sinister Obamacare provision; it is the virtually unchecked power the IPAB has. This law delegates Congress' Constitutionally based legislative power to an unelected panel, and it is nearly impossible for anyone, including Congress, to stop them:

★ The national healthcare law requires the secretary of HHS to implement the IPABs' proposals, making them law automatically unless Congress replaces the IPAB proposal with its own. And if Congress' substitute proposal is more costly than the IPAB proposal, Congress can only pass its own law on this subject with a 3/5 majority vote in the Senate, a majority vote in the House, and the President's signature.

★ Obamacare prevents Congress from repealing the IPAB except during a short window in 2017, and even then, the law requires a 3/5 supermajority vote in the Senate and the House, and the President's signature.

★ If Congress does not repeal the IPAB in 2017, the next sinister provision is that as of 2020, Congress loses any and all power to restrain these unelected panelists/legislators.

Ladies, you do not need to be a lawyer or a politician to see this law as the truly oppressive power grab that it is. One Congress is not actually permitted to bind future Congresses, so we can all hope that the courts would strike down this attempt in the healthcare law to limit future Congresses' right to to limit or eliminate the IPABs. But please let it sink in—today's Democrat leaders in Washington are utterly determined to inflict absolute federal control of the healthcare system on future Americans, regardless of what their elected officials want. Sinister is not a strong enough word for this kind of ruling class tyranny

Another Reason Government-Run Healthcare Always Brings Suffering

Ladies, there is another thing that is really important to understand -- and that shows so clearly the need to get government out of the healthcare system as much as we can: *the best quality service will always come when there is a direct connection between you and your healthcare provider, and you and your insurer.*

The "middleman" controlling the dollars and the care hurts you (and your children, your parents, everyone). This is such an easy concept to understand—and a great practical insight you can share with friends who (ignorantly) think that government provided/paid for healthcare is a great idea. In short, if you want great care – advocate for freedom and free markets—get government out of the way!

The value of direct connection between you and your "provider" or—insist on being in charge of your life—insist on freedom!

Think of it this way: when you hire a hair stylist to cut your hair, and she does a lousy job, you would "fire" her, meaning you would never go back to her again. You control the quality of the services you choose to buy. And a stylist who is repeatedly fired would take steps to improve: she might go back to school, or practice listening better to what the customer wants. She is incentivized to respond to you and her other customers, because you pay her.

If someone else were paying her, say the government, to cut your hair, and all she had to do was keep the government payer happy, she would care a lot less about what you think about your haircut. And if you had nowhere else to turn for haircuts, you would keep going back for another lousy haircut.

This is the "third-party payer" problem. Under the "government pays for your haircuts" approach, there is a disconnect between the provider (hair stylist) and the recipient of services (you). You and every consumer would be better off, more in control of your life, if you had more direct control over, or connection with, your insurance provider and your healthcare provider.

Insurers and Healthcare Providers and Getting the Best Service.
Get Freedom—Get Better Insurance and Better Care

Insurers

Right now insurance companies cannot sell insurance across state lines. Congress could fix that in a very short bill—one that authorizes selling insurance across state lines. The immediate impact of that would be that individuals and businesses looking to buy health insurance could shop for the best insurance policies, the ones that best fit their needs. Insurance companies would likely respond with more policy choices, especially if state legislatures were inspired to reduce mandates on insurance companies.

Right now, insurance companies are highly regulated by the states, and many states mandate insurers to provide coverage for all sorts of things that most consumers do not want or need, and do not wish to pay for. Some states have more regulations than others. If purchase across state lines were permitted, the free market would bring about changes that benefit consumers—including probable changes in the mandates some states impose. You the consumer would have more choices, as would employers who purchase insurance for their employees.

This free market solution is, as you likely are by now guessing, supported by conservatives and opposed by liberals, because liberals like to control everything, people and businesses alike.

Healthcare providers

The more government gets entangled in the healthcare system, the more restrictions and limitations are established that keep you, the consumer, from choosing the healthcare provider you want. When you have fewer healthcare provider choices, fewer doctors or specialists, you have less power to hire and fire because you don't have other back-up provider choices.

Again, re-instituting free market principles that would provide the consumer more choices is a basic policy goal of conservatives, and as you likely have guessed, intolerable to liberals who want to make all important choices for you, and everyone.

Caring for Those Who Cannot Afford Insurance or Healthcare

The decision to push socialized medicine through Congress in 2010 despite massive opposition from the American people was, in my view, all about the Democrat goal of larger and more centralized big government, controlling more and more aspects of our American life. The "crisis" was manufactured, and the number of uninsured grossly and intentionally overstated. Most Americans at the time the healthcare takeover passed, and still today, do not want a healthcare system controlled by the federal government.

Concern for those individuals who cannot afford or choose not to buy, health insurance was "sold" as the justification for the takeover.

It's important to separate the issues of the lack of insurance, and the alleged lack of access to healthcare.

No system on earth is perfect, but America already provides access to healthcare for the poor through Medicaid, and to seniors, through Medicare. We have historically, and still do today, cared for our most vulnerable. We will undoubtedly continue to refine and improve those programs throughout our history. But creating a massive coerced-insurance purchase legal and administrative mess was completely unjustified.

When 89 percent of Americans who were polled in June 2008 said they were satisfied with their healthcare, there was no honest justification for the complete conversion of the healthcare system to the socialized medicine model the Democrats rammed through in 2010. That was nothing short of a power grab—and we must stand up against it!

Did You Know?...Stories and Facts to Share Chapter Five

When someone says "the healthcare system was broken…we had to do something."

You can say:

"Do you know what percent of Americans were happy with their own healthcare system only a year before the healthcare takeover by Congress? Well, in June of 2008, a large survey found that 89 percent of Americans were satisfied with their healthcare!

"But after a year of Democrat-led crisis creation, another poll found that 87% of Americans believed that the healthcare system needed to be fundamentally changed or completely rebuilt."

When someone says: "But socialized medicine works 'over there'—in England, Cuba, and Canada!"

You can say: "But when the rich and famous from around the world are sick, they come to America for the best help—400,000 people a year do that! Not to Cuba or France, but to the United States! People "vote" on the best healthcare system every day, by where they choose to come for care. Why would we ruin ours and make it more like the systems people try to get away from?

"And America has the most modern and best healthcare equipment in the world. Like the MRI machines: the U.S. has 27 MRI machines per million Americans, while Canada and Britain have a mere six MRI machines per million people. Same for CT Scanners---the free market system works better!

"And American survival rates for cancer are much higher than in Cuba or France."

When you hear, "But the new healthcare system will save money, and my healthcare will be free," be ready with the facts.

You can say: "Nothing is free—the taxpayers will always be paying for the healthcare system. And once it's free more people will take advantage and find more services they want, and we the taxpayers will pay more.

"Seventy five percent of the costs of Obamacare will fall on the backs of Americans earning $120,000 a year or less. (http://www.humanevents.com/2012/06/30/wsj-chief-economist-75-of-obamacare-costs-will-fall-on-backs-of-those-making-less-than-120k-a-year/; accessed July 8, 2012) (Remember the president who promised that taxes for those earning less than $250,000 a year would not go up?)

"The Congressional Budget Office (CBO) is already doubling its estimate of what the national healthcare takeover will cost, acknowledging that the new law will cost taxpayers $1.76 trillion between now and 2022, and the full accounting for it, including implementation costs, is $2.6 trillion. (http://www.humanevents.com/2012/03/15/obamacare-twice-as-expensive-as-promised-and-getting-worse/ Accessed July 8, 2012).

"The national healthcare takeover will cost American taxpayers trillions and at the end of the day, we'll have worse and more expensive coverage. You see how well the government manages the Post Office and the DMV, and you want to put them in charge of healthcare?"

"That death panel talk was just ridiculous—no one would do that!"

"The IPAB—Independent Payment Advisory Board—indeed is part of the healthcare bill. The IPAB's job is to restrain Medicare spending—the spending we do to care for the health of our senior citizens who have paid into the system for their whole working lives. The IPAB has authority even Congress cannot override—and their job is to keep costs down. One way or another, the job of reducing costs must include limiting care."

Ladies, your compassion may have caused you to support or at least consider supporting the national healthcare law. If so, I hope this chapter will inspire you to question why, if it is truly a noble and good idea, the supporters resorted to the tactics they used to get it passed: the arm-twisting, manipulation of public thought, gross misrepresentation of data and facts, and why they were impelled to include onerous provisions designed to prevent future Congresses from representing the will of the people in making changes to it.

★ ★ Chapter Six ★ ★

Who Cares Enough to Help the Needy?

Social Justice, Charity, Social Spending, and Dependency Creation

Can We Talk…About How to Really Help All Americans

Compassion for the needy drives some women to vote on the liberal side, because they see support for social and government assistance pro-grams as an effective means of helping others. But shouldn't we look at the outcome, the actual impact of that government spending? And what kind of society it is creating?

Since the Great Society was launched in 1964, America has, through our tax system, transferred $16 trillion from taxpayers to recipients, and we have more poverty today, nearly 50 years later, than we did then. Not only that but the devastating impact on families and children has been and continues to be staggering.

Social spending is one area where political correctness silences discussion about what really is the best way to help people, because any opposition to ever increasing government assistance is denounced as selfish or calloused. But if we really want to help, don't we have to start with honest conversation? Let's talk about it!

> *"The assumption that spending more of the taxpayer's money will make things better has survived all kinds of evidence that it has made things worse.*
>
> *The black family-- which survived slavery, discrimination, poverty, wars and depressions-- began to come apart as the federal government moved in with its well-financed programs to "help."*
>
> —Dr. Thomas Sowell, Ph.D., Conservative African American
> economist, author, and columnist

Topics We'll Talk About in Chapter Six
The Charitable Goodness of Americans

What Does Private Charity Have to Do With a Policy Discussion on Social Spending?

How Private Charity Information Impacts Social Spending Policy

The Big Picture on Taxpayer-Funded Government Assistance Programs in America Today

Assistance for Our Most Vulnerable

How Did America Get to This Point of Massive Reliance on Government?

The Brutal Impact on Families of the Welfare Programs

A Tale of Two Approaches the PDI and a NYC Welfare Office

Meet Two Friends of Mine, Linda and Laurie

Did You Know?...Stories and Facts to Share

The Charitable Goodness of Americans

Women Care

When women are polled about what inspires their vote, one of the most common answers is their concern for the needy and wanting to be sure society looks out for the most unfortunate. Compassion inspires our votes, as does our yearning for a fair and just society.

That's why I am going to share with you some big picture ideas about charity and society before we delve into the politics and economic realities of social spending and social justice.

The Three Sectors (Sources of Funding) in American Society

American society includes three "sectors" or sections that provide financial support for charitable causes. Those are the private sector (individuals and businesses), the public sector (government at all levels, funded by taxpayers), and the nonprofit sector, (the churches, charities, foundations, etc., funded by donations almost entirely by individuals and businesses).

Massive, Voluntary, Nongovernmental Charity

While the American political discussion normally focuses only on government spending, over the decades and even more so today, nonprofit foundations, church-based charities, other large private charities, and individual/personal charity, taken together, amass *literally billions of dollars annually.* These funds are meant to help Americans facing the challenges of poverty, illness, hunger, homelessness, domestic violence, natural disasters, and every other conceivable difficulty.

It's vital to know about and consider the impact of this nongovernment generosity, for several reasons. This information on charity puts in a more factual and accurate light the condition of our society in terms of need, as well as in terms of whether wealthy Americans are the greedy and miserly folks that some politicians accuse them of being.

But even more importantly, the kind of society and culture that is created, promoted, and protected by the fact of profound, generous charitableness is very different, and much better, than a society that creates and promotes forced collectivism by a powerful centralized government as the primary means of helping those in need.

Just How Charitable are Americans?

America the beautiful is also America the astoundingly generous and charitable.

If you doubt that, I urge you to read a book called *Who Really Cares* by Arthur C. Brooks. (*Who Really Cares*, by Arthur C. Brooks, published in 2006 by Basic Books, a member of Perseus Books Group.) You'll learn that Americans are more generous as individuals than are the citizens of virtually all other nations on earth. Arthur Brooks is a former Syracuse University professor of business and government policy. The book is a heavily researched and thoroughly footnoted catalog of studies on charitable giving in the United States.

American citizens make private charitable donations that add up to about a quarter of a trillion dollars, every year. That's a total of private donations in the amount of $250 billion a year. (Ibid p. 3) This does not include donations by foundations or corporations or from bequests, and it does not include any monies contributed by the government from tax revenues.

But Which *Americans are charitable?*

When Professor Brooks set out to do his in depth study of charitable giving in America, he assumed that he would find, consistent with traditional stereotypes and his own views at the time, that "political liberals" genuinely cared more about others than conservatives do, and that therefore the liberals would turn out to be the most privately charitable people. (Ibid, p. 12).

The most surprising outcome of this research

What Professor Brooks found surprised him so much that he re-ran the analyses on the research results. The answer was astonishing to him, because the truth was exactly the opposite of the stereotypes, assumptions, and firmly held opinions prevalent in our culture.

The short answer to his question *Who Really Cares?* After studying mountains of data and rechecking it, Professor Brooks found:

> **Which Americans are the most frequent and generous donors to charities of all kinds?**
> *"Political conservatives, cultural conservatives, Republicans, people who are skeptical of the government interfering in our nation's economic life, those in strong families, those with religious faith, and those who embrace personal entrepreneurism, by every measure, are by far the most generous and charitable Americans.*
> *"These facts hold true regardless of race, ethnicity, gender or income level."*
> —*Arthur C. Brooks, Who Really Cares? 2006, pp. 1 to 11*

The Giving Patterns of Liberals Versus Conservatives

In the year 2000, "households headed by a conservative gave, on average, 30 percent more money to charity than households headed by a liberal." (Ibid pg. 21) Even more amazing, the liberal households earned on average more money, but donated less money, than the conservative households. (p. 22)

The Giving Patterns of Democrats Versus Republicans

The pattern remains the same when the researchers looked at political party affiliation. Republicans consistently are more likely to donate to charity than Democrats, and to donate more, even when researchers controlled for income level. (p. 22)

Even Blue States Versus Red States

The Red State versus Blue State election outcome in 2004 offers further evidence of the same pattern. Red States are those that went Republican, so in 2004 supported President Bush, while Blue States went with the Democrat candidate Senator John Kerry. To summarize the research results, "the red states are more charitable than the blue states." (Ibid 23) By a lot: "of the twenty-five states that donated a portion of household income above the national average, twenty-four gave a majority of their popular votes to George W. Bush for president; only one gave the election to John F. Kerry." (Ibid 23)

Professor Brooks fills 160 pages with details about the many studies on this subject, and raises, addresses and refutes every single imaginable liberal argument against his findings. Quite simply, he proves that it is undeniably true that conservatives and Republicans are more generous, much more generous, with their money, time and efforts to help charitable causes, than are liberals and Democrats, regardless of race or ethnicity, or differences in income levels.

Those are the facts, and they are important to keep in mind as we go forward looking at the battles over budgetary priorities.

What Does Private Charity Have to Do with a Policy Discussion on Social Spending?

These research results are helpful to the American political discussion for several reasons:

1. Facts matter. When political debates occur on the subject of spending and budget cuts, one of the most common tactics the Democrats use is to say that Republicans, or conservatives, do not care about others. At a minimum, this research should put a complete stop to this obviously false argument. Tell your friends. They may not believe it, but tell them anyway.

2. When you do hear someone claim that Democrats must care more because they support social spending by the government—which is a form of wealth redistribution— challenge them, nicely. Ask why is it, if they care so much, that Democrats donate so much less of their personal money than Republicans do, even in studies when the Democrat has the higher income level.

3. Recognize that when Democrats clamor for more social spending by the government, they are agitating for the

government to spend other people's money. Supporting increased government spending is not an act of personal charity.

4. The breadth and depth of private charitable donations in America is a mostly untold story. Professor Brooks's book goes even deeper into the subject of charity in terms of nonmonetary donations. The same givers who donate money, also donate time to good causes, and are actually even more likely to donate blood. Most of us do charitable work already, out of compassion, and find it greatly rewarding. Challenge those who have supported ever increasing government-based social spending in the past to redirect some of their fervor toward direct support for private charity efforts, and encourage them to discover the society-enriching and personally satisfying results.

Societal Impact of Voluntary Charity versus Taxpayer-Funded Assistance
The "vote myself benefits" impact

Consider the creation, structuring, and cementing of political power that happens under ever-growing government assistance programs. Liberals and Democrats create and grow social spending programs, funded by the shrinking number of Americans who work and pay taxes. The proceeds of those spending programs go to an ever-larger group of Americans who do not work, or work little, and who live in dependence on those programs. Is there any question how the recipients of those dependency-creating programs will vote? Does this "voting myself benefits from the government" *approach serve the best interests of a prosperous and self-reliant American future?*

The growing givers-versus-takers divide

There are other consequences to society of a bigger and bigger government using its power to tax, and then to redistribute the wealth.

Government assistance engenders resentment among taxpayers, an impersonal or nonexistent connection between the recipients and donors, a sense of entitlement among recipients, and as we have clearly seen in the last 40 years, a growing class of dependent citizens who live and function by relying on government assistance. These recipients are precious Americans who are being deprived of the joy and dignity that only self-reliance can bring.

The Societal Cohesion Created by Charitable Giving

Contrast that with the dynamics and consequences for society of private and foundation-based charity. Charity by citizens toward other citizens leads to awareness on the part of more people about the challenges others in society face, involvement and connection by donors and recipients, and compassion by many for the real-life challenges others face, which are invisible to them under the government assistance model. Private charity creates a more connected society.

"Charity makes you happy, healthy, and rich"

That's the title of Chapter 7 in Professor Brooks' *Who Really Cares?*

There is a profound positive impact flowing from charitable giving, not just on the recipients, but on the givers too.

Here is a snapshot of America's generosity and who in America makes monetary contributions to others:
- About 3/4 of our American families choose during the year to make charitable contributions, and the average amount contributed per family is around 3.5 percent of their income, or $1,800.
  - Charitable donations annually run around $250 *billion* a year in America.
  - Only about 1/3 of those donations go to churches or religious activities.
  - While 225 million Americans make monetary charitable contributions each year, another large swath of Americans, around 75 million, do not ever give any money to charity.

• The same folks who donate money each year—the Givers—also are far more likely to donate time to community activities, to help friends informally, to donate blood, and even to return excess change given to them by a clerk at a store.

• Givers are more tolerant, less prejudiced, and more sympathetic.

• Neither race, ethnicity, income level, nor gender correlate to the likelihood of being a Giver.

• But political and religious leanings are very good predictors of whether a person will be a giver or not:

a. "Culturally traditional people—are the biggest givers in America today." (Brooks, p.11)

b. Political "conservatives are, on average, more personally charitable than liberals." (Ibid p. 11)

c. People who oppose the idea of government redistributing wealth are *twice as likely* to make charitable donations than people who support wealth redistribution. Even more amazing, wealth redistribution opponents (conservatives/Republicans) 'give away more than *one hundred times* as much money per year' than the person who supports the coerced government redistribution of wealth." (Liberals/Democrats) (Ibid p. 10)

—Arthur C. Brooks, *Who Really Cares*, 2006, Basic Books, p. 1–21.

How Private Charity Information Impacts Social Spending Policy

For one thing, it tells us more about where we are starting.

When the politicians argue about whether or not to increase social spending, we are rarely offered a factually accurate context for making that decision. Instead, advocates for increasing spending share unsubstantiated numbers about poverty, and truly heart-rending stories about the sufferings and plight of our fellow citizens. The easiest answer and seemingly most compassionate answer is to just simply agree with all requests for increased social spending, because no one wants to tolerate suffering, if we can prevent it.

But isn't both fair and in fact responsible to put requests for increases in social spending in some context? For example, doesn't it matter (1) how much our society is already donating via private charity to address these problems (2) what percentage of our current tax dollars already go to assistance programs as opposed to, for example national defense and other budgetary necessities, and (3) how much overall we are currently spending—where are we on the debt and deficit?

The family budget analogy

As we turn now to looking at where we are as a nation in terms of our social spending, it is helpful to consider comparing the federal budget with your family budget. Just as in a family when we need some adult to put the brakes on spending that will bankrupt the family, you'll see as we review our spending on social programs, it is only the Republican Party making any effort to address the situation responsibly. The consistent answer from most elected Democrats when anyone points out that our spending on government assistance programs is out of control, is "tax the greedy rich more," and advocacy for more spending.

The Big Picture on Taxpayer-Funded Government Assistance Programs in America Today

Anyone looking at the information in the following chart can figure out that things in America must change. Not a tiny tweak here and there, but big time. Let's at least start with acknowledging that the picture presented is screaming at us "We need to do something!"

Let's start by clearing up the myth that we Americans spend more on our defense budget than our social spending budget...

But, Don't We Spend More on Wars than Welfare?

Democrats and liberals regularly claim that America spends too much on national defense and too little on government assistance and social welfare programs of various kinds. Republicans argue the opposite. This is a "facts matter" issue. While waste of government money no doubt occurs

---

• *Since 1964 America has spent $16 trillion on the War on Poverty. We have more poverty today than in 1964.*

• *Social Security is broke: Social Security (SS) pays out more in benefits than it takes in through taxes. Both the Social Security Administration and the Congressional Budget Office (CBO) agree this is a permanent situation—because of the sheer number of retirees. Medicare is equally "broke."*

• *Over the next quarter century, 77 million baby boomers will start collecting SS checks and Medicare benefits.*

• *More than 70.5 percent of all federal spending is on dependency programs, up from 48.5 percent in 1990.*

• *America spends more on government assistance (welfare) than on national defense. This welfare spending includes TANF, Medicaid, SNAP (food stamps), Head Start, public housing, and Social Services Block Grants.*
• *In 2010, 98 million individuals, or 32 percent of our population, were enrolled in Medicare, Medicaid or CHIP (Children's Health Insurance Program). That's one in three Americans relying on government for their healthcare.*

• *One in seven Americans is on food stamps.*

• *By 2049, Medicare, Medicaid and Social Security will consume 100 percent of the federal tax revenues—no money will be left for anything else.*

• *Over the next 10 years, the cost to taxpayers for all welfare spending combined, will be an anticipated $10.3 trillion.*

(The 2012 Index of Dependence on Government, Heritage Center for Data Analysis, February 8, 2012; accessed May 14, 2012)

---

throughout the federal budget, and should be addressed and corrected, what's the truth about how our spending breaks down?

The liberal leaning Center on Budget and Policy Priorities (CBPP) provided a summary in 2012 of our nation's fiscal year 2011 spending. (http://www.cbpp.org/cms/index.cfm?fa=view&id=1258; accessed May 14, 2012. The information in the chart below is taken from their summary.)

From the chart you can see that 20 percent of the federal budget goes to national defense, while the combination of Social Security, Medicare,

Category	percent of Budget Dollars
Defense & Security, including the Iraq & Afghanistan conflicts:	20 percent/$718 Billion
Social Security:	20 percent/$731 Billion
Medicare, Medicaid and CHIP: (nearly 2/3 to Medicare)	21 percent/$769 Billion
Government Assistance/Safety Net/Welfare Earned income tax credits, cash payments to individuals or households, Supplemental SS, In-kind assistance for low-income families such as food stamps, school meals, housing assistance, child-care assistance, energy bill help, aid for abused and neglected children, unemployment insurance, free cell phones:	13 percent/$466 Billion
Interest on the debt:	6 percent/$230 Billion
Benefits for Federal employee retirees & Veterans:	7 percent
Transportation & Infrastructure:	3 percent
Education	6 percent
Science & Medical Research:	2 percent
Non-Security International:	1 percent
Other:	4 percent

(Rounding causes total to be higher than 100 percent.)

Center on Budget and Policy Priorities (CBPP) (http://www.cbpp.org/cms/index.cfm?fa=view&id=1258; accessed May 14, 2012)

Medicaid, CHIP, government assistance/welfare spending, is more than twice that high, amounting to 54 percent. We spend much more on dependency creating programs than on our national defense.

But what if we just cut ALL defense spending—then couldn't we keep up this pace on social spending?

Defense spending makes up only 20 percent of the federal budget, and providing for our national defense is the government's number1 job in America. This is not to say that the defense budget should never be cut, or that defense spending is never wasteful, because surely it is, sometimes. Republicans and Democrats have periodically pointed to some particularly egregious wasteful spending in the military budget and demanded that the problem be resolved.

> A recent scholarly study shows that "even eliminating vital defense spending completely *would not solve the entitlement spending problem."* (http://www.heritage.org/federalbudget/defense-spending-entitlement-spending-problem: accessed May 14, 2012)

Understanding of this point is key: If we stopped defense spending completely in 2012, the massive growth of entitlement spending would still result in enormous fiscal disaster. Gals, it is time for us to open our ears and learn the facts to that we can open our mouths and do something about this!

So let's look at our nation's social spending.

What Are Dependency Versus Nondependency Programs

Nondependency federal spending is on things the Constitution requires the government to do, such as providing for our national defense, and oth- er areas where all Americans know that individuals cannot carry out these tasks (individuals are not going to start ordering new submarines for the Navy). These are areas where only the government can, and they must, provide these things. Of course, government uses the people's money collected in taxes to do them. Note that only 30 percent of our federal budget goes for these basic, Constitutionally mandated expenditures.

Dependency programs are federal government spending programs that cover people's personal life needs and that the communities, charities and other societal institutions also assist in providing, such as food, shelter, etc.. These also include farm subsidies and other agricultural spending.

Within Dependency Programs, Means-Tested Versus Not Means-Tested

Dependency programs include some that taxpayers pay into, and from which they are eligible at a certain age to receive benefits such as Social Security and Medicare. These do not involve means testing.

Others dependency programs are means-tested (available only to lower -income Americans), and were created or expanded largely in the 1960s.

Ladies—I discuss the Social Security and Medicare programs in Chapter Seven on Government, as they involve some different dynamics because they are programs recipients have already contributed toward throughout their working lives in anticipation of receiving benefits after retirement.

Assistance for Our Most Vulnerable

"Means-tested" dependency spending is, put simply, the social spending offered only to Americans below a certain income level.

How much are we talking about?

For 2011, America spent $466 billion on the government assistance of various kinds including SNAP (food stamps), earned income tax credits, school meals, housing assistance, and a host of other programs where tax dollars are distributed to lower income Americans.

Just the 13 percent spent on government assistance/welfare, is more than one out of every 10 dollars we spend. In addition, both Medicaid and CHIP are means-tested programs on which we spent something in the range of $256 billion in 2011.

What are all these dependency programs?

A typical family receiving government assistance can receive money or help from at least six or seven programs, such as SNAP (food stamps), public housing, TANF (Temporary Assistance for Needy Families), Medicaid, CHIP, and social services block grants.

Free cell phones for the poor?

Under a federal government program called Universal Service Fund, Pennsylvanians on public assistance now get free cell phones, with 250 minutes a month for "free." (http://www.nypost.com/p/blogs/capitol/free_cell_phones_are_civil_right_htTMcKQFrjdvyl9A6NHPdP; accessed on May 14, 2012)

By the way, how poor is "poor?"

Again, women's hearts intuitively respond to human suffering. We really do not want anyone to be hungry or in misery.

But have you checked out what "poverty" means in America, today? (http://www.heritage.org/research/reports/2011/07/what-is-poverty; accessed May 14, 2012)

- *74 percent of the "poor" own a car or truck*
- *70 percent own a VCR*
- *64 percent own a DVD*
- *63 percent have cable or satellite*
- *53 percent have a video game system*
- *50 percent have a computer*
- *30 percent have two or more cars*

And,

- *on an average day, just 1 percent of households have someone who is forced to miss a meal*
- *only ¼ of 1 percent, or .25 percent of children on any given day are hungry*
- *96 percent of poor parents say their children are never hungry during the year because they could not afford food*

No one wants anyone to be hungry or to suffer, but we also need to know enough of the facts to recognize what "poverty" is and is not, in America.

"Free" is in quotes because, as we learned in our discussion in Chapter Four, there still is no such thing as a free anything. Either taxpayers will pick up the tab because government is paying for this, or if the phone providers are forced to "donate" the units and minutes, their paying customers will pick up the cost in the form of higher rates. Girls, I don't know about you, but I wish someone else would pay my cell phone bills, but I doubt that will happen anytime soon.

Food stamps as just one example of skyrocketing dependency

America nearly doubled spending on food stamps between 2008 and 2011—in three short years. The food stamp outlay for just FY 2011 is estimated at $78.5 billion.

How Did America Get to This point of Massive Reliance on Government?

The brief history below tells you how America got to the point that we are on track today to spend over $10 trillion dollars on welfare programs over the next 10 years. But the core of the explanation is that creating and cultivating dependency among America's poor, besides being a cruel suppression of their growth into responsible, participating and self-reliant citizens, is the ticket for the Democrat Party to millions of votes every single election year. People have, in the prescient words of Benjamin Franklin, found out that they "can vote themselves money," and the ending of Franklin's warning was that once we arrived at that point, "that will herald the end of the republic."

Ladies, our votes of support for ever-growing government assistance, made out of compassion, will trigger a most unhappy future for America if we cannot make fundamental changes to that system very soon. And you only need read the remainder of this chapter to figure out that the Democrat Party cannot and will not ever make any such reforms, because those reforms would enrage their dependent voting base.

How Democrats structure welfare—the handout mode

Democrat President Johnson launched the War on Poverty in 1964. Since then, America has spent $16 trillion on that war. In 1962, about 11.7 percent of Americans received government assistance through the programs that existed at that time, and in 2010, nearly a full 50 years later, that percentage has nearly doubled, to 21.8 percent. (The 2012 Index of Dependence on Government, Heritage Center for Data Analysis, February 8, 2012; accessed May 14, 2012)

Let that sink in: $16 trillion later, neediness in America has gone up, not down. The percentage of Americans receiving assistance went from 11.7 percent to 21.8 percent. This giant wealth transfer program that took American taxpayers' money and redistributed it to other Americans; it not only failed to solve the poverty problem, it made it worse. More people were impoverished.

How Republicans structure welfare—the hand-up mode

Thirty-two years later in 1996, the Republican-led Congress passed the Welfare Reform bill (PRWORA), which among other things, swapped out the AFDC (Aid to Families with Dependent Children) program for the newly created TANF (Temporary Assistance to Needy Families) program. (The 2012 Index of Dependence on Government, Heritage Center for Data Analysis, February 8, 2012; accessed May 14, 2012)

The essential differences between AFDC and TANF were…?

The Republican-supported TANF imposed time limits on how long recipients could remain on the receiving end of government handouts, while the Democrat-supported AFDC had included no limits on how many years Americans could remain on the welfare rolls. TANF imposed new requirements that recipients demonstrate that they were looking for work, or were at least taking part in work-related activities.

In short, TANF made self-sufficiency the goal, whereas AFDC had lacked practical incentives to inspire self-sufficiency. In fact, AFDC had cultivated if not encouraged growing dependence on government.

Republican-backed welfare reform had as its primary goal to move people from being reliant on government to functioning self-sufficiently. And it worked! Welfare caseloads declined, from 4.4 million families, down to 1.9 million families between 1996 and 2010.

Republicans made further reforms to TANF in the 2006 TANF reauthorization, and in part those reforms were targeted at reducing unwed motherhood, and supporting stable family units. (The 2012 Index of Dependence on Government, Heritage Center for Data Analysis, February 8, 2012; accessed May 14, 2012)

Democrats undid welfare reform aimed at self-sufficiency the first chance they got.

As soon as Democrats regained control of the White House and Congress, in early 2009, they reversed key components of welfare reform. Specifically:

".... in February 2009, the Democrat-controlled Congress and the new Obama Administration enacted legislation that essentially overturned the fiscal foundation of welfare reform and reverted to an AFDC-style funding scheme. States now receive cash bonuses when they swell the welfare rolls. Moreover, covering 80 percent of the cost of new welfare caseloads, the federal government is giving states much more money than it did under the old welfare program. The legislation clearly undercuts the incentives wrought by welfare reform to move individuals into work and self-sufficiency." (My emphasis). (The 2012 Index of Dependence on Government, Heritage Center for Data Analysis, February 8, 2012, page 16; accessed May 14, 2012.)

Further, in July of 2012, the Democrat-run Department of Health and Human Services issued an Information Memorandum that "guts" the work requirements that were established in federal law under welfare reform. (http://blog.heritage.org/2012/07/12/obama-guts-welfare-reform/) Accessed August 16, 2012). No public discussion, no national debate, just a memorandum that tells the states "never mind about those federal work requirements—you can do whatever you want" (my words, not those of HHS). (http://www.acf.hhs.gov/programs/ofa/policy/im-ofa/2012/im201203/im201203.html Accessed August 16, 2012)

Note the difference in how the two parties went about making the policy changes they preferred in welfare reform.

Republicans openly and repeatedly advocated for the welfare reform provisions that eventually passed in 1996, and they made their case to the public and in public about the need to reverse the trend of the creation of long-term government dependency. President Clinton vetoed the bill twice, and finally signed it the third time, stating that the reform bill would take an historic chance "to make welfare what it was meant to be, a second chance, not a way of life."

By contrast, the Democrats pursued their welfare policy outside of the limelight of public debate, and via administrative fiat. The legislative undermining of the welfare reform provisions were quietly added into a catchall stimulus bill in February of 2009, and it was weeks before most folks even found out that the hard-fought-for and successful reforms had been largely eliminated. .(http://www.nationalreview.com/articles/226878/ending-welfare-reform-we-knew-it/editors#; accessed May 14, 2012) It is very questionable whether HHS had authority under federal law to cut the heart out of the requirement that recipients of government assistance make attempts to find work. Making that change in the law should have been the job of the United States Congress, as it was in 1996 when the welfare reform legislation passed. But this is another example of the manner in which today's Democrat Party operates. The 1996 Welfare reform legislation was popular with the American people, and Democrats did not have the backbone or moral courage to openly advocate for its repeal, so they just did administratively/authoritatively. (http://blog.heritage.org/2012/08/08/morning-bell-obama-denies-gutting-welfare-reform/ Accessed August 15, 2012

You have to ask yourself why. Why do elected Democrats prefer social programs that mire people in helpless dependence? Why wouldn't they pursue programs that lead Americans to self-sufficiency? They have access to and awareness of the same information you are reading here, and much more. It's not like they don't know.

One final point: We talked earlier about the hidden path to socialism, marked not by loud pronouncements but instead by a series of regulations and policy changes that weaken the freedom and free markets on which our unparalleled prosperity is based. Swelling the ranks of the dependents both justifies higher taxes on the hard working Americans to pay for the assistance programs, and creates a larger class of people more dependent on the government. The more folks are dependent on government and not self-sufficient, the more power and control government has and must exercise over the people.

Still doubting that Democrats try to increase dependence on government?

Ladies, I know that for many of us the idea that one political party would actually try to increase the number of people who are dependent on government seems so sinister that you may be thinking it just couldn't be true. But consider this:

A Food Stamp Party???

In 2012, under a Democrat administration, the USDA (United States Department of Agriculture) spent between $2.5 and $3 million dollars running radio ads urging food stamp (SNAP) recipients to host social events, including games, activities, food and entertainment, *for the purpose of urging their guests to sign up for food stamps!* They spent your tax dollars on ads imploring more people to sign up for food stamps. A pamphlet on the USDA website contains the same message— try to grow the food stamps program! This from an administration that has already brought us a huge increase in spending on food stamps!

This is not just a totally irresponsible expenditure of your hard earned tax dollars, it is proof if you possibly needed more, that the Democrat party's leadership in 2012 desperately wants more Americans to become helplessly reliant on government. http://dailycaller.com/2012/06/27/usda-suggests-food-stamp-parties-games-to-increase-participation/ accessed July 13, 2012.

The Brutal Impact on Families of the Welfare Programs

Beyond immersing Americans in long-term dependency, the decades-long welfare state has had another devastating impact on America's most vulnerable population: the massive breakdown of families resulting in fewer children being raised in the safety and security of an intact family unit. Although divorce is sometimes the best choice, and many single moms or dads are wonderful parents, study after study proves that children thrive best in a home with two parents who are married.

Substituting the responsibility of parents to supply family income and support, with free stuff from the government, greatly degrades the quality of life for women and children, and for the men who abandone their families, too.

The data below are about the impact on children of the breakdown of the family. Note the timing: the breakdown of the family parallels the timing of the rise in Great Society, and the massive social spending that was meant to help.

"The erosion of marriage and family is a primary contributing factor to child poverty and welfare dependence, and it figures significantly in a host of social problems. A child born out of wedlock is seven times more likely to be poor than a child raised by married parents, and more than 80 percent of long-term child poverty occurs in broken homes or homes where the parents never married. Moreover, unwed parents and the absence of fathers in the home negatively affect a child's development, educational achievement, and psychological well-being, as well as increasing a propensity toward delinquency and substance abuse.

"For the past four decades, the unwed birth rate in America has been rising steadily, from 5.3 percent in 1960, to 41 percent in 2009. Among blacks, 72.8 percent of children born in 2009 were to unmarried parents; among Hispanics, the percentage was 53.2 percent. Although the pace of growth in the proportions of births to unmarried women slowed in the immediate years after welfare reform, more recently, it has risen rapidly. From 2002 to 2009, the share of nonmarital births increased by one-fifth.

"In 2009, 1.7 million children were born to unmarried parents."

(The 2012 Index of Dependence on Government, Heritage Center for Data Analysis, February 8, 2012, p. 15; accessed May 14, 2012.)

The loss of individual self-worth and the loss to society-more negative side effects of decades of government assistance

Did you ever think about the fact that the creation of the massive dependency class not only hurt the individual recipients who never learned the satisfaction of self-reliance, but that society lost out too, in never realizing the value of the creativity, ingenuity, products and services those who do not participate in the economy, might have brought? Who knows all the progress and products our society would be enjoying if the fruits of the labors of those who have not participated in our economy were suddenly available.

How Is the Impact of Welfare a Conservative Versus Liberal Issue?

Two quotes from prominent spokesmen from the conservative versus liberal side, say it all.

George McGovern, Democrat standard-bearer and leader, former Democrat candidate for U.S. President, and U.S. Senator from South Dakota, wrote a book published in 2011 called *What it Means to be a Democrat.* In that book he speaks proudly and supportively of the Democrats as the party of "…Lyndon Johnson's Great Society," and describes with unswerving determination the goal of the Democrat party to be the party that will continue to support and boost government funding for virtually all existing social programs.

In pertinent part, Senator McGovern speaks of one portion of the welfare programs he helped to create, saying:

"As one of the senators who originally proposed WIC (Women, Infants, and Children) and saw it into law, I feel a father's pride that it has fed roughly 177 million low-income hungry children and mothers—and a father's grief that it has been so drastically cut." (Ibid page 7.)

Ladies, absolutely, in all 237 pages of Democrat McGovern's book, there is no reference of any kind to the undeniable fact that welfare programs trap millions in helpless dependence on government, parallel the destruction of the family, and wreak havoc on children growing up in the welfare society. McGovern, like many Democrats, is content with a good motive and lots of taxpayer money spent, without regard to the impact—the long-term dependency and misery those programs create. It's the Fish-Giver (from Chapter Three) mentality.

Dr. Thomas Sowell, the conservative African American economist, author, and columnist, by contrast, says:

"The assumption that spending more of the taxpayer's money will make things better has survived all kinds of evidence that it has made things worse. The black family—which survived slavery, discrimination, poverty, wars, and depressions—began to come apart as the federal government moved in with its well-financed programs to 'help.'" (http://chicago-freedom-forum. blogspot.com/2009/06/great-quotes-from-thomas-sowell.html; accessed May 15, 2012)

A Tale of Two Approaches, the PDI and a NYC Welfare Office

Ladies, sometimes a short story makes a point better than a thousand-page textbook ever could. In that spirit, I want to share with you two "short stories." One is about a Dallas-based charity, and the other is actually a transcript of an interview. These "stories" offer a contrast between the impact, power and "outcomes" of long-term government assistance programs, as compared with personal charity.

The New York City Welfare Office
Alexandra Pelosi (daughter of Democrat Congresswoman Nancy Pelosi) shot a video documentary made up of "interviews" of people in New York City in line to get government assistance. She spoke first to the doorman of the building, and then to several different men, and one woman, who were in line at the "welfare office."

Ms. Pelosi aired the interview on the Bill Maher show, and it is available online. (http://www.youtube.com/watch?v=c2kGPdxkofo; accessed June 4, 2012)

Alexandra Pelosi: Hey, Bill! I'm in New York City. This is where I live. Across from the welfare office. Meet Joe, the doorman.

Doorman: For 16 years, I have been working at this address, and for 16 years there are people walking by this building with a white piece of paper in their hand, looking for (Flex?) and they come up freely and say "I'm looking for the welfare office" or "I'm looking for social services" or "I'm looking for food stamps."

I see that most of them are able-bodied (camera pans to young man in welfare line doing pretty crisp push-ups on the sidewalk). They don't look like they are handicapped in any way. They just look like they don't want to work, and it's really, really hard to look at this and say "I come to work every day, why can't you?"

(Camera turns to interviews of people in line at the welfare office.)

Guy: I am here to try to get some Obama-bucks. That's what I want to try...some Obama bucks.

Another Guy: I am here to get some benefits; you know what I mean (blowing smoke out) to get a check. I want a check.

Alexandra Pelosi *(to woman):* Tell me why you like Obama.

Woman: Because he gives me stuff!

Alexandra Pelosi *(to guy):* Who you gonna vote for in this election?

Guy: Obama.

Alexandra Pelosi: Why?

Guy: Because he's black.

Alexandra Pelosi *(to different guy):* What do you get from the government? Tell me everything you get from the government.

Guy: All I get...stamps...we call it money in the palm...we call it money in the palm.

Alexandra Pelosi: What kind of benefits are you getting?

Guy: Let's see, whatever the hell they got to offer...it ain't like they got a checklist like you can go "this" "this" and "that." I'm just here to get what I can get.

Woman: Food stamps. It's just food. It's like food.

Alexandra Pelosi

(to guy):   When's the last time you actually worked?

Guy: Aw…I'd say about half a decade.

Alexandra Pelosi

(to different guy):   But you're a perfectly healthy young man; why aren't you working right now?

Guy: My background. Once you go to jail it's hard to get a job.

Alexandra Pelosi

(to different guy):   Why should I help you? Why should my tax dollars be going to you?

Guy: Only cause my ancestors came here…helped build this place.

Alexandra Pelosi: What do you mean?

Guy: My ancestors…the slaves.

Alexandra Pelosi: How many kids do you have?

Guy: I have five.

Alexandra Pelosi: How many mothers?

Guy: Four baby mothers.

Alexandra Pelosi: Four baby mamas?

Alexandra Pelosi

(to different guy):   Do you really want to work or do you just want to get a free check?

Guy: I just want the check.

Alexandra Pelosi: There is a sign behind you that says Waverly Job Center. Do you have any intention of going in to get a job? Or are you just going to get the food stamps?

Guy: Not looking for a job. Maybe a career, but not a job. (To passing woman) How you doin? You're lookin' good today!

Alexandra Pelosi: It sounds like you're looking for a date.

Guy: Hey, single, ready to mingle.

Ladies, let's contrast that picture of the life created by a far-away face-less government in Washington handing out checks, food stamps and benefits to dependent people around the country, with the PDI program in Dallas.

PDI/NLO: Changing lives of those suffering in prostitution

The Dallas PDI/NLO—Prostitute Diversion Initiative/ New Life Opportunities ("PDI")—program works to help lift women out of the dangerous, degrading and destructive life of prostitution. PDI started back in 2007, and was the brainchild of a thoughtful Dallas police officer who saw that repeatedly arresting prostitutes, who were also almost all suffering with drug and alcohol addictions, was not actually helping them, neither was it remedying the violence, drug abuse, and the spreading of disease that are part of the cycle of prostitution.

He shared his idea with the director of a nonprofit detoxification and drug treatment center called Homeward Bound and together they devised a first-of-its-kind initiative that took social services directly to the streets where these women were being arrested.

The Dallas area is home to several large truck stops along major interstate freeways, and those stops also serve as gathering places for prostitutes and their customers, and drug dealers. Officers regularly patrol these stops, and arrests for prostitution are common.

On an October night in 2007, the Prostitution Diversion Initiative was born and this one officer arranged for five of the prostitutes arrested to be evaluated by volunteer clinicians and taken before a local magistrate to be sent to Homeward Bound for detox and trauma counseling in lieu of going to jail that night. Homeward Bound was at that time a "live-in for 45 days" drug detoxification and treatment center. Those five women all eventually gave up prostitution, and were able to transition into a new life off the streets of Dallas. And a new idea took off.

This initial effort evolved into what is now a nationally recognized and highly impactful program that combines the resources of the Police Department, Sheriff 's office, the courts, other law enforcement, and a few dozen social service and faith-based organizations.

Once monthly a group of 60 or so volunteers meets up at a truck stop or other pre-determined location, and assists in the processing of the women who are arrested for prostitution. Those arrested can choose the diversion program (NLO) or jail, and for those who choose diversion, they are placed in available beds in local treatment centers, and a whole host of services are offered. Once they are clean, another niche of volunteer organizations works to help the women find jobs and teaches them how to interview. Another group offers gently used professional clothing for the women to wear to interviews.

Of those 60 or so people who show up every month at the truck stop, most of the social service and law enforcement officials are volunteering their time. In fact, many of the patrol and vice officers who are actually on-duty, have requested to participate in the PDI. The others are just acting out of the most basic and noble American instincts: the instinct to love and help your fellow man. They are motivated by the desire to help lift others up. Additionally, there are several "peer advocates" (women who have suc- cessfully exited the life on the streets) and come back to work with the PDI to help reach out to their "sisters" from the streets and encourage them to seek help.

PDI does not "rescue" every single woman who comes through the program. There are dropouts and failures—but also brilliant successes. PDI symbolizes the American spirit of goodness and generosity that exists all over this country. Neighbors and communities come together to help, because this nation is one founded on values arising out of our Judeo-Christian heritage. Every community in America is filled with loving and caring Americans who work to help their neighbors in their own unique ways.

Meet Two Friends of Mine, Linda and Laurie

My good friend Linda, who lives in North Texas, agreed to be interviewed for this book. Her life story tells about as much about America's greatness as it does about her. Linda's life simply defies compartmentalization or accurate labeling.

You will just love how she took life on with feistiness and ingenuity.

Linda did not graduate from college, though she attended Fisk University, one of the "Ivy Leagues" of the traditionally black colleges that was rated in the top 15 percent of American colleges by Princeton Review. Linda learned after two years at Fisk that college required more studying and less enjoying life than she had engaged in, so left Fisk to go out on her own in life.

What follows is remarkable only in today's world: It was quite common only a handful of years ago. Linda first settled in Houston where she found some odd jobs, including working at a news station writing stories. She was making very little money, so she began contemplating what kind of business she could start. She learned about a class where she could learn how to get started in the world of making bids for large janitorial contracting jobs.

When Linda began thinking through what kinds of businesses she could create, she first considered opening a salon that offered manicures, pedicures, and similar services. Enticing as that idea was, she was persuaded by a friend that a more pragmatic and realistic idea was to pursue a simple service business.

So back she went to the janitorial contracting class. Linda could not afford the fee ($300) but bargained with the teacher, offering to do a news story about her class in exchange for taking the class. The deal was done, and Linda emerged with basic knowledge of the janitorial business, but no cleaning supplies, no cards or brochures, and no clients.

Linda quit her daytime employment a couple of years later and resourcefully turned to the Yellow Pages in search of her first client for her as yet non-existent janitorial service. She opened to an ad for a Firestone Tire store, called the manager and asked "Is your current janitorial service doing an absolutely fantastic job? "When he replied "no," she asked if she could come over and talk about that.

They met at the store 20 minutes later, he explained what was needed, and asked her to make a bid; she gave him one (made up out of thin air), and she had her first client. Before she left Firestone that day the manager asked if she could handle his four other stores also, to which she of course replied, "Sure!"

Next came her dilemma of locating cleaning supplies and a worker, so Linda called people she'd met in her janitorial contracting class, found one man with supplies and willingness to work, and hired him to do the Firestone stores.

From there, and using the same personable, one-on-one approach, Linda secured contracts for cleaning four Exxon service stations, and then an electrical supply company that was her largest business—a 10,000-square-foot place. She found through family contacts a woman who needed the work and Linda hired her to carry out some of these jobs.

After running this business a few years, Linda closed it and moved to Atlanta, where she worked two full-time jobs for three months just to make ends meet. She described her thoughts at this point in the mid-1980s: "you just do what you have to do" in terms of finding legal and legitimate work.

It then occurred to her that she could teach people in Atlanta how to do the janitorial contracting work she did in Houston, so she whipped together some class materials and a formal training program, ran an ad in a local paper, and started holding classes, charging each student $125 for a one-day class. She had 15 to 20 people in each class. Linda also ran a word processing business out of her apartment while in Atlanta.

Linda's resourcefulness in one more aspect of life is important to our discussion. She took a job at one point as a debt collector for a credit card company. She found this rather ironic as she had frequently felt financially pinched and was behind on her bills. She saw the job as an opportunity to put into practice something of what she had learned in her early religious training and in her love for mankind. She said she always treated people with respect, always worked in her heart and thoughts to love her neighbor as herself and tried not to judge them. Her kinder demeanor seemed to resonate with many people she called because she had an exceptionally high rate of success in getting folks lined up and signed up to pay their bills.

The debt collection business transferred her (at her request) to Dallas where she has had several businesses, one current and very successful one being a mediation service. She began that service in 1997 and developed her own mediating approach about which she wrote a book called "Playing the Resolution Card: Mediating Disputes with the Thought Resolution Protocol™, that was highly acclaimed as "not short of ingenious" in a Texas Bar Association, ADR Division 2009 book review. She has trained approximately 300 mediators to qualify them to mediate court-annexed cases in Texas, and employed many others as mediators.

The biggest distinctions between the welfare office line and the PDI effort are the presence or absence of the truly healing impact of person-to-person support and concern, and the sense of a temporary handout or a permanent hand-up.

What does Linda's life have to do with our social spending crisis?

Linda is extraordinary but at the same time ordinary. You know people just like her. Everyone does. Making your way in life by either locating a job or creating one by creating a product or offering a service was just the expectation for everyone in life, for most of America's history.

Part of the reason to tell Linda's story is that it so deeply conflicts with the worldview that current Democrat leaders in Washington try to sell America about how impossible it is for Americans, especially minority Americans, to find jobs, and that their only hope is to collapse into the abyss of dependence on government.

Linda's life story is the American story and is just as available today. One of our country's great needs is for leaders who will speak to the goodness and greatness of our American free market economy and its capacity to grow and multiply and divide businesses and jobs if we will only use our resourcefulness and energy. Linda and thousands like her are the antidote to dependence. Political leaders need to believe in and share the Linda stories and not the "you are a victim and you need government" stories.

Meet another Dallas friend of mine, Laurie

My friend Laurie is in my view, brave. During her childhood years she was the victim of repeated sexual abuse by her dad. Her mom was no help at all. Lots of women who endure such pain, trauma, confusion and sense of betrayal end up living troubled lives. Remember the Prostitute Diversion Initiative (PDI) I mentioned earlier? I learned through volunteering in that program that, as impossible as it may seem to imagine, many of those women ended up on the dangerous streets as prostitutes because that was a safer place for them than the abusive homes where they grew up.

But back to Laurie. She struggled too as a result of the abuse during her childhood. She found it hard to trust people, especially men, and had some pretty serious personal missteps along the way. Today, she is an extraordinarily successful entrepreneur. And she is a happily married mom with two fine young adult sons.

But the most important work she does, and I think she would say this, is to share her personal story with other women, to inspire them, to help them know that they too can triumph over the deepest and most painful of life's challenges. She shares her understanding that faith in God is vital to the healing path she found, and she inspires other women to find that path too.

Laurie's life story is a testament to the goodness of America and her people, and to the importance of faith and of religious freedom in America. Laurie's life did not get "rescued" by government-funded social programs on which we have spent trillions of dollars. Real turnarounds happen on a personal level, between people who care. In Laurie's case, long into adulthood, and still struggling personally, she connected with a woman who shared with her how faith in God, actual genuine faith, can heal. Laurie spent the next few years of her life finding and growing in that faith. God turned out to be the only place she could turn for lasting healing of guilt, pain, shame, bitterness and sadness.

There are several reasons I am telling you about Laurie. America is filled with good, generous and loving people like the woman who brought Laurie to God, and like Laurie herself who didn't stop at appreciating how her life was transformed, but who is in turn giving back by sharing with others her life journey. Impersonal, government-funded, bureaucratically run programs cannot compete with the power and effectiveness of the individual American reaching out to help her fellow American. Life stories like Laurie's are an utter rebuke to the characterization of our precious country by too many on the liberal Democrat side who paint America as a cold, "unfair," "greedy" country, and a testament to the goodness of the American people.

Did You Know?...Stories and Facts to Share Chapter Six

Ladies, support for social spending is among the key drivers of the women's vote. We want to take care of people, and we want to try to make life fairer. Thank goodness for the heart of women in America, whose charitable generosity is incalculable. I hope this chapter has helped to inspire you to consider whether our intuitive generosity is misspent when directed toward government-run, long-term, dependency-inducing, family-destroying government assistance.

Some quick facts

★ When liberals say "but the Democrats care about the poor, and Republicans don't ever want to help them", please, I implore you ladies, share the facts. Tell them that massive studies undertaken by people who set out to prove that Democrats care and Republicans don't, found out that exactly the opposite is true. It is Republicans, conservatives, those opposed to unlimited big government social spending programs, religious Americans, who do the vast majority of the donating, sharing, giving and caring in charitable America, regardless of income level, race, ethnicity or gender. Truly, most people have no idea.

★ Only 20 percent of the federal budget goes to national defense, while the combination of Social Security, Medicare, and government assistance/welfare spending, is more than twice that high, amounting to 54 percent. So when a liberal tries to say that America spends too much on national defense and too little on helping people, offer some truth. Facts matter!

★ America spent over $16 trillion on the Great Society social spending programs since 1964, and there is more poverty today, nearly 40 years later, than there was when we started. And worse, those programs directly parallel the destruction of the nuclear family unit (guys abandon families when government takes over as the "big daddy"), and that hurts children. We all have compassion, but let's be honest enough to admit that these programs do not solve the problems they are intended to solve, and brave enough to withstand the assault by the left wing political correctness crowd who will surely claim that any effort to reform those programs is selfishly motivated. If people really care about children and the poor, they'll support policies that actually lift them up and make a successful and self-reliant life possible.

★ One in five Americans is reliant, right now, on the federal government, not even counting all of the employees of the federal government. One in seven Americas is on food stamps. We spend more on welfare than we do on our national defense. No nation can continue on this trajectory. We need to unite as a nation around the goal of changing this trajectory—moving Americans back toward self-reliance. And at the same time, moving our government back out of our lives and wallets!

★ Share the news with people you talk to that the United States Department of Agriculture, (USDA) spent between $2.5 and $3 million dollars in 2012 running radio ads urging food stamp recipients to hold parties and other social events for the purpose of encouraging other people to sign up for food stamps. This Democrat administration is spending your tax dollars urging more people to become dependent on your tax dollars.

More Insights from Mei

My friend Mei came to America (from China via Dubai) to start working as an assistant to an older woman who owned a small store in Dallas. Mei first began working for her, and eventually bought the business from her. Through her hard work, Mei developed the business from a one-store shop that did $100,000 a year in business, to a four-store enterprise that grossed $5 million dollars annually. She did that between 1990 and 2001.

Mei still speaks with a heavy accent, though she tenaciously studied English when she came to America, and yet was able to succeed and build her "American dream." She now runs her own business, and during our recent two-hour lunch, was interrupted repeatedly by calls from employees and customers. She abhors the idea of becoming dependent on government, like so many of her countrymen in China are forced to be, under the communist government there.

She is not unique in her success. She followed the path of many Americans before her who figured out that America was the land of opportunity for anyone willing to work hard, and she made her way by doing just that. Nothing has changed about the ability and opportunity for Americans to do that, but the long-term trap of economic dependence has dampened the confidence and enthusiasm for too many, who may question whether they can make it on their own.

American leaders should inspire self-reliance, not dependence!

Ladies, think about what your parents encouraged you to do, and what you encourage your kids to do. Did they or you encourage becoming independent, pursuing your dreams and self-reliance, or did they and you encourage pursuing weakness, helplessness and dependence? There is too much talk out of Washington Democrats encouraging people to buy into the state of victimhood and helplessness, and too little inspired American leadership that animates the human spirit to seek and find the independence and satisfaction borne of self-reliance.

Our politicians, as national leaders, should be encouraging Americans to jump into the American Dream, as Mei did. The only way out of our economic mess is economic growth—so let's encourage everyone to engage their entrepreneurial spirit, and pursue their dreams.

America needs national leadership that encourages and inspires the American spirit of freedom and self-sufficiency. Ladies, it is only the Republicans speaking those messages. Their message honors the genuine goodness of the American people and the greatness of our country's free market and freedom-based opportunities.

Chapter Seven

I Already Have a Big Brother, Thank You!

Big Government—Protection and Limits

Can we talk…About Why Big Government Is Such a Big Deal?

Ladies, concern about big government isn't at the top of the list for most women when it comes to issues that drive our votes. But the rising cost of government, as well as its sheer number of employees and programs, is making people feel concerned. Does bigger government mean more protection for people, or is it a problem?

The size and power of public unions is also a big issue in the news, but why are they a problem?

Finally, there is so much concern about two of our most important programs—Medicare and Social Security—both run by the government. Are they really in trouble and, if they are, how can we fix them?

And how are any of these Republican versus Democrat issues?

"If you have ever seen a four-year-old trying to lord it over a two-year-old, then you know what the basic problem of human nature is - and why government keeps growing larger and ever more intrusive."
—Dr. Thomas Sowell, Ph.D. Economics, Author, Columnist, Political Philosopher

Topics We'll Talk About in Chapter Seven

So, How Big is our Government, and Why Does That Matter?

How Do Public Unions Add to the Problem?

Big Government Ganging Up on Americans? The NLRB and the Card Check

The Medicare and Social Security Programs–Protecting Them from Bankruptcy

Isn't "Too-Big Government" a Democrat and a Republican Problem?

Did You Know?...Stories and Facts to Share

★ ★ ★

How Big Is Our Government, and Why Does That Matter?

Most women I know, conservative or liberal, do not honestly seem to care that much about the size of government as a political issue. And I understand that ambivalence because it is one of those hidden-from-everyday-life issues and we only become aware periodically, ususaly because of some narrow individual experience. It is similar with union-related matters. Unless you are a union member, or deal with unions at your workplace, what difference does it make to you whether government workers are unionized? As a former labor attorney, I am probably more tuned in to these issues than some folks, but I can totally understand the ambivalence.

This chapter is deliberately short, but I urge you not to skip over it. The simple and short answer about why the size of the government matters, and the size and influence of the private and public sector unions matter, is that both involve a strain on the economy. Both operate outside of the basic laws of free market economics that keep most things—salaries and prices—in some natural balance. And bigger government necessarily means less freedom.

How many people employed, how much money?

Many sources offer employment data measured in different ways, so sometimes numbers conflict. The U.S Census Bureau report for 2010 says that the federal government directly employed 3,007,938 individuals that year, at a total cost for one month's payroll of $16,238,227,775. (http://www2.census.gov/govs/apes/10fedfun.pdf; accessed May 15, 2012) The Census Bureau Summary report on public employment in 2010 is also available. (http://www2.census.gov/govs/apes/g10aspep.pdf)

Also according to the census, state governments together employed 3.8 million people in 2010 at a monthly cost of over $17 billion. (http://www.census.gov/govs/apes/ ; accessed May 15, 2012.)

Local governments added another 10.9 million full time employees (http://www.census.gov/govs/apes/; accessed May 15, 2012)

Conservatively, the employment numbers above total nearly 17 million people directly employed by government.

Plus the military and the contractors and grant recipients

Those numbers do not include Americans paid to serve in our military, or the number of individuals and entities being paid by the government as independent contractors, or those whose incomes depend entirely upon grants from the government. Iain Murray in his 2011 book reported that Professor Paul Light of New York University attempted to calculate the actual number of people who are compensated by the government. Light calls his number the "true" size of government and by 2005 he estimates that the true size of government was around 14.6 million.

Extrapolating from that calculation, author Murray calculated conservatively that by 2011 the real size of the government-funded workforce *was around 40 million, or roughly 26 percent of the workforce!* (Iain Murray, *Stealing You Blind*, 2011, Regnery Publishing, pages 19-20)

What does big government mean for election outcomes?

Just think, that is 40 million Americans who have a vested interest in opposing cuts in the size of government. Compound that with their likely similarly-motivated spouses and partners, and we are already looking at a sizeable mass of voters who may believe that their personal well-being is best served by maintaining and growing government (until the government goes bankrupt, of course).

Surely government shrank, too, during the recent recession?

Nope!

★ In the three plus years between the start of the recession in December 2007, and January 2011, 7.5 million private sector jobs were lost, which represented about 6.6 percent of the private sector workforce.

★ In that same time period the federal government workforce enjoyed healthy *growth*: government added 230,000 jobs, an 11.7 percent increase in those employment ranks. (http://blog.heritage.org/2011/02/22/federal-workforce-continues-to-grow-under-obama-budget/; accessed May 15, 2012)

And this is one example of a phenomenon that just goes with the territory of public sector entities: they do not even remotely fall under the same set of naturally existing free market rules that govern the people and businesses who work in the private sector.

Although this may be obvious, consider for a moment the impact of the recession on your average private sector business. People got fearful about spending money, so they held on to their cash and spent less money at the local shoe store. As business dropped off, the shoe store owner could try to hold on for a while and dip into savings, or cut prices in an attempt to bring business in, but eventually, if the recession lingers he is forced to lay off employees or cut pay, or both. He may have to close the business if things do not improve because other than sales of shoes, he has no source of revenue.

The government, by contrast, always has more sources of revenue, both because it can always levy taxes (it can make you pay taxes, while the shoe store owner cannot make you buy shoes), and the government simply continues rolling along using deficit spending—spending money it doesn't have because it can borrow and borrow and borrow. Hence our national debt. (This is a short digression from our subject of the size and power of government, but it seemed like a fortuitous opportunity to throw in a good private sector/public sector comparison.)

How Do Government Salaries Compare With the Private Sector?

For decades, the common and true wisdom was that going to work for the government as opposed to the private sector was a tradeoff: Government workers were traditionally paid less than their private sector counterparts but they had better benefits, shorter hours, and a little more job security because the government was recession-proof.

Recent studies have proved that only half of that traditional equation is true today. *Government employees still get better benefits, more vacation, and much better job security (more on that in a moment), but times have changed and now, government employees also earn more than their counterparts in the private sector.*

The American Enterprise Institute, along with the Heritage Foundation, conducted an in-depth study in 2011 of wage/benefit comparisons between public and private sector employees. (http://www.aei.org/files/2011/06/08/AEI-Working-Paper-on-Federal-Pay-May-2011.pdf; accessed May 15, 2012) That survey was conducted in part to refute claims by both sides of the political aisle as to whether federal employees were overcompensated in comparison to private sector employees. That report found:

> *"Public sector compensation has come under increased scrutiny from politicians and the media, but comprehensive technical comparisons of federal and private compensation have been largely absent from the discussion. Drawing from the academic literature and using the most recent government data, this report measures the generosity of federal salaries, benefits, and job security.*
>
> *"Compared to similar private sector workers, we estimate that federal workers receive a salary premium of 14 percent, a benefits premium of 63 percent, and extra job security worth 17 percent of pay. Together, these generate an overall federal compensation premium of approximately 61 percent. Reducing federal employee compensation to market levels could save taxpayers roughly $77 billion per year."*
>
> *(http://www.aei.org/files/2011/06/08/AEI-Working-Paper-on-Federal-Pay-May-2011.pdf; accessed May 15, 2012)*

That research by the Heritage Foundation and the American Enterprise Institute apparently inspired the Congressional Budget Office (CBO) to engage in a similar study, which resulted in similar findings.

(http://www.heritage.org/research/reports/2012/02/federal-pay-is-out-of-line-with-private-sector-pay-cbo-supports-heritage-aei-conclusions; accessed May 15, 2012)

How's Job Security as a Federal Government Employee?

USA Today reported in 2011 that job security among federal government employees was *extraordinarily high* as compared with the private sector. In the year ending September 2010, the Federal Communications Commission, and the Federal Trade Commission had zero ("0") people fired or laid off. A Housing and Urban Development spokesman said his department's 99.85 percent job security rate merely reflects a skilled and committed workforce. The federal government fired just over one half of one percent (0.55 percent) in the year leading up to September 2010, and by contrast, the termination rate in the private sector in that same time period was about 3 percent who were fired for poor performance. (http://www.usatoday.com/news/washington/2011-07-18-fderal-job-security_n.htm; accessed June 5, 2012)

Nearly 60 percent of government firing happens within the first two years of the government job and those who keep their job past that initial phase have almost total job security. (Ibid)

As we discussed in Chapter Four, the only way government has any money to pay federal employees is by collecting taxes from the private sector, the small businesses and large companies, and the individuals who work for them, so the growth of government impacts everyone. While we all know we need to fund the federal government to do at least those things spelled out for it under the Constitution, we also know that government today has become massive and does far more than the limited Constitutionally-required tasks. The historic trend has always been toward bigger government.

Does Big Government Really Hurt Anything?

Big government is not just an expensive proposition, it is ultimately one of the clearest indicators of how much power government has and, consequently, how much liberty the people do not have.

As Thomas Jefferson wisely noted:
"The natural progress of things is for liberty to yield,
and government to gain ground."

(http://www.monticello.org/site/jefferson/natural-progress-things-quotation;
accessed May 15, 2012)

Big government hurts us in another way: Countries that have higher rates of government spending and "larger public-sector payrolls—have higher unemployment" in the private sector. (http://www.heritage.org/research/reports/2011/02/heritage-employment-report-january-report-shows-some-thawing; accessed May 15, 2012) [FN-Based on information from: Yann Algan, Pierre Cahuc, and André Zylberberg, "Public Employment and Labour Market Performance," *Economic Policy,* Vol. 17, No. 34 (2004), pp. 7–66; Jim Malley and Thomas Moutos, "Does Government Employment 'Crowd-Out' Private Employment? Evidence from Sweden,"

Scandinavian Journal of Economics, Vol. 98, No. 2 (1996), pp. 289–302; Horst Feldmann, "Government Size and Unemployment: Evidence from Industrial Countries," *Public Choice*, Vol. 127, No. 3 (June 2006), pp. 443–459.) And that makes sense, because the more tax dollars taken out of the private sector to pay for government employees' salaries and benefits, the less money out there for individuals and businesses to start or build businesses and hire people.

What are all those government employees doing? Sure some are doing important work to protect America and keep government running smoothly but necessarily, the more government we have, the more regulators, the more enforcers, the more rules, and the higher costs to employers to follow those rules. And the more the country continues the slide from free market economics to the American style socialism the Democrats advocate, which is enforced by high taxes and oppressive regulation.

But federal employees pay taxes, too—so the economics balance out, right?

No, not really. Picture the money flowing in our tax system. You pay taxes to the federal government and government uses that money to pay federal government employees. Those employees receive federal government money (your tax dollars) in the form of paychecks and then return some of that federal government money (your tax dollars) back to the government in the form of paying income tax. It's just a giant loop with no "new" money or value added to the economy. (There is value to the extent that federal employees are adding non-monetary value in their work, but in terms of dollars circulating it is just the federal government recirculating money earned in the private sector and paid in taxes.)

Significant increase in regulations over the last few years

A lengthy report called "Red Tape Rising: Obama's Torrent of New Regulation" that was produced in 2010 documents the great growth in federal government regulation that has occurred in the last several years. The report documents not only the number and kind of regulations that have vastly increased under Democrat control, but also the cost of those regulations to the American economy and to businesses. In short, the cost to American businesses and their customers of major new regulations in fiscal year 2010 was $26.5 billion, up from under $13 billion in FY 2009. Among the most costly of the FY 2010 regulations were those arising out of fuel economy and emission standards, limits on effluent discharges at construction sites, and renewable fuel quota requirements. (http://www. heritage.org/research/reports/2010/10/red-tape-rising-obamas-torrent-of-new-regulation; accessed June 5, 2012)

Why do liberals assume federal government employees can do things better? Why does anyone assume that?

Ladies, there is an assumption that has wormed its way into political discussions that must be debunked. And that is that the federal government is to be trusted more than the state governments and local governments to do important things. Did you ever think about the fact that the federal government is made up of people, Americans mostly, educated in America, who happen to be employed by the federal government? And the employees of every state and local government in America are just people, Americans mostly, educated in America, who happen to be employed by those state and local governments. No one magically becomes smarter, more ethical or moral or better informed, by virtue of becoming a federal government employee. In fact one could argue that those closest to the "situations on the ground" in the states are better informed, more in touch, more aware of what solutions will work, on various issues.

This is a major point of distinction between the parties today. Republicans frequently advocate for putting some policy areas and issues back under state or local government control and Democrats regularly and ardently insist on seizing more and more areas of regulation and placing them under federal control. Environmental and educational policy matters are good examples. The determination of Democrats to keep more and more policy areas under federal control and their skepticism about the capacity of state governments to handle important decisions and policies are inexplicable unless you recognize that a primary Democrat goal is the consolidation of power at the federal level, because that is how they can keep more control over society. That can sound more sinister than is meant. Even the most pro-big government Democrat thinks he or she is doing a good thing for society by keeping tight control over people and businesses all over the country and that, in part, stems from the elitism that has overtaken today's Democrat party. They really do think they know more and better than the rest of us about how things should be.

How Do Public Unions Add to the Problem?

Most Americans know that many public employees are members of unions, from schoolteachers to office workers. (And this is nothing against the members of public unions; this is about the dynamics of the money flow.)

Remember we talked earlier about the circular money flow of your federal tax dollars going to pay public employees' salaries, whose income tax payments are then just a recycling of those same tax dollars you paid, back to the government?

Well, consider the additional wrinkle that the existence of public unions adds to that cycle. Your tax dollars go to the government, that pays its employees, who then make mandatory dues payments to unions using the money in their paycheck that came from your tax dollars, and the public union uses that money to pay negotiators to negotiate with the government to pay the government employees higher salaries and bigger benefits, which will come from your tax dollars. Your tax dollars pay the salary of the negotiator who is negotiating to increase government spending in the form of higher salaries and benefits, which your future tax dollars will pay for. Such a deal for them, not such a good deal for you!

Follow the (union) money

And there is a political wrinkle here too. Unions, public and private, donate money to political campaigns. Tons of it, and it almost all goes to Democrats, not Republicans. (See data below.) So Democrats in government are in NO position to stand firm against union demands for higher salaries, etc. In fact the Democrats if anything are in a position of needing to support their union donors by conceding to their union demands for pay and benefit increases, which is exactly the opposite of the motivation the government (the employer) should have in negotiations with unions.

Unions are becoming rare in the private sector in America, but the great increase in unionization rates and in their power is in the public sector. But consider:

★ The impact of *public* sector unions on our economy and government is enormous, both in terms of employment-related costs including pension fund obligations, and because they make it difficult or even impossible to make necessary reductions in the size of government.

★ *Private* sector unions have great political power over elected Democrat public officials, resulting in the ongoing effort to crush the rights of individual Americans (through efforts such as the Card Check legislation) who do not wish to join unions.

★ While only 11.8 percent of the American workforce are unionized, *12 of the top 20 biggest multimillion dollar campaign donors in the United States are unions*, and they donate virtually all of their money to Democrats.

★ This is a small segment of society with enormous political clout.

How many Americans are in Unions?
Unions in Decline—Especially Private Sector Unions

In 2011, only 11.8 percent of American workers, or 14.8 million Americans, were union members. That is a drop off from the first year such statistics were kept, in 1983, when 20.1 percent or 17.7 million Americans joined unions.

But it is the growth in public sector as opposed to private sector unions that is most striking. Union membership rates are five times higher among public versus private sector employees.

Public sector employees had a 37 percent union membership rate, as opposed to only 6.9 in the private sector.

Bureau of Labor Statistics- January 2012 report, for 2011 (http://www.bls.gov/news.release/union2.nr0.htm; accessed May 20, 2012)

Campaign Donations by Unions

In the list of the 140 "Top All-Time Donors, 1989-2012" to political parties and candidates, which includes corporations, foundations, unions, and any other donors, 12 of the top 20 are unions.

Of those 12 unions that are generous in campaign donations, three are public unions and nine are private.

And of those 12 top-level union donors, all gave overwhelmingly to Democrats and nothing, or almost nothing, to Republicans. Four gave 0 percent to the Republicans, and half gave over 90 percent to Democrats.

(http://www.opensecrets.org/orgs/list.php; accessed May 20, 2012)

Big Government Ganging Up on Americans? The NLRB and the Card Check Scheme

Ladies, one last point about big government and its impact on your lives. It involves the intersection of big government and big unions.

Here is the scoop:

★ Unions are losing elections in America, especially in the private sector, big time. Those would be elections involving a secret ballot that obviously allows each individual to vote the way she or he wants to, meaning "yes" or "no" on a union.

★ So unions came up with a proposal about a replacement for secret ballot voting called Card Check, or the more outrageously dishonestly named "Employee Free Choice Act."

★ The union "vote" under Employee Free Choice Act eliminated the secret ballot, and replaced the whole system with a new idea, which was that union officials could just go around to employees and ask them if they wanted to organize, or join the union, and once the union officials had managed to get a majority of the employees to sign a card saying the "yes, I want to join the union," the union got certified. No secret ballot. No ability to say no.

★ Now I don't think it will take any of you brilliant ladies more than a nano-second to figure out that employees approached by some union thug in the parking lot, at home, at night in an alley, wherever they could find you, have no choice but to say yes. And imagine the workplace opportunity to harass the person who would not sign.

★ The bill was just a Union Thug Empowerment Act, or a Crush the Right of the Individual to a Secret Ballot Vote Act.

★ Unions brought this idea to the Democrats in Washington, who, immediately embraced it and began trying to "sell" it in Capitol Hill.

★ This union bullying was even too much for most Democrats and the bill never passed, though public opposition to it was so strong that it may have been constituent pressure against it rather than virtue that prevented the bill's passage.

★ Undeterred, the Democrats pursued having this same idea passed via rule making and regulation by the Democrat-dominated (National Labor Relations Board.) The NLRB has not passed all the steps along the way yet to enforcing the Employee Free Choice Act via regulation, and I'll spare you the other steps along the way except to say the NLRB has now required employers to supply union organizers with the names and home addresses of every employee, and the employees have no right to opt out of this.

★ The latest is that the NLRB passed the "election ambush rule" that says unions can work to organize a particular employer's workforce and give the employer only ten days' notice before the announcement of a unionization election. This is such an obvious further union empowerment tool that many employers objected.

★ In May 2012 the Senate voted on a bill to overturn the NLRB's ambush rule, based on the view that it was grossly unfair to the employer. Every single Democrat in the US Senate voted against, the idea, meaning voted to let the ambush rule stand. All Republicans voted to overturn the ambush rule.

Two Points on Democrat/Union Politics and Card Check:
Democrats who are going around Congress to the NLRB to ask it to do what Congress did not dare do is a Constitutional problem—a thumbing of the nose at Congress and, therefore, at the America people.

And realize—the Democrats are not standing up for the little guy here, they are standing up for the right of the unions to bully the little guy.

Ladies, I know that big government and big unions do not even make the list of issues that drive the women's vote. But because both are such "big" issues in American life in these early years of the 21st century the issues surrounding them deserve your thoughtful attention.

Big unions

Most of you probably watched the Wisconsin elections in June 2012, in which voters refused to recall Republican Governor Scott Walker. Public sector unions organized and galvanized the recall election, in reaction to

Walker's legislation greatly diminishing the power of public unions in that state. Voters sided with Governor Walker and against the unions, after millions of dollars and hundreds of hours of television and radio ads saturated the state.

Three issues surrounding unions are likely to be in the public spotlight going forward, and all seriously impact the American economy and political landscape.

Public sector unions

First, some debate is ongoing about whether public sector employees should be able to unionize at all. One reason for doubt about their propriety relates to the cyclical pattern of taxpayer money they necessarily involve, discussed above. It is almost Orwellian, and at least bizarre that you are paying tax dollars that are used to fund negotiations that result in higher wages that will require you to pay higher taxes. And you, the taxpayer, the real employer, the payer of wages, have no place at the negotiating table.

Unions are tax exempt and can monopolize

The second issue is that unions are tax-exempt. They are organized under 501 (c)(5) of the Internal Revenue Code, and they pay no taxes. In 2010, the combined assets of all labor unions and farm bureaus in the U.S. were over $32 billion dollars. The businesses those labor unions negotiate with/against pay taxes, but the unions do not. Unions are also exempted from the anti-trust, anti-monopoly laws, so that they can monopolize entire industries. This makes them a formidable force, to say the least. It is unclear why they should be exempt from taxes and from the anti-trust laws, today.

Unions can lobby and make political contributions, unlike some other tax-exempt organizations

The third point is that there is serious question about whether there is any good reason unions should be permitted to lobby, and/or to make political contributions. It is no secret that unions make massive campaign contributions, they are among the largest contributors in the country, and almost all of their contributions go to Democrats. If unions were confined to representing their union member employees in collective bargaining, they would be less of a divisive political force. It has long been a source of contention that unions forcibly collect dues and then make contributions to political candidates that their dues-paying members may not support.

Unions and Socialism—BFFs

Unions and socialism have a great deal in common:

1. They are a stellar example of group rights and the power of the group over the individual;
2. They are premised on a basic class-warfare model; and
3. Their representation is dedicated to group benefits and to equality of outcome in workers' pay, rather than to rewarding the individual's unique and actual achievement and hard work;
4. A small group of highly paid elites runs them, and those elites do not live under the terms of the contract they negotiate/inflict/impose on the masses.

Unions and socialism share the collectivist, coercive mindset that elevates groupthink and group power over the freedom and growth of the individual. No wonder the Democrats love them!

One purpose of this book is to urge American women to see the issues we face in the broader context of where we are headed as a nation. In Wisconsin, the voters in June 2012 convincingly turned down the invitation of the public unions to recall elected Republican Governor Scott Walker, who followed the path he promised to follow during his campaign and legislatively reined in the expenses associated with public unions in that state. Union reaction was swift and harsh but ultimately unsuccessful because voters chose to stand with the ideas of freedom and fiscal responsibility, instead of yielding to the angry demands of the public unions. The vote was not anti-teacher, but pro-American and pro-fiscal responsibility. Another whole book could be written about the fiscal peril many local, county, and state governments face due to benefits negotiated with public unions that contain completely unsustainable, unaffordable expenses associated with pension and other benefits. More states are going to need to follow Wisconsin's lead and stand up for fiscal responsibility.

The Medicare and Social Security Programs Who Will Protect Them from Bankruptcy?

Social Security—Who Will Protect Our Seniors?

As you all likely know, Social Security is the taxpayer funded retirement system, which working Americans pay into, and from which citizens are eligible to begin receiving benefits at age 65. Social Security, along with Medicare and Medicaid make up 42 percent of total federal spending. (The 2012 Index of Dependence on Government, Heritage Center for Data Analysis, February 8, 2012, at http://www.heritage.org/research/reports/2012/02/2012-index-of-dependence-on-government; accessed May 14, 2012)

The combination of the facts that:

★ Millions more baby boomers and retirees will soon move into retirement and Social Security eligibility (77 million over the next 25 years),

★ Fewer and fewer Americans are paying taxes,

★ Social Security already pays out more than it takes in every year, and

★ Congress used previous excess Social Security trust fund money to pay for other government programs instead of preserving, protecting and investing it (They did deposit special-issue U.S. Treasury bonds into the SS Trust Fund.)

means that our Social Security system is broke and has no means of becoming solvent without some reform. Making Social Security financially stable is vital, in part because half of retirement-aged Americans do not have any private pension coming to them from their former employers.

Everyone who is focusing on these serious issues (which is mostly just the Republicans) is working to find ways to save and protect Social Security for our senior citizens.

This is one example among many where today's Republican Party, and the conservative side, is acting responsibly, and the Democrat Party is truly doing nothing, unless you count their efforts at scaring seniors by falsely claiming that Republican efforts to solve our Social Security funding problems are meant to harm seniors.

Republican U.S. Representative Paul Ryan worked tirelessly to come up with a plan to address the Social Security funding shortfall, which along with other proposals to bring federal entitlement spending under control, became known as the Roadmap for America's Future.

The basics, from Representative Paul Ryan's website, are these:

"The proposal strengthens this important retirement program and makes it sustainable for the long term.

★ Preserves the existing Social Security program for those 55 or older.

★ Offers workers under 55 the option of investing over one third of their current Social Security taxes into personal retirement accounts, similar to the Thrift Savings Plan available to Federal employees. Includes a property right so they can pass on these assets to their heirs, and a guarantee that individuals will not lose a dollar they contribute to their accounts, even after inflation.

★ Makes the program permanently solvent – according to the Congressional Budget Office [CBO] – by combining a more realistic measure of growth in Social Security's initial benefits, with an eventual modernization of the retirement age." http://www.roadmap.republicans.budget.house.gov/Issues/ Issue/?IssueID=8521.roadmap.republicans.budget.house. gov/Issues/Issue/?IssueID=8521, Accessed May 14, 2012

Democrat responses from top leaders including Representative (and former Speaker of the House) Nancy Pelosi include that the Ryan plan must be "snuffed out, " and that she is repeating "the most important" part of her 2005 strategy (dealing with another Social Security reform proposal) of *not offering a competing Democrat proposal*. She said "…we're saying that we have a proposal on the table. It's called Social Security." (http://www.huffingtonpost.com/2011/04/06/pelosi-ryan-budget-plan_n_845692.html; accessed May 14, 2012)

Ladies, stand up for our Seniors!
*We cannot let this "head in the sand…we just won't deal with our problems",
"trample by bullying without fixing anything"*

*Democrat mind-set rule this country. Democrats have clearly decided that
winning current elections by glossing over and failing to acknowledge serious
fiscal problems is more important than taking the political risk of telling
the truth and proposing a solution.*

So there you have it. An already broke Social Security system and an impossible set of real-life factors adding to the financial strain on SS, and the Democrat strategy is to "snuff out" any proposals to fix the system. And Pelosi's "strategy" is most unfortunately repeated over and over again by the Democrats who lead their party in Washington.

Medicare—Should Millionaires Get the Same as the Poor?

Congress created Medicare in 1965, and today it faces underfunding for many of the same reasons that Social Security does—a huge number of Americans approaching retirement age and therefore Medicare eligibility, rising costs, and insufficient contributions to cover the costs. The 2011 report of the Medicare trustees shows that Medicare faces $24.6 trillion in unfunded obligations currently, and that Part A is already running deficits.

(The 2012 Index of Dependence on Government, Heritage Center for Data Analysis, February 8, 2012; accessed May 14, 2012)

When Medicare was started in 1965 life expectancy in the U.S. was a little over 70, and now it is almost 79. The program "planned" to cover healthcare for on average five years, and now it must do so for 14 years. And in 1970, there were 20.4 million Americans enrolled in Medicare, as compared with 47.5 million in 2010. Baby boomers have just started rolling into the program in 2011, and they will just keep on coming.

Just as with Social Security, the Republicans and conservatives are offering solutions to deal with the predicted shortfalls, and the Democrats are offering up scare tactics, and no solutions.

In addition to Representative Paul Ryan's Roadmap plan to fix the entitlement programs, other conservative (read: actually responsible) organizations are also studying and trying to come up with solutions for these programs, to protect what needs protecting and to reform where that is needed. The Washington D.C based think-tank Heritage Foundation created a thorough, detailed proposal that addresses the national debt, cuts spending, and restores our economy, called *Saving the American Dream*. It is brilliant and thoughtful: Google that if you are interested.

Back to the other responsible proposal by Paul Ryan in his Roadmap: Here, from his website, is what his plan would do:

"The Roadmap secures Medicare for current beneficiaries, while making common-sense reforms to save this critical program.

★ It preserves the existing Medicare program for those currently enrolled or becoming eligible in the next 10 years (those 55 and older today) - So Americans can receive the benefits they planned for throughout their working lives. For those currently under 55 – as they become Medicare-eligible – it creates a Medicare payment, initially averaging $11,000, to be used to purchase a Medicare certified plan. The payment is adjusted to reflect medical inflation, and pegged to income, with low-income individuals receiving greater support. The plan also provides risk adjustment, so those with greater medical needs receive a higher payment.

★ The proposal also fully funds Medical Savings Accounts (MSAs) for low-income beneficiaries, while continuing to allow all beneficiaries, regardless of income, to set up tax-free MSAs.

★ Based on consultation with the Office of the Actuary of the Centers for Medicare and Medicaid Services and using Congressional Budget Office (CBO) these reforms will make Medicare permanently solvent.

★ Modernizes Medicaid and strengthens the healthcare safety net by reforming high-risk pools, giving States maximum flexibility to tailor Medicaid programs to the specific needs of their populations. Allows Medicaid recipients to take part in the same variety of options and high-quality care available to everyone through the tax credit option." (http://www.roadmap.republicans.budget.house.gov/Issues/Issue/?IssueID=8520; accessed on May 14, 2012)

Ryan's Roadmap protects current Medicare recipients, and those 55 and older, leaving their benefits unchanged. For the future, for those now under 55, the program is in part "pegged to income, with low-income individuals receiving greater support." Given that we do not live in a utopia where all the money for everything everyone wants simply grows on trees, isn't there wisdom in making health benefits more available to lower-income people, and requiring those with more financial security to pay more of their own healthcare costs? You would think that would make Democrats happy, but this too has earned nothing but hostility from them.

Actually, to be fair to the Democrats, they do commonly offer one approach, a highly provocative tactic that Nancy Pelosi and other Democrats often take when they do not want to admit that the federal entitlement programs are broke and must be reformed. They fire off some verbal missile at one of the villains they have created such as "tax subsidies for big oil" or "defense spending" or "tax cuts for the rich." Note there is never an accounting of how adjusting these other areas could possibly remedy the long-term viability of programs whose fundamental financial structure simply cannot support them.

Isn't "Too-Big Government" A Democrat and a Republican Problem?

Yes. It is most certainly true that Republicans and Democrats have contributed to the growth of government, both in terms of size, and spending. Regulations proliferated under some Republican administrations, but not nearly at the rate or scope as under Democrat ones.

But the Democrats problem is that they have no way—politically speaking—to reduce spending in any area of the budget except in military/defense spending. That is because too much of their voting base consists of unionized America, recipients of the massive government assistance programs the Democrats perpetually create and fund (with the tax dollars working Americans pay in), those lobbying for more handouts (such as women getting "free" contraception), and the extremist factions in the environmental movement, all of whom count on the Democrats to fund their lifestyles and causes. Even when genuine and irrefutable proof is right out there for everyone to see that reforms are needed to save Social Security and Medicare, the top leaders of today's Democrat Party can offer nothing except irrelevant accusations and fear-mongering. It is like there are no grown-ups left in the leadership of the Democrat Party.

Americans, those who still work, pay taxes and support themselves, are a dwindling segment of society. Not one of them, in light of where we stand today, should be remotely considering voting Democrat. America cannot afford it.

Did You Know?...Stories and Facts to Share Chapter Seven

Quick Facts to Share

★ How big could government be? Try scholarly estimates of 40 million Americans, or 26% of our workforce, directly employed by government or in government-funded jobs. That leaves the rest of working Americans laboring to pay taxes to support this ever-growing government workforce.

★ Compound those massive numbers with the unionization rates among public employees---much higher than in the private sector AND working hard to increase their salaries and benefits so you can pay higher taxes to pay them more!

★ Public employees have significantly higher salaries, benefits and job security than their equivalent counterparts in the private sector. It didn't used to be this way, and it is a bad sign for America's economic stability.

★ In the political sense, the unions "own" the Democrat party due to their massive campaign donations almost exclusively to Democrat politicians.

When your less-than-informed liberal friends say the usual liberal dribble that Republicans just want to destroy Social Security and Medicare and the Democrats are fighting to save them, remember to say, "Read the Roadmap!" Then insist and persist in telling the truth.

Those programs are on fiscal life-support and Republicans are trying to preserve them by modifying them, while protecting seniors and especially lower income seniors, and Democrats are performing their head-in-the-sand act ignoring the problem, while occasionally emerging to sling some meaningless and irrelevant slogan. Again, facts matter…urge the uninformed to look online at the Ryan plan and then look (in vain) for proposals by the Democrats to solve these problems.

Big government—can't we at least agree to reduce/eliminate duplication?

The United States Government Accounting Office (GAO), a nonpartisan organization, issued a report in March of 2011 about the number and scope of duplicative government agencies. One Senator estimated that the overlap/waste costs taxpayers between $100 and $200 billion dollars a year.

Here's a short list of some of the areas of duplication:

★ There are 82 different programs that are designed to improve teacher quality.

★ Eighty programs to help disadvantaged individuals with transportation;

★ Fifty-six programs to help people to understand finances;

★ Eighteen programs on food and nutrition assistance;

★ Eighty economic development programs

Cutting redundant government programs is an area where the two political parties could agree, and there is no reason for either party to reject the concept on philosophical grounds. And fewer programs should cut the cost of government!

★ ★ Chapter Eight ★ ★

Two Plus Two Always Equals Four

Can We Talk...About the National Debt, in Numbers We Can Follow?

One of the great conversation silencers is the fear of being thought ignorant. And there's something about the sheer size of America's debt numbers that so defies comprehension that we almost instinctively default to silence as the better course.

The numbers are big, but that just can't be an excuse to walk away from the subject in 2012. The numbers can be brought down to household size—and then the numbers are not so incomprehensible.

What's incomprehensible is that we could have had generations of politicians who checked their common sense at the door of Congress and placed this country in a financial condition that none of us would (or could) tolerate at the household level.

We really need to talk about this.

Much has been written about the nearly $16 trillion dollar U.S. national debt. For years I would hear news reports about the federal debt and deficit and not pay too much attention, and for sure I didn't worry about it. Huge as they are, our national debt and annual budget deficits remain areas of American political life that most people do not follow closely.

Topics We'll Talk About in Chapter Eight
No More "But I'm Not a Numbers Person"

Comparing Our National Budget to a Family Budget

The "De-Sensitizing" Problem

How Much Does the Debt Cost Us, Annually?

Republican Versus Democrat Approaches to Solving the National Debt and Annual Budget Deficit Problems

Did You Know?...Stories and Facts to Share

No More "But I'm not a Numbers Person"

Those of us who say (and this includes me!) "I'm not a numbers person" especially seem to have accepted that we cannot put these large national debt and deficit numbers into any meaningful context, or that we can't do anything about the debt anyway. Unfortunately, women tend to do this more than men, and studies on women's voting show that most women place little importance on debt and fiscal issues in making voting decisions.

But that's just not good enough anymore. And, ladies, serious fiscal/economic problems in America will hurt women just as much if not more as they'll hurt men, so it is in our best interests to get on top of this!

In 2012, more Americans than ever, myself included, are tuned in to the federal budget, and with very good reason. Many Americans sense that we are in "way over our heads" and we know that the spending trend is going in the wrong direction.

Comparing Our National Budget to a Family Budget

Part of the problem is that the numbers are too big to fathom. I'll keep this chapter short, and make only two points on this (literally) massive subject:

★ Compare the national budget to your family's budget. It is easier to understand the amount of money we are talking about when we say that the U.S. is nearly $16 trillion in debt, if we transpose the discussion down to the "local level" of your family budget. It seems that is the only way any of us can begin to grasp how wildly out of bounds our national debt and federal spending are.

★ Ending annual budget deficits and eliminating the national debt requires something the Democrat Party simply can never do—cut spending. Our national *spending* levels created our annual deficits and our national debt problem. There is a huge difference in the way that Democrats and Republicans approach the national debt. Democrats are genuinely politically powerless to reduce spending in the areas where reductions are needed. They literally *cannot* solve the problem because they won't get re-elected if they do. Read Chapter Seven to find out why.

Comparing Family Versus National *Debt* Levels

Your family "debt"

Let's talk about your family budget. (Or, in the words of a good friend whose family sat down with a financial counselor to help them through some financially tight times, the "b" word.)

Let's start with a simple example. Let's say that your total family income is $100,000/year. (Yes, I know that's more than the average American family income, but it helps me—a non-numbers person – keep it simple!) Taking out a mortgage to buy a home is the most common reason Americans borrow money and acquire debt.

The 3-to-1 rule. The historic rule of thumb was that a family or individual could afford to handle, at the most, a mortgage (which is taking on debt) that is about three times the family's combined or total annual income. So if you earn $100,000 a year, you could afford to borrow, and handle, a mortgage of about $300,000.

It's important to realize that this 3-to-1 ratio was not arbitrarily selected; it is the result of years of bank and mortgage loan practical experience, that proved that people spend money in relation to their earnings, and it is risky for people to take on mortgages higher than three times their earnings, since people obviously have expenses other than their mortgages that rise with their incomes.

Let's just call this 3-to-1 ratio, debt-to-income.

America's Debt

Now let's compare that with our national debt. The federal debt and our federal spending rise so dramatically and quickly that it is difficult to pin down specific and current numbers. All numbers in these examples are taken from an informative and detailed website called www.usgovernmentspending.com. I strongly encourage you to visit that website and inform yourself about our federal budget situation.

Total revenues to the U.S. government in 2011 were $2.3 trillion dollars. (Those revenues came in to the federal government from personal income taxes, social security tax, ad-valorem taxes, fees and charges, and business and other taxes.)

Our national debt in 2011 was $14.7 trillion.

That's a debt-to-income ratio of 6.39 to 1, *well over twice* the widely accepted "highest safe level" of the 3-to-1 ratio.

Back to the family budget, that would be like the family that earns $100,000/year taking out a mortgage of $639,000. Of course, the family earning that $100,000 would never find a bank willing to make a mortgage loan of over half a million dollars. Banks serve as a voice of reason outside of the family, preventing irresponsible borrowing.

And most of us would not even need a bank to tell us "no."

Ladies, if you're married, and your family income were $100,000 but your husband demanded that the family take on a $650,000 mortgage, most of us would be able to say "no," without the bank's advice. Because most of us want to be sure that our family's budget leaves room for the family's needs and the future needs of our children. And if you are single, you would stand up for your own financial health and resist the temptation to take on debt far outside your ability to repay it.

But the U.S. government can literally vote itself the higher debt to income ratio, every time Congress votes to raise the debt ceiling. There is no similar voice such as the bank or the wise woman—the outside voice of reason with authority—to tell Congress to stop borrowing money, except of course the well-informed voters. That would be you and me, and all of the American women who are going to talk to each other!

Comparing Family Versus National *Spending* Levels

Let's compare family spending versus income ratios, with federal government spending versus income ratios, as another gauge on the spending that has brought us to the point of the national debt crisis.

Total spending by the U.S. government in 2011 was $3.6 trillion, while total "income" (or tax revenues) was only $2.3 trillion.

So the government spent $1.3 trillion dollars more than it took in, which is the annual budget deficit for 2011. Put another way, in 2011, the government spent 156 percent of its "income," or more than half again what it took in.

That would be like a family earning $100,000 a year, and spending $156, 000 a year. You and I both know that no family can function like that. Families who do spend more than they earn, end up with high debt (often on credit cards) and eventually in bankruptcy and financial ruin.

But the federal government rolls along, increasing debt year after year, proposing new and expanded spending programs, seemingly with no consequence. That is because politicians make promises to have the federal government fix things and spend money, and then those politicians find it more expedient, and preferable, to continue the spending spree to keep their voters happy, than to keep spending within the limit of the tax revenues the government takes in.

Voters must take charge!

The "De-Sensitizing" Problem

Remember the research a few years back that showed that children in America have become desensitized to violence because they watch so much of it on television? The result was that kids were abnormally unalarmed by real-life violence, less concerned about it, less repulsed by it.

That same phenomenon has happened with the debt. We are so desensitized to big numbers, so inundated with news stories about billions and trillions of dollars, that the numbers no longer faze us.

But that has to stop. We need to recognize that our national debt is real, enormous, threatening to our country's economic stability, and utterly "defeatable." We can and must take on our national debt. Congress needs to know that the voters are insisting that spending cuts must happen.

How Much Does the Debt Cost Us Annually?

Do you know how much money the U.S. government spent in 2011, just on *interest* payments on the national debt? A whopping $230 billion—that's $ 230,000,000,000—in one year! That is money that we'll never get back, that is entirely spent paying for the fact that we borrow.

Let's Not Be Greece

Most of you likely followed the news over the last few years about the country of Greece and its financial condition. The Greek government fell into severe financial crisis in large part due to enormous national debt, a dependent, aging, and low birth rate population that had become accustomed to government assistance at an unsustainable level, and the ultimate unwillingness of the European Union to keep the Greek economy afloat without major reforms. Greek citizens protested in masses against the government's austerity measures, taking a more or less I-don't-care-if-we-can't-afford-it-you-can't-cut-spending attitude.

The longer America perpetuates spending we cannot afford, the more we create dependency and weakness, the higher the risk we follow in Greece's footsteps. We create a nation dependent on spending we cannot sustain, and a debt we cannot repay.

Republican Versus Democrat Approaches to Solving the National Debt and Annual Budget Deficit Problems

Let's all agree that both Democrats and Republicans are at least partly responsible for the current national debt. Both parties have had elected officials in Congress and in the White House as the debt grew.

While this book is encouraging women to vote Republican, I am really urging women to vote conservative and, therefore, not to support Republicans who are part of the big-spender, debt-builder crowd. And there are a few of them! But the Washington, D.C. Democrats are nearly entirely part of the big-spender, debt-builder crowd. It is just where the Democrats live politically today.

The parties offer two very different paths out of the debt and deficit mess. Put simply, Republicans know we have to reduce federal spending over the long term, and Democrats continue to insist that we can raise taxes enough to maintain federal spending levels, although they are always willing to talk about cutting defense spending.

The Balancing Acts: How Are Current Federal Tax Dollars Spent, *and* Should We Try Tax Increases or Spending Cuts?

There are (at least) two broad balance issues on how to address our national debt and annual budget deficit issues. They are:

★ The balance between defense and other spending essential to meet the federal government's responsibilities set out in the Constitution, as compared with social program/individual payout-based expenses.

★ The balance between raising taxes and/or reducing spending as the means to get to a balanced budget annually and ultimately to eliminating the national debt.

Finding the right balances depends on the actual facts of where we are as a nation, now, in our spending and taxing.

Where are we as a nation spending our tax dollars?

This discussion necessarily overlaps with issues covered in Chapter Six on Social Spending and Social Justice, concerning the number of people currently dependent on government, and the size and scope of federal spending on dependence-inducing programs.

To review, in 2011, the federal budget breakdown was:
- 20 percent—Defense spending
- 20 percent—Social Security payouts
- 21 percent Medicare, Medicaid, and CHIP
- 13 percent—Safety Net programs such as earned income and child tax credits, unemployment insurance and other cash payments to eligible individuals, food stamps, school meals, low-income housing assistance and assistance to pay for child care and home energy costs, free cell phones, and other similar programs.
- 6 percent—Interest on the debt
- 7 percent—Benefits for federal retirees and veterans
- 3 percent—Transportation and infrastructure
- 2 percent—Education
- 2 percent—Science and medical research
- 1 percent—International, non-security
- 4 percent—other

(Data from the liberal Center on Budget and Policy Priorities, http://www.cbpp.org/cms/index.cfm?fa=view&id=1258)

We spend one-fifth of the budget on the main job Congress has, defending the country, and well over twice that on individual benefit programs such as Social Security, Medicare and Medicaid, CHIP, food stamps, housing assistance, etc.

How Expensive and How Financially Secure Are Our Current Social Spending Programs?

On our present path, by the year 2049, Medicare, Medicaid, and Social Security will consume *all* federal tax revenues. No money for anything else. Social Security is already broke (paying out more to recipients than it is taking in). (http://www.heritage.org/budgetchartbook/entitlements)

Americans' financial dependence on the U.S. government is at an all-time high

★ Nearly 15 percent of Americans were on food stamps (SNAP) in 2011, which brought the number of recipients to over 45 million. That 15 percent means almost 1 in 7 people are on food stamps. (http://money.cnn.com/2011/08/04/pf/food_stamps_record_high/index.htm)

★ One in five Americans (67.3 million people) receives financial or in-kind subsidies from the federal government, including assistance with housing, food stamps, healthcare, retirement assistance, and college tuition.

★ And 49.5 percent of Americans do not pay any federal income tax. At all.

(http://blog.heritage.org/2012/02/08/dependence-on-government-at-all-time-high/ accessed June 5, 2012)

From Where (or From Whom) Are We as a Nation Collecting Our Tax Dollars?

For data on who pays taxes and how much, check back in Chapter Four, under Universal Truth Number Nine.

Our tax system is already heavily weighted to having the "rich" pay nearly all of the taxes that are collected. And recall also Hauser's Law, also discussed in Chapter Four, also under Universal Truth Number Nine, which is essentially that regardless of the tax rates the government comes up with, it collects slightly under 20 percent of the nation's GDP in taxes.

In plain English this means that the government has no ability to extract endless higher amounts of tax dollars from citizens. This is true because sane people will not work hard to make money that the government is just going to take away, so they either refuse to work hard and earn, decline to build new businesses, or in other ways act in a manner that allows them to circumvent the tax collectors.

> In quick summary, nearly half of all Americans pay no tax at all, the top 1 percent of income earners pays 40 percent of the tax burden, and the top 5 percent of income earners pays over half of all taxes collected.

What do all these data and numbers have to do with eliminating the national debt and ending our annual budget deficits?

Whatever your political background, the numbers and statistics above shout out "we have to cut spending." We spend more than we take in, by a lot, and our taxpayer base already consists of a small percentage of Americans who shoulder the entire tax burden. All responsible Americans need to be pressuring Congress—both sides of the aisle—to make meaningful and long-term spending cuts. Just as in our household budgets, we need to cut spending, even on things we used to think of as useful or helpful. We need to cut back closer to what is necessary.

Here's the bottom line, ladies: We Americans cannot continue to spend 156 percent of what we take in, and we cannot continue to shoulder a debt-to-revenue ratio that is more than twice the highest safe level. If we all get on board and say so, we can get moving back along the path to economically rational spending.

Did You Know?…Stories and Facts to Share Chapter Eight

Girls, I am not a numbers person myself, so I will keep the quick facts very short and crisp. Hopefully these are numbers and facts you can remember and share with your friends who don't yet know how big our debt and spending problem is.

America is $16 trillion in debt. Don't get de-sensitized by hearing big numbers or decide it must not matter. We do NOT want to be Greece.

Just in 2011, the United States government "earned," meaning took in revenues (taxes, fines etc) of $2.3 trillion, BUT it spent $3.6 trillion. The government spent (and that really means we the American people spent) 156 percent of our income. No family could afford to do that, and neither can America.

In 2011, America spent $230 billion on interest on our debt. That is money spent that we will never get back AND that bought us no value.

Be ready with some simple facts about our national spending priorities! We spend more on social spending than on national defense! More Americans than ever before are relying on government programs, rather than on the opportunities and blessings of the free markets for their basic needs.

On our present path, by the year 2049 Medicare, Medicaid, and Social Security will consume all federal tax revenues. No money for anything else. That means that unless we actually fix these programs and our spending problems, by the time kids born in 2012 turn 37 years old we will have no money to pay for anything except Medicare, Medicaid, and Social Security (http://www.heritage.org/budgetchartbook/entitlements).

When people tell you that we could fix our national debt problem if we would just tax the rich more, tell them: the top 1 percent of Americans already pays 40 percent of the tax revenues. Remember Hauser's Law: people will not let the government squeeze them dry.

We do not have a taxing shortfall in America; we have a spending problem!

★ ★ Chapter Nine ★ ★

The Race for Fairness

Who Stands Up for *Fairness* in Amerca?

Can We Talk…About What Standing Up for Racial Equality and Fairness Should Mean in American Society Today?

"We hold these truths to be self-evident, that all men are created equal, that they are endowed by their Creator with certain unalienable Rights, that among these are Life, Liberty and the pursuit of Happiness.

That to secure these rights, Governments are instituted among Men, deriving their just powers from the consent of the governed…."
—Declaration of Independence, July 4, 1776

When asked what issues drive their votes, many women include the desire for fairness in society and concern for racial equality. These ideas are among the noblest sentiments on earth, but the question is how to get there? What are the best ideas and, really, what is the best mindset to help Americans along the journey of furthering fairness and promoting genuine equality?

Let's talk about it.

"I have never had a feeling politically that did not spring from the sentiments embodied in the Declaration of Independence."
—*Abraham Lincoln, Republican, 16th President of the United States, Author of the Emancipation Proclamation, the Decree Freeing Slaves in America*

We'll talk in this chapter about the role each party played to protect black Americans historically, who pushed through and passed Civil Rights legislation, where the parties stand today, who stands for genuine equality, and whose policies and ideals are most helpful, fair, and productive for all Americans.

Topics We'll Talk About in Chapter Nine

The Tenderness and Importance of the Conversation about Race Relations in America

Historical Truth On Republicans Versus Democrats On the Issue of Race Relations

Legal Equality

Where Do We Stand Today?
What is the Best Way to Unite Americans?

Playing the Race Card

Meet Some Stellar Conservatives of Color Brave Enough to Push Back Against Political Correctness

Did You Know?...Stories and Facts to Share

The Tenderness and Importance of the Conversation about Race Relations in America

America was founded around ideas like limited government, all men having equal rights from our Creator, a government of laws and not of men, and not around the perpetuation of ancient kingdoms or particular ethnicities or races. We are blessed as a nation with a population comprised of individuals of nearly every background on earth.

Discussing the concepts of "fairness" and "equality" is deeply important to me on a personal level. I think the idea of equality comes from the absolute truth that man (all people) was created in God's image and likeness and therefore we are all inherently equal. While we are each unique and individual, we are all children of God, with individual rights coming to each of us from our Creator. Many Republicans I know believe the same thing. A central obligation of government based on America's Judeo-Christian heritage is to support that truth.

Race and race relations are also among the most tender, sensitive and important issues in America going forward, as we strive to make America an even better country. From conversations with dear friends of different racial and ethnic backgrounds it is clear that it is difficult to impossible for anyone to put himself or herself completely in someone else's "shoes." Past wrongs, hurts and misunderstandings are deeply felt and challenging to overcome. And suspicion, justified or not, about the motivations others have for their political views, can be a stumbling block to finding unity on policy decisions.

Perceptions about society vary, but in my experience most Americans of every background are intuitively fair-minded and want racial harmony and fairness. That is not to say that real racism doesn't exist in America: of course it does, and under every skin color. But American culture has developed and blossomed to the place where the norm is to recognize that each individual deserves respect as an individual, and that generalizations based on race or ethnicity are repugnant and unacceptable. That's a great thing.

Historical Truth On Republicans Versus Democrats On the Issue of Race Relations

A very short American history of Republican versus Democrat Party conduct concerning race relations and equality

America's history on the subject of race relations and the pursuit of legal equality for all is not perfect, but is, among the nations, exceptionally noble. Much has been said and written about the brilliant system of government our founding fathers created in the Declaration of Independence and the Constitution. But of course the Constitution as originally written acknowledged and therefore accepted slavery in the southern states. That along with its failure to recognize the equal rights of women and men were of course egregious lapses in what was still the most advanced and thoughtful, rights-creating document in human history.

To the credit of our ancestors, Americans in the early nineteenth century began to speak out against the horrors and evil of slavery. The abolitionist movement, joined by black and white Americans, led the way to the Civil War, which was fought to end the institution of slavery. Over half a million Americans, approximately 620,000 people, died in the Civil War. I mention that to give tribute to the goodness of our forefathers who stood up for a repressed segment of society that had no capacity at that time to stand up and demand freedom. That selfless willingness to stand up for the rights of others is in my view a hallmark of American society, then and now, and it springs from our nation's grounding in values that are derived from the Judeo-Christian heritage.

The Republicans who made equality the law..

You likely know that U.S. President Abraham Lincoln was a Republican, and that it was through his leadership, courage, and vision that America embarked on the path to freeing the slaves.

But did you know that the 13th Amendment to the Constitution that banned slavery, and the 14th Amendment that extended the Bill of Rights to the States, *and* the 15th Amendment that gave voting rights to blacks, were *all, repeat all*, enacted by what was then called the Radical Republicans, and that it was the Democrats who fiercely opposed all of them? [Back to Basic for the Republican Party, by Michael Zak, 2003, First Edition Thiessen Printing, Second and Third editions, Signature Book Printing, page 1.]

But that was all 150 years ago, right? Consider who brought about the 20th century advances in equal rights protection.

The 1964 Civil Rights Act, outlawing discrimination against blacks and women, came about in great part due to the brilliance and determination of Martin Luther King, Jr. and the nonviolent protests he led. That bill, the Civil Rights Act of 1964, passed in the U.S. House of Representatives with 80 percent of Republicans supporting it, and only 63 percent of Democrats voting for it. On the Senate side, the "vote was 73 to 27 (for passage), with 21 Democrats and only 6 Republicans voting no."

Of great importance is that *Democrats in the U.S. Senate "filibustered"*— used the tactic of standing to speak and refusing to stop, in order to prevent a vote from occurring— to try to stop the passage of the 1964 Civil Right Act. (Ibid, p. 195) Among the Senate ringleaders of the Democrat opposition to the bill were Albert Gore Sr., and a Democrat Senator from West Virginia named Robert Byrd, who was a former member of the KKK (the "Klan").

Legal Equality

Today powerful federal and state laws outlaw discrimination on the basis of race, sex, national origin, religion, age, and disability. Federal and state agencies enforce these laws, and file lawsuits on behalf of the individuals who believe they have suffered discrimination. While there is always room for improvement, America as a nation stands as a world leader in demanding equality in race relations.

Neither party can claim a perfect record on race relations by every elected official. But the above history makes clear that the Republicans "own" the moral high ground on the issue of pursuing and defending racial equality in America: the fact that anyone thinks otherwise is a product of Democrat spin and Republican failure to communicate.

Space considerations prevent me from setting out a more complete history of the roles the two parties played historically in moving America toward racial equality, but there is so much more fascinating history you could read if you are interested. One book, *Back to Basics for the Republican Party,* by Michael Zak, is filled with facts and historic information that will leave you wondering how you ever got convinced that it was the Democrats who stood for equality in American history.

The more you learn about this history, the clearer it will be to you that the right values in terms of embracing genuine racial equality have their roots in the Republican Party. Historic southern racism, the battles over school desegregation, suppressing voting rights, denial of equal access to public restaurants and facilities, and other very ragged and painful episodes in our nation's history, happened under Democrat control of the southern states. Democrat opposition to racial equality in America's south throughout the mid-20th century is what fanned the flames of those battles.

Where Do We Stand Today?
What Is the Best Way to Unite Americans?

Should America Build Unity Around Ideas, Or Around Race and Ethnicity?

The Democrats' Approach: Unite Around Race and Ethnicity

The Democrat Party and its leaders see America, define America, and function politically in America, in hyphenated groups. Rights are defined and discussed, and support groups for candidates are organized, around skin color and where your grandparents were born. Hispanic or Latino-Americans, African-Americans, Indian-Americans, Asian Americans, etc. are commonly spoken of within the liberal Democrat lexicon as defined groups in our society. Democrats extend this group-division crusade by consistently speaking of some Americans as "the rich," and amplifying "the 1 percent versus the 99 percent," type thinking., thus creating division among Americans along socio-economic lines.

This Democrat view, assigning political identity to individuals by their race and ethnicity, is on display in liberal political events and speeches, and even on President Obama's reelection campaign website, which includes support groups such as Latinos for Obama, and other ethnically based groups. Same for Democrat Senate candidate for United States from Massachusetts, Elizabeth Warren, whose website features groups of supporters based on ethnicity.

But the most irrefutable evidence that Democrats approach politics by looking at Americans in racial and ethnic categories instead of as unique individuals, was the statement by the head of the Democrat National Committee, Debbie Wasserman-Schultz, who said:

"..the Democratic Party is....the natural home, politically on major issues to Hispanics, to women, to Jews, to Asian-Americans, the diverse spectrum—to African Americans... we stand up for the issues that matter to those communities..." (http://www.realclearpolitics.com/video/2012/01/13/wasserman_schultz_natural_home_for_minorities_is_the_democratic_party.html) Accessed August 11, 2012

The question for every American thinker is: why does anyone assume that an individual's race or ethnicity determines his or her views on political issues? Don't individuals think for themselves? Isn't a very basic part of respect for our fellow Americans the notion that we respect the intelligence and ability of each individual to for her or himself and arrive at his or her own views? Who has the right or authority to decide for people based on their skin color what they think about anything? And then to abashedly announce to the world what those group members think? And don't statements like the one above create or add to the political pressure on minorities to keep quiet if they don't support the Democrat values?

Given the Democrat party's main goals in the last several years, why would anyone assume that any group based on race or ethnicity would prefer bigger and more controlling government, higher taxes, and strangling business regulation, and the proliferation of government assistance programs and massive increase in social spending and dependency creation? Why should those freedom-crushing ideas be viewed as appealing to anyone?

The Republicans' Approach: Unite Around Ideas

Republicans come from a different perspective. While all of us respect the many varied racial and ethnic heritages represented among the American people, at our core in America, we are citizens abiding under one set of laws, one Declaration of Independence and one Constitution. Our highest sense of unity in America should be, and I would argue can only derive from unity around ideas such as freedom, the rule of law, equal rights for all, and rights from our Creator that government exists to protect. These ideals and ideas apply equally to all and have no divisions. It's not a "help one group as opposed to another group" approach. This is how the Republican leaders I know, (and I know a few), think.

Republicans advocate for unity around ideas, while Democrats urge individuals to join competing groups that are based on ethnicity or race, and to identify their political views with those of similar backgrounds. Generalizations are never 100 percent fair, but I urge you to watch the conduct and listen to the words spoken by our elected officials and candidates, and you'll see how often they follow these two different paths.

Playing the Race Card

Openly claiming or subtly implying that racism is an underlying factor in the actions or policy proposals by politicians or just regular American citizens is of course a deeply offensive accusation, and should never be made without some genuine and legitimate basis. Especially when real discrimination still does occur, the use of the "racist" label solely as a weapon to silence political opponents is truly evil. Falsely raising the suggestion of racism, or implying it, is called "playing the race card," and it involves not just raising claims of racism where the facts do not justify it, but also raising that claim to stir up the passions, suspicions and anger of voters. Truly offensive, but it still happens.

Voter ID laws

You likely have heard that there is a controversy surrounding Voter ID laws. The entire issue concerns whether or not states can require a potential voter to show a picture ID before being allowed to cast a vote. You know, like you and every American show at the bank and dozens of other places all the time. It's not just a license that can be used—any official picture ID works. The purpose of these laws is to prevent voter fraud: it will prevent in-person voter fraud, where someone walks into the voting location and votes under someone else's name.

Democrats oppose these laws, and claim without any rational explanation that the laws have a racist purpose, to prevent minorities and the elderly from voting. Democrat U.S. Attorney General Eric Holder has barred Texas from enforcing its new Voter ID law, and the case is making its way through the courts as this book is being written. For supporters of voter ID laws, it seems that the only genuine reason liberals fight against these laws, is to protect and enable voter fraud. The discriminatory purpose/racist charge just does not stand the test of logic.

Holder and other Democrats claim that there is no basis for concern that in-person voter fraud even happens, so there is no need for these laws. But check out the box called "So you say there is no in-person voter fraud in America?"

So you say there is no in-person voter fraud in America?

Remember that AG Holder said that there was no evidence that in person voter fraud was happening? That is a common point made by liberals and Democrats: that voter ID laws are unnecessary because in person voter fraud isn't really happening in America.

So it was particularly ironic that after Holder's initial ruling against Texas, an imposter, armed with a hidden video camera but absolutely no identification, entered the polling location in Washington D.C., where Attorney General Holder himself is registered to vote, and asked the election clerk if they had an Eric Holder listed in the voter registry. That clerk confirmed that Holder's name was in the registry, made a check mark by Holder's name, offered the imposter the pen to sign next to Holder's name and was ready to hand the imposter Holder's ballot.

The imposter even offered "I left my ID in the car—I can go get it" to which the clerk responded that no ID was necessary. You can still watch the video of this "sting" online at http://blog.heritage. org/2012/04/09/video-voter-id-sting-targets-eric-holder/; accessed June 17, 2012) (The imposter left and did not return: he did not vote Holder's ballot.)

I tell this story to make two points: This escapade is living proof of what everyone already knows: it is simple to commit voter fraud if no ID is required. It is unconscionably dishonest for any elected official to claim otherwise.

And the second point is that it is even more reprehensible for elected Democrat officials to claim that voter ID laws have a racially discriminatory purpose. The officials making those claims may know better, but lots of less-informed Americans do not, and the citizenry suffers from an unjustified deepening of racial suspicion and tension.

The Way the Left Treats Black Conservatives

Blacks in America have historically tended to vote Democrat since the 1960's, which is not news. Obviously every American is free to vote as he or she chooses—this is a great country!

But it is a fair and in fact morally compelling question why black conservatives are so vilified by Democrats in elected office and in the media's political conversation. Liberals treat black conservatives with disdain because liberals think they know better what is better for blacks (and everyone!) and they are shocked and appalled when intelligent black Americans choose conservative views.

Consider just a few among many examples:

★ Former Maryland Lt Governor Michael Steele, the first black man to win a statewide election in liberal Maryland, was pelted with Oreos during a campaign appearance in his race for the U.S. Senate. (If you don't know the Oreo's significance, it is that they are black on the outside and white on the inside—an inference that Steele was acting "white" by running for federal office as a Republican). How dare that man think he is allowed to choose his own political party, based on what he believes? Democrat Party leaders in Maryland were reported to have called the Oreo attack "fair" and "pointing out the obvious."

★ Try Googling the name "Justice Clarence Thomas," who is a conservative black justice on the United States Supreme

Court. Among many vicious attacks, he has been criticized as "self-loathing" because of a ruling he made against the constitutionality of a particular college affirmative action program.

Ladies, consider what the left wing world is saying: because Justice Thomas is black, he is required to be pro-affirmative action. He could not possibly enjoy the right to sit on the Supreme Court and decide cases on the merits, or be allowed to hold a view different from what the political correctness police have decided he is allowed to think. Deeply offensive, yet that view is widely held in liberal circles.

Meet Some Stellar Conservatives of Color Brave Enough to Push Back Against Political Correctness

Ladies, conservatives of color deserve our admiration and support, regardless of whether we agree with what they are saying, just because they have been brave enough to speak up in a political climate where they are vilified for doing so. I'll just run through a short list here, and urge you to read more about them.

(1) The Honorable Artur Davis, a black former Democrat Congressman from Alabama, who supported Barack Obama in his first bid for the White House and who was the person who seconded Obama's nomination at the Denver Convention. Davis publicly announced in August of 2012 his shift from the Democrat to the Republican Party, saying:

> "I made a decision that on every single issue we're debating in the country right now, what Republicans were saying made more sense to me than what Democrats were saying,"
> "I saw a Democratic solution that always amounted to 'Let's take more money from people that are successful and grow the

footprint of government... That became the two-pronged, all-purpose solution to every economic problem.

http://campaigntracker.blogspot.com/2012/08/man-who-seconded-barack-obamas-2008.html#storylink=cpy
Accessed August 11, 2012

(2) Star Parker, black American author, founder of CURE, the Center for Urban Renewal and Education (http://www.urbancure.org/starparker.asp), Republican candidate for United States Congress and outspoken advocate for reducing the size of government and for reducing dependency on government programs. Star wrote "Uncle Sam's Plantation" which is her first hand description of the misery created by dependency on government.

(3) Allen West from Florida, a black Republican Congressman and candidate for re-election, and a leader in standing up for fiscal conservatism, personal responsibility and the need to reduce the size and scope of government. He has been particularly harshly criticized for his outspoken defense of conservative ideas.

(4) More conservative black authors: Dr. Ben Carson (America, the Beautiful, Rediscovering What Made This Nation Great), Dr. Thomas Sowell (Economic Facts and Fallacies, and Black Rednecks and White Liberals, and other books), Angela McGlowan (Bamboozled), Larry Elder (What's Race got to do with it?), John McWhorter (Losing the Race, Self-Sabotage in Black America). Dr. Walter Williams (Liberty versus the Tyranny of Socialism, More Liberty Means Less Government Our Founders Knew This Well).

(5) Indian-born American conservative Dinesh D'Souza, wrote The Enemy at Home, What's So Great About America, The Virtue of Prosperity, and The End of Racism, and other books.

(6) Hispanic conservatives are emerging in a more focused voice in America, on websites, and in elected office. The Texas State legislature has a

new Hispanic Republican Caucus and has seen the very positive experience of numerous elected Democrat Hispanic representatives converting to the Republican Party. You can read about them at www.texasgopvote.com.

Girls, I included this section in an effort to commend these brave conservatives, but also to inspire each of you who finds it impossible to imagine telling your longtime Democrat friends that you are no longer comfortable continuing to support that party. Lots of longtime Democrats are feeling the same way. And it is not that you are leaving the party, it is that the Democrat Party has left mainstream America, and wandered way down the far left path. We as a nation just cannot go there with them.

The "Fairness" Club

"Fairness" is the new Democrat theme-word used to justify or explain demands for tax increases, increased regulation, and just about any other policy they support. Everyone is naturally in favor of fairness. Everyone.

The question is how you define fairness.

Absolute fairness in all things is of course a fairy tale never achieved in all of human existence. I urge you to closely examine what politicians are asking you to accept, in the name of fairness. Democrats today pursue ideas and programs with goals similar to the socialist goal of equality of outcome, through pushing for higher, "fairer" taxes on the successful, to be used to spread wealth around. When Democrats and liberals lament income disparity, they are attacking freedom and free markets. More and more experts are recognizing that the use of the term "fair" is an alibi for instituting wealth redistribution, increased taxes and growing regulation. Let's not let politicians bully us with the "fairness" club!

> "Critics of capitalism often complain that the distribution of income generated by the market system is unequal.
> Talk of equity and fairness generally means wealth redistribution."
> —Meltzer, Allan H. (2012). Why Capitalism? New York,
> Oxford University Press page

Did You Know?…Stories and Facts to Share
Chapter Nine

Share a little history! It was the Republican Party that formed and coalesced around opposition to slavery and that fought for and led the way to passage for nearly every significant advancement in the civil rights arena from the time of the Civil War until the Civil Rights Acts in the 1960's.

Don't let the Left's proclivity to too frequently hurl the "racist" label at anyone who won't agree with them, cause you to think that the idea or person they are labeling with that ugly term, necessarily deserves it. It is permissible to view the healthcare takeover as unconstitutional and a bad idea beside, and to hold the opinion that the government assistance/entitlement programs need to be reformed, and none of us should be bullied or silenced from expressing those views, out of fear of being labeled.

The emergence of the Tea Party in America in 2009 was a direct challenge to the big government leftists in America. The Tea Party stands for limited government, adherence to the Constitution, personal responsibility and opposition to ever-growing government programs and spending. The Tea Party opposes everything that today's Democrat Party stands for, and the response by Democrat leaders was…you guessed it…to label the Tea Party as racist! Ladies, we cannot allow this verbal intimidation to impact our views. It is not "racist" to disagree with the Democrats!

It is obviously my view that the Republican approach of urging unity around ideas, rather than the Democrat approach of unity around skin color or ethnicity, best serves the interests of all Americans and the American culture going forward.

One very helpful perspective on the relative merits of each view is to consider what is the ultimate "end game" of each approach. How does the ever-growing divisiveness and division promoted by today's Democrats ever get us to a better society, a unified people? The answer is that of course it cannot unify us as a nation. Unity is contrary to divisions.

The end game of the Republican approach of unity around ideas is the promotion of the timeless ideals and virtues set out in our founding documents that offer all equally the opportunity to pursue life, liberty and happiness. Ladies, I love that we women care so deeply about racial equality and fairness. I hope you will consider whether supporting a party that organizes its supporters and policies around individual races and nationalities, is helping or hurting American unity.

I hope you'll consider that uniting around ideas that apply equally to all is a more unifying and in fact progressive step. And that is just another reason for you and more American women to vote conservative, to vote Republican. The only political "home" for those who embrace equality and fairness in America is the conservative side of the aisle.

Getting America on a more even keel, a more trustful keel, in terms of race relations, is vital. Race relations are such a tender, personal and yet society-impacting set of concerns. America could, should and will be the land of increased racial harmony as we all insist on following the inspiration of Dr. Martin Luther King, Jr., who urged that his children (and all men) not be judged - and I would add not be labeled, hyphenated or categorized—by the color of their skin—but by the content of their character. A related notion is that respect for the individuality of each person must mean at least that we respect the right of each person to think and reason for himself and herself, and arrive at the ideas we each believe in.

What a great way forward for America!

★ ★ Chapter Ten ★ ★

Weird Science

Why Are Energy Development and the Environment *Political* Issues?

Can We Talk...About America's Energy Needs and Environment? And How Odd It Is that Science Has Become Political?

Many women hold stewardship of the environment front and center in their hearts and thinking on Election Day.

Every American I know, of any political persuasion, wants clean air, pure water, a clean environment and access to enough energy to travel freely and live comfortably.

Doesn't it seem odd that energy and environmental issues, that are technology-based, involve politics? The "politicizing" of energy and environmental issues makes little sense from a scientific perspective, but a great deal of sense from a political power perspective. He who controls energy access, controls the country. And the world.

We may find talking about energy and environmental issues a little daunting, and think we should just rely on the "experts." But ladies: (1) the experts disagree, even on big issues like the global warming theory, (2) we *can* understand important basics, and (3) we need to recognize the political motivation behind some "expert" opinions, so we can play our part in shaping America's future.

Let's talk about it.

★ 233

Ladies, I am serious in my question that serves as the title of this chapter. Why should the two related issues of energy development and environmental policy be considered nearly entirely political, instead of mostly scientific and a little bit political? The answer is that the manmade global warming theory (aka climate change) is itself a political issue, and in fact a political cause, as well as a scientific question, and manmade global warming theory literally drives the entire energy and environmental debate in America and the world today.

The way that America's two political parties approach energy and environmental issues parallels their approach on other issues. Both parties support basic environmental protection, of course. But Democrats trust government, and pursue extensive regulation and government control of energy production, the economy and the choices consumers are permitted to make, including standing in the way of energy development that Americans want and need. Republicans trust the free markets, the goodness and freedom of the American people and the businesses they build, and support the people's right to pursue energy production.

But in this particular issue of energy and the environment, the differences between the parties are even starker, and relate to how the parties view America's abundance, prosperity and continued development and growth. Today's liberal Democrat Party leaders view our nation's abundance with disdain, guilt and embarrassment, and want to reduce America's prosperity to bring it more in line with other nations. The Democrats goals in the climate change issue parallel their domestic policy approach: they support expanding government control and redistribution of "wealth" on terms they decide. Republicans see America's abundance as a blessing based on our system of government and free markets, and are eager to perpetuate this system and to share it and the blessings it brings with other nations.

Here is what we'll talk about in this chapter:
*Putting Energy and Environmental Issues in Manmade Global Warming
  Perspective*

The Manmade Global Warming Controversy – The Environmental Issue that Defines All Others

Serious Experts Questioning the Climate Change Theory

The Climate Alarmists' Political Agenda Climate, The UN, Agenda 21 and Sustainability

Now We Can Talk about the Environment, Energy Development and Energy Independence

EPA Under Democrats as Major Political/Governmental Bully

Back to the Question That is the Title of This Chapter—Why Energy and Environmental Issues Are, Today, Political Issues

Did You Know?...Stories and Facts to Share

Putting Energy and Environmental Issues in Manmade Global Warming Perspective

The overarching environmental and energy issue in America and the world today is the manmade global warming theory, so that is the primary subject of this chapter. Before you flip to the next chapter without reading another word of this one, please know that I have presented some very basic information, lots of references to sources so you can read more, and I did not get so technical that it will put you to sleep, I promise.

We all know that all Americans need clean air and clean water. These are givens and all sides are in substantial agreement about them. These simply are not the environmental issues of consequence today.

The major source of political disagreement in the energy and environmental arena is the difference of opinion about the existence and/or extent of manmade global warming and possible harm arising out it. Manmade global warming theory impacts:

★ Whether we will drill for oil and develop other natural resources.

★ How much pressure Congress puts on car manufacturers to develop cars that meet extreme fuel efficiency standards, and to produce cars that no one wants

★ Our national security, as we refuse to develop our abundant, untapped resources at home so we remain dependent on foreign oil produced by countries that are our enemies

★ The kind of light bulbs we are allowed to buy

★ The kind of meters the power companies want to put in our homes, the "smart meters" that will allow the power companies and the government to monitor and eventually control our power usage, in our own homes

★ The willingness of those on the America Left to submit American sovereignty to international bodies that exist to set international standards about where and how people can live, under the United Nation's Agenda 21 project (if you haven't heard of this, read more in this chapter).

The Manmade Global Warming Controversy: The Environmental Issue that Defines all Others

It is rather amazing to think that twenty years ago, almost no one was worrying about global warming, and now it is the subject of heated controversy, international activity and pressure, and mocking ridicule by the American Left directed at anyone who will not agree with the theory and comply with the extremist policies that flow from it.

What is Manmade Global Warming (MGW) Theory and where did it come from?

The basic premise of the MGW argument is that the earth's temperatures are rising due to the concentration of "greenhouse gases" which are gases that absorb and emit radiation. The primary greenhouse gases in Earth's atmosphere are naturally occurring elements: water vapor, nitrous oxide, methane, ozone and carbon dioxide. The burning of fossil fuels (oil/gasoline) emits carbon dioxide, which is, by the way, also what all humans breathe out with every breath, after we breathe in oxygen.

Vice President Al Gore introduces global warming theory

Most of us first heard about the supposed dangers of global warm- ing due to increasing levels of CO2 in the atmosphere, when former Vice President Al Gore published his book "An Inconvenient Truth" in late spring 2006, and also produced a documentary by the same name.

In a New York Times interview Al Gore gave around the time he published his book, he said that "polar bears have been drowning in significant numbers" as melting ice forces them to swim longer and longer distances," and that the Emperor penguin population "has declined by an estimated 70 percent over the past 50 years." And, said Mr. Gore, the penguins and the polar bears and lots of other animals will suffer and die under global warming's impact. (http://www.nytimes.com/2006/05/23/books/23kaku. html?pagewanted=all; accessed May 30, 2012)

Those who predict dire harmful effects from global warming claim that increased CO2 levels due to human activity will result in the sea levels rising, expansion of deserts, increase in precipitation, hurricanes, melting polar ice caps and glaciers, and all sorts of drastic weather pattern changes.

The solutions proposed by global warming "believers" are equally drastic. Al Gore and other climate change believers say that in order to remedy the impending disaster, the world needs to take extreme steps to reduce CO2 emissions, including drastically cutting back on our use of fossil fuels, and heavily regulating industry emissions. It is notable that while Mr. Gore and other climate change believers clamor for immediate reduction in the use of fossil fuels by others, he and they continue to jet around the world to warn others to stop burning so much fossil fuel. Mr. Gore justifies this by saying that he buys carbon setoffs, but that raises the question: so only those who are wealthy enough to be able to buy carbon setoffs will be free to travel, but the lowly individual American will not have that opportunity?

By the way, you probably know that CO_2, carbon dioxide, is a natural compound made of oxygen and carbon, right? Do you know what percent of the CO_2 in the world is manmade? Three percent. Yep, a measly little 3 percent of all the CO_2 in our atmosphere is manmade – and all the rest is "natural," and beyond our control.

This is as good a time as any to point out that Al Gore is not a climatologist. In fact, he got a "D" in Natural Sciences 6 at Harvard, and a C+ in Natural Sciences 118. He dropped out of law school to run for Congress.

Global Warming Theory Instantly Becomes Left Wing Gospel, So Don't You Dare Question It!

Many real climatologists began to examine the evidence on global warming, and some of these real experts disputed Al Gore's theory and findings. I will report more below on that.

The American Left immediately adopted Al Gore's theory, and global warming "science" has become such a political hot button that America's Leftist leaders call anyone who does not fall into step with the manmade global warming (MGW) theory right down the line, a "denier." The MGW orthodoxy that must be accepted includes the need to immediately reduce greenhouse gases, radically reduce the emissions by power plants, eliminate large vehicles like SUVs, shun or severely limit new oil exploration, and a whole host of other new and strict environmental regulations. In case that "denier" analogy was not familiar to you, they are equating any skepticism over the question of whether MGW is real, dangerous and requires immediate and drastic cutbacks and other steps by all nations, with the truly evil people who deny the reality of the Nazi Holocaust.

The fact that the American Left resorts to mocking and derision against anyone who questions the global warming theory and agenda is cause enough for rational people to take a second look. Since when do genuine scientists who are confident of their theory and data attempt to silence people on scientific subjects?

If we think, "how could so many experts who accept global warming be wrong," it is equally logical to ask, "how could so many skeptics be wrong?" Why accord only those with dire predictions the presumption of accuracy? And before we make truly radical changes in our lives and our freedoms, shouldn't we at least look at the facts, the science, the information and the bases for the views of those scientists who do not agree with the MGW theory?

Global Warming Becomes Climate Change: Conveniently for Climate Change Believers, All Weather Patterns Prove Climate Change

Global warming true believers changed the name of this theoretical phenomenon from "global warming" to "global climate change" as they attempted to take into account temperature and precipitation occurrences that deviated from their prognostications. That is one of the reason many experts and nonexperts respond with skepticism, as the theory morphs into one that now points to any weather pattern, temperature adjustment, and fluctuation, as proof of CO_2 related global climate change.

Too hot? Climate change! Too cold? Climate change! Too dry? Climate change! Too much rain? Climate change! Every possible weather pattern proves the theory; it's a great gig if you can get it!

So What do the Manmade Global Warming skeptics say?

I have presented here just a smattering, a very small amount, of the vast amount of information that any of you could find out on the Internet and in books. Honestly, choosing among the many data sources and points to raise in this section was difficult. This book is not a global warming treatise, but the more I researched the more I realized how much information exists in the genuinely scientific world to refute the MGW theory, and how very political, rather than scientific, the MGW advocates are.

The UK Government Uncovers a Few Inconvenient Al Gore Not-Truths

Some British schools considered including Al Gore's *An Inconvenient Truth* movie in their curricula. The High Court in London required the British government to accompany that movie distribution with a "corrected guidance note" that let the schools know that a significant number of the claims Gore makes needed correction or were unproven (read: false or mere conjecture). Failure of the government to "send that notice would otherwise constitute contravention of an Act of Parliament prohibiting the political indoctrination of children."

Ladies, I will not repeat these Al Gore "not-truths" here, but I have provided in the footnotes the link to the online article by Lord Christopher Monckton that enumerates "35 inconvenient truths" about the movie.

The *Inconvenient Truth* movie was propaganda, not science. (http://science- andpublicpolicy.org/monckton/goreerrors.html; accessed May 30, 2012) And many of Al Gore's and other alarmists' dire prognostications and assessments have been completely debunked.

Just a few "but that's not happening" examples—bears, penguins, and hurricanes

One reason the number of climate change skeptics is growing is that so many of the drastic predictions made by the global warming alarmists just are not coming to pass. Plus, the clearer it becomes that the climate alarmists have political, professional reputation and monetary incentives impelling them to stand with their climate change story, and the more and better information real experts gather, the more those experts and just everyday citizens conclude we do not have the problem the alarmists forecast. And we really do not want the solutions they would impose.

The Bear Truth

You might recall that Al Gore mentioned to the *New York Times* that polar bears were threatened by global warming: nearly all of us have watched with a cuddly soft spot reaction the picture of a polar bear floating helplessly on a tiny piece of glacier ice. The truth? According to data reported in 2007, the world's population of polar bears has "increased dramatically over the past decades, from about five thousand members in the 1960's to twenty-five thousand today" (that's 5,000 up to 25,000) "through stricter hunting regulation." [*Cool It—the Skeptical Environmentalist's Guide to Global Warming*, by Bjorn Lomborg, Borzoi Book, published by Alfred A. Knopf, 2007, page 5.]

Author Bjorn Lomborg explains also that the Polar Bear Specialist Group that reported a reduction of polar bears in 2001 was actually only reporting on one or two of the 20 distinct subpopulations of polar bears, and that among the remaining groups, more than half were stable, and two of the subpopulations were increasing in size. (Ibid) The hardest fact for the alarmists to swallow may be this: the declining populations live in areas where it has been getting colder, while the growing bear populations live where average temperatures are increasing. (Ibid)

The penguin truth

And those adorable penguins? Again, the global warming alarmists predicted the impending devastation of penguins, but facts defeat hysteria. The Antarctic Emperor penguins (and there are no penguins in the Arctic) live in a colony near a French research station called Dumont d'Urville, so that particular population happens to be the subject of the most study. That population has decreased from 6,000 breeding pairs between 1952 and 1970, to about 3,000 pairs, where it has remained steadily for decades. But the Emperors near Dumont d'Urville are not the only penguins down there. There are about 40 colonies in the Antarctic, and some of the larger colonies have 20,000 pairs each. And another Antarctic penguin, the Adelie, has increased in population more than 40 percent in the last 20 years. (Lomborg, *Cool It*, *page 66*.)

It also turns out that recent improved quality satellite mapping has allowed researchers to get a far more accurate penguin count than previously possible, and the "good news" is that the team found that the Antarctic emperor penguin population numbers about 595,000, "nearly double previous estimates." (http://www.reuters.com/article/2012/04/13/us-antarc-tic-penguins- idUSBRE83C0A220120413; accessed May 31, 2012)

The hurricane truth

Another global warming alarmist prediction is that more hurricanes will occur due to supposed manmade global warming phenomena, but that has not been borne out by the facts either. The National Weather Service reports that since 1851, through today, the decade with the most hurricanes was 1941-1950, and the decade with second highest number of hurricanes was between 1881-1890. The years between 1851 and 1950 have many more decades above the average per decade, than do the decades since 1950. (*The Politically Incorrect Guide to Global Warming and Environmentalism*, by Christopher C. Horner, Regnery Publishing, 2007, page 156.)

Serious Experts Questioning the Climate Change Theory

A Longer Climate History

Try reading *"Unstoppable Global Warming—Every 1,500 Years,"* written by renowned climate physicist and environmental science professor Dr. S. Fred Singer, and senior State Department analyst, author and columnist Dennis T. Avery. The title of the book gives away the entire plot, but I'll mention the opening paragraph in Chapter One in which the authors say that the earth is currently warming, but that physical evidence tells them that CO2 has only a minor role in that warming, and that the current warming is part of a natural 1,500-year climate cycle that goes back in earth's history for at least 1 million years. [FN= *Unstoppable Global Warming Every 1,500 Years*, by S. Fred Singer and Dennis T. Avery, Rowman & Littlefield Publishers, Inc., 2007, p. 1.]

Among the many fascinating things in the book are detailed descriptions of the inconsistencies between the greenhouse gas theory and the actual temperature fluctuations in history. For example, most of the current warming happened before 1940, which means that warming occurred before the great increase in the number of vehicles on America's roads. Then, between 1940 and 1975, as the numbers of our vehicles increased, there was a decrease in temperatures. This data fits well in the 1,500-year fluctuation cycle and not at all in the Al Gore greenhouse gas theory. [Ibid, p. 10]

And Some Very Recent Climate History

Additionally, actual recorded temperatures show that, quoting Randall Hoven's 2011 article summarizing NASA and GISS data:

• "The trend of annual mean temperatures since 1880 is warming of 0.59 degrees Celsius per century

• The trend over the last nine years (since 2002) is one of cooling and

• There has been no statistically significant warming in 14 years (since 1997)."

(http://www.americanthinker.com/2012/05/global_warming_melts_away.html; accessed May 30, 2012)

But I thought there was a "consensus"!

Lord Christopher Monckton has written and spoken extensively on the MGW theory, and one of his often-repeated points is that when defenders respond to questions or skepticism about the MGW theory by saying that "there is a consensus!" on that, they are engaging in "intellectual baby-talk." More precisely he points out that asserting "there is a consensus" as a substitute for factual argument is a "violation" of one of the basic rules of logic. Claiming "everyone agrees" does not prove anything. In fact the repeated "there is a consensus" mantra signals that supporters of the MGW theory are at a loss to defend their theory or to answer a question.

In fact, it is the record number of scientists denouncing the MGW theory that if anything, signals a "consensus."

★ The Global Warming Petition Project: A large and scholarly group of American scientists have signed on to what they are calling the Global Warming Petition Project, which is an online project that involves having educated American scientists sign a petition that debunks global warming. It says:

"We urge the United States government to reject the global warming agreement that was written in Kyoto, Japan in December, 1997, and any other similar proposals. The proposed limits on greenhouse gases would harm the environment, hinder the advance of science and technology, and damage the health and welfare of mankind.

"There is no convincing scientific evidence that human release of carbon dioxide, methane, or other greenhouse gases is causing or will, in the foreseeable future, cause catastrophic heating of the Earth's atmosphere and disruption of the Earth's climate. Moreover, there is substantial scientific evidence that increases in atmospheric carbon dioxide produce many beneficial effects upon the natural plant and animal environments of the Earth."

To date, 31,487 American scientists have signed onto this petition, including 9,029 Ph.Ds.! That is over 31,000 scientists are willing to put their names out there in the world stating that "There is no convincing scientific evidence that the human release of carbon dioxide…or other greenhouse gases is causing catastrophic heating of the Earth's atmosphere…."

★ In September 2011, Nobel Prize winning physicist Dr. Ivar Giaever resigned from his teaching post at Rensselaer Polytechnic Institute (RPI) out of dismay over the school's official stated policy "that global warming is occurring." He especially objects to the use of the expression that global climate change evidence is "incontrovertible." Giaver founded and writes the website Climate Depot, where he expands on his debunking of the theory of man-made climate change. For loads of information and links to other information, check out his website, http://www.climatedepot.com/.

Fears of Climate Change are not new

Fears of climate change are hardly novel. Check out just a few headlines from American history in the last 60 or so years:

★ "Winters Since '40 Found Colder In Studies by Weather Bureau: Data Indicate, a Reversal of a Warming Trend That Began in 1888 by Walter Sullivan, January 26, 1961 (http://select.nytimes.com/gst/abstracthtml?res= F30F11F83C5D1 B728DDDAC0A94D9405B818AF1D3&scp=155&sq=Climate+change&st=p; accessed May 30, 2012)

★ "Ice in Antarctic Reported on Rise; Sheet Growing at Rate of 293 Cubic Miles Yearly, Soviet Expert Says; IGY Data Disclosed; Hoarforst is Said to Fall the Year Round in Heart of Polar Continent; Ice in Antarctic is Found Piling Up,

By Walter Sullivan, Special to the New York Times, August 4, 1960 (http://select.nytimes.com/gst/abstract. html?res=F10814F63D581 A7A93C6A91783D85F448685F9&scp=179&sq=Climate +change&st=p;accessed May 30, 2012)

★ "Climate Warming in the Antarctic 5-Degree Rise over the last cen- tury is Recorded at Little America; ICE is FOUND THICKER; Director of U.S. Program Says Sheet Drops 10,000 Feet in Many Areas, by Walter Sullivan, May 31, 1958. (http://select.nytimes.com/gst/abstract. html?res=F2091FFA 3555127B93C3AA178ED85F4C8585F9&scp=25&sq=Climate+change&st=p; accessed May 30, 2012)

The CO2 and Warming Relationship—Which "Started It"?

The argument of the climate change alarmists is that the increased level of CO2 in the atmosphere is causing annual temperatures to rise. (And the CO2 levels are due to or caused by human existence, cars and other indicia of modern civilization.) But climate scientists on both sides of the question readily admit that historically, *it was the increase in temperatures that occurred first, which then caused the CO2 levels to rise.* Then after that, the CO2 levels acted as a "feedback," amplifying the temperature change.

But what is viewed as the likely cause of the temperatures rising? One likely cause is the "Milankovich cycles," which is the "precession of the equinoxes, and variations in the eccentricity of the Earth's orbit and in the obliquity of its axis with respect to the plane of the ecliptic." [http://www.cfact.org/a/2102/Moncktons-Schenectady-showdown] Accessed May 31, 2012.

Ladies, I know this is "eyes glazing over" stuff, but I included it just to be sure you know how twisted the alarmists' arguments are. Historically everyone can see that temperature increases came first, then increased CO2 levels, but now that the climate change paradigm has been imposed on the truth, we all are supposed to believe that CO2 (produced by human breathing and human activity) is causing the temperature increases.

And stop thinking; just believe!

And it Gets Worse!
Science Abandoned: Some Climate Change Supporters Actually Manipulate Data to "Prove" Climate Change is Real

Ladies, this is where this climate change issue gets honestly creepy. There are numerous instances of scientists who have engaged in deception and dishonesty to prop up this climate change theory that cannot stand on its own.

Let's start with the famous "Hockey Stick" scandal.

The IPCC "Hockey Stick" Scandal – a Big Climate Not-Truth
Because the Intergovernmental Panel on Climate Change (IPPC) "hockey-stick" episode was so widely reported, I will not go into great detail, but in case you do not know about this…you need to!

The IPCC was formed in 1988 by two organizations within the United Nations, the World Meteorological Organization and the United Nations Environment Programme. While their charter may have been to study and provide accurate information on the climate change theory, they soon evolved into an advocacy organization, no longer dedicated to science, but instead dedicated to advocating for the acceptance of the climate change theory.

One episode/scandal was the IPCC's outright revision of temperature history to buttress their claim that modern temperatures are undeniably warmer.

Compare:

• In the IPCC's 1995 Climate Change report, they showed a temperature change chart that accurately showed a Medieval Warm Period, from 1,000 AD to around 1,500 AD, when the earth was very warm, much warmer than it is now! There was a Little Ice Age between 1,500 AD to 1,700 AD that was also shown on their 1995 chart, when the earth was colder than it is now.

• In the IPCC's 2001 Climate Change report, the IPCC simply presented false temperature data from both the Medieval Warm Period and the Little Ice Age, showed instead a nearly flat temperature line between 1,000 AD all the way up to around 1910, and then showed a sudden and drastic shooting up of the temperatures into ranges not reflected in the chart before that time. (The shape of the new line looks like a hockey stick.)

• The IPCC changed the "facts" of the earth's temperature history, to fit their political agenda! The utter determination to convince the world that global warming was real and alarming overcame the scientific integrity of the IPCC.

For many, the hockey stick scandal helped open eyes to the realization that climate change is not about science at all. It is a left-wing political movement. (More on that later.)

Unstoppable Global Warming—Every 1,500 Years by S. Fred Singer and Dennis T. Avery, pages 68-69.

The "Climate-Gate" emails

You may have heard about the "Climate-Gate" emails and even read a bit, and again, I will offer only the briefest summary on what was a major episode in the further unraveling of the climate "consensus" farce.

In November 2009, an unknown person hacked into the computers of the Climatic Research Institute of the University of East Anglia, in England.

This hacker downloaded and then dispensed around the world the contents of literally thousands of emails sent between climate scientists work- ing on climate change.

These email authors were not run-of-the-mill climate scientists. They were the "tiny international clique of climate scientists, centered on the Climate Research Unit at East Anglia, that has been the prime mover in telling the world that it is warming at an unprecedented rate, and that humankind is responsible." (http://wattsupwiththat.com/2009/12/01/lord-moncktons-summary-of-climategate-and-its-issues/; accessed May 31, 2012)

Lord Christopher Monckton of the UK wrote a brilliant summary of the emails, and he describes them this way:

Who are the Authors of the Climate-Gate emails?

"A tiny clique of politicized scientists, paid by unscientific politicians with whom they were financially and politically linked, were responsible for gathering and reporting data on temperatures from the palaeoclimate to today's climate. The "Team", as they called themselves, were bending and distorting scientific data to fit a nakedly political story-line profitable to themselves and congenial to the governments that, these days, pay the bills for 99 percent of all scientific research."

http://wattsupwiththat.com/2009/12/01/lord-moncktons-summary-of-climate- gate-and-its-issues/ Accessed May 31, 2012

You may have read that some climate change advocates dismissed the Climate-Gate emails as "taken out of context," misunderstood, misinterpreted etc. I will include a few summaries below, to give you a flavor.

More "Climate-Gate" Emails

A second batch of East Anglia emails was anonymously released to the world two years later in November 2011. They were equally damaging to the climate change cabal, and revealed further the effort to shape truth rather than report it. You can read summaries of the emails in question, or the actual emails, but it is simply fallacious for the climate change alarmists to imply that these were innocuous emails.

Here is one summary of some of the first batch of emails, by Lord Monckton:

• "The Team had tampered with the complex, bureaucratic processes of the UN's climate panel, the IPCC, so as to exclude inconvenient scientific results from its four Assessment Reports, and to influence the panel's conclusions for political rather than scientific reasons."

• The Team had conspired in an attempt to redefine what is and is not peer-reviewed science for the sake of excluding results that did not fit what they and the politicians with whom they were closely linked wanted the UN's climate panel to report.

• They had tampered with their own data so as to conceal inconsistencies and errors.

• They had emailed one another about using a "trick" for the sake of concealing a "decline" in temperatures in the paleoclimate.

• They had successfully leaned on friendly journal editors to reject papers report- ing results inconsistent with their political viewpoint.

(http://wattsupwiththat.com/2009/12/01/lord-moncktons-summa-ry-of-climat- egate-and-its-issues/; accessed May 31, 2012)

Ladies, the emails described in these boxes are representative of many similar ones. This email scandal was devastating to the credibility of the climate change advocates. You can go online and read the second batch from November 2011 yourself if you are interested, at http://foia2011.org/.

I do not support email hackers, but I do urge you to consider that the tone and content of these emails tells you more about the motives of the cli- mate change advocates than any feel-good, save-the-planet, love the earth message they send.

A Forbes magazine article reported on the second batch of Climate-gate emails:

"Emails between Climategate scientists, however, show a concerted effort to hide rather than disseminate underlying evidence and procedures.

"I've been told that IPCC is above national FOI [Freedom of Information] Acts. One way to cover yourself and all those working in AR5 would be to delete all emails at the end of the process," writes Phil Jones, a scientist working with the United Nations Intergovernmental Panel on Climate Change (IPCC), in a newly released email.

"Any work we have done in the past is done on the back of the research grants we get – and has to be well hidden," Jones writes in another newly released email. "I've discussed this with the main funder (U.S. Dept of Energy) in the past and they are happy about not releasing the original station data.""

http://www.forbes.com/sites/jamestaylor/2011/11/23/climategate-2-0-new-e- mails-rock-the-global-warming-debate/ Accessed May 31, 2012

Why Are the Climate Change Believers So Insistent—What's in it for Them?

Americans intuitively want to trust fellow Americans, and their government, so it is hard for most Americans to dismiss the climate change alarmists, even with all of the evidence of the contortion, hiding and misrepresentation of data by climate scientists. Because the question nags, why would Al Gore and the other leftists claim that radical change is needed in greenhouse emissions or the whole world will be in deep trouble, unless it is true? What's the point in making stuff up, or in continuing to ignore legitimate questions and to advocate for an idea that has been quite seriously undermined by facts and genuine climate experts?

A group of 16 scientists submitted an editorial to the Wall Street Journal in May 2012 called *"No Need To Panic About Global Warming—There's No Compelling Scientific Argument For Drastic Action To "Decarbonize" The World.*

The scientists, after completely dismissing, in fact eviscerating, the idea that "increasing amounts of the 'pollutant' carbon dioxide will destroy the civilization" go on to point out that the number of publicly dissenting scientists is growing, but that young scientists who also doubt the global climate change alarmists are fearful about speaking up because they fear they will lose jobs, or be passed over for promotions, for not towing the global climate change left wing party line. That phenomenon—not wanting to be the one who says, "the emperor has no clothes"—explains the unwillingness of more to speak up. (http://online.wsj.com/article/SB1000142405297 0204301404577171531838421366.html)

There is also the related idea (my thought, not that of the WSJ writers) that those who have invested their professional reputations and life's work to studying global climate change theory, have spoken publicly and taken a firm position, want to stand their professional ground because it seems preferable to admitting a pretty big mistake. When we are talking about billions and billions of dollars of expense retrofitting factories and businesses, major increases in costs for power for the average citizen, foregoing drilling for oil when America needs jobs and plentiful oil is available, scientists' egos need to take a back seat to their obligation to speak up and speak truth.

So who are these 16 scientists who spoke out in the WSJ?

They are from all over the world, from renowned schools such as Princeton and Cambridge, and from countries including Holland, Australia, Israel, Switzerland, and the United States, all holding degrees or positions of authority in relevant scientific endeavors.

Making Money off of Global Warming. Who Knew?

But there is another and more mercenary explanation that rings deeply true. And that boils down to "follow the money." To quote these WSJ editorial-writing scientists: "Alarmism over climate is of great benefit to many, providing government funding for academic research and reason for government bureaucracies to grow. Alarmism also offers an excuse for

The Conclusion of These Sixteen Scientists Whose January 2012 Wall Street Journal Editorial Set Off a Firestorm Among Global Climate Change Believers

"Speaking for many scientists and engineers who have looked carefully and independently at the science of climate, we have a message to any candidate for public office: There is no compelling scientific argument for drastic action to "decarbonize" the world's economy. Even if one accepts the inflated climate forecasts of the IPCC, aggressive greenhouse-gas control policies are not justified economically.

A recent study of a wide variety of policy options by Yale economist William Nordhaus showed that nearly the highest benefit-to-cost ratio is achieved for a policy that allows 50 more years of economic growth unimpeded by greenhouse gas controls. This would be especially beneficial to the less-developed parts of the world that would like to share some of the same advantages of material well- being, health and life expectancy that the fully developed parts of the world enjoy now. Many other policy responses would have a negative return on investment. And it is likely that more CO2 and the modest warming that may come with it will be an overall benefit to the planet.

Every candidate should support rational measures to protect and improve our environment, but it makes no sense at all to back expensive programs that divert resources from real needs and are based on alarming but untenable claims of "incontrovertible" evidence."

(http://online.wsj.com/article/SB10001424052970204301404577171531838421366.html; accessed May 31, 2012)

governments to raise taxes, taxpayer-funded subsidies for businesses that understand how to work the political systems, and allure for big donations to charitable foundations promising to save the planet." (Ibid)

There are other financial ties as well. Al Gore makes money off of having America "buy into" global warming. In fact, he could become the "world's first carbon billionaire" because he founded a company that loans and invests in green-energy and energy-saving technology, and when the government announces that grants and other monies will go to companies in which Mr. Gore's company has invested, he and his partners prosper. Especially because Mr. Gore is so actively promoting the climate change agenda, he is talking America into investing in a theory and into entities from which he will make a profit. And conversely, if Mr. Gore's chosen green companies flounder and wither without U.S. government assistance, he stands to lose on the investments he has made. (http://www.telegraph. co.uk/earth/energy/6491195/Al-Gore-could-become-worlds-first-carbon-billionaire.html; accessed May 31, 2012)

But What is the Bottom Line?
Is there Global Warming at All?

The sixteen scientists who submitted the WSJ editorial said it well. Their views are in accord with other global climate change skeptics, such as Lord Monckton. Yes, there is regular temperature variation on the planet, yes we are in a slightly warming period, and yes, some of that warming is due to human activity and to CO_2. But CO_2 is a natural and needed element to survive on earth, the warming is and will be slight and inconsequential, and no radical environmentalist actions are needed. A more accurate term for those who oppose the radical environmentalist alarmists and their agenda is "global warming realists."

To repeat the WSJ editorial authors' words:

> ...nearly the highest benefit-to-cost ratio is achieved for a policy that allows 50 more years of economic growth unimped- ed by greenhouse gas controls. This would be especially beneficial to the less-developed parts of the world that would like to share some of the same advantages of material well-being, health and life expectancy that the fully developed parts of the world enjoy now. Many other policy responses would have a negative return on investment. And it is likely that more CO_2 and the modest warming that may come with it will be an overall benefit to the planet.

Why Do Climate Change Alarmists So Harshly Attack Those Who Do Not Agree with Them?

Again, ask yourself in what other context in the study of science do institutions fire people for entertaining or discussing varying scholarly points of view? The global warming alarmist fallacy is, in the eyes of the believers, an infallible truth, which may not be questioned.

★ In 2008, Lord Christopher Monckton's paper Climate Sensitivity Reconsidered was published in Physics and Society, and it showed that even a doubling of CO2 concentration which is expected by the year 2,100, would cause less than 1 degree Celsius of temperature increase. Both the Commissioning Editor who asked for the paper, and the review editor who was an eminent Physics professor, were dismissed for publishing it. (http://texasgopvote.com/voice-conservative-vote-lord-christopher-monckton; accessed May 31, 2012)

★ "In September 2006, on CNBC's Global Players program, the CEO of a solar power company called for a fellow guest on the program, ...Fred Smith... to be locked up in jail for the crime of expressing doubt about climate alarmism and schemes offered in its name."(*Red Hot Lies: How Global Warming Alarmists Use Threats, Fraud, and Deception to Keep You Misinformed* by Christopher C. Horner, Regnery Publishing, 2008, page 105-106.)

★ "Canadian alarmist David Suzuki...wants all politicians who oppose the global warming agenda to be thrown in jail." (Ibid, page 106]

Recognize the political manipulation practiced by the MGW alarmists

Some of the Political Manipulation Tactics described in Chapter Three are in play here:

★ Tactic One—my motive is good (I am trying to save the planet!), so don't question my "facts";

★ Tactic Three—the impossible choices (agree on the whole MGW theory or you are a heartless or ignorant "denier");

★ Tactic Four—my opponent (anyone who will not agree with the MGW agenda right down the line) is an idiot (the ad hominem attack);

★ Tactic Eleven—the mockery tactic (you can't seriously be questioning MGW—"there is a consensus!"…); and

★ Tactic Twelve—political correctness—it is simply not permissible for anyone to challenge the MGW "gospel."

The Climate Alarmists' Political Agenda
Climate, the UN, Agenda 21, and Sustainability

A full discussion of the climate change alarmists' international plans and goals is far beyond the scope of this book, but there is one last important point I need to share with you. And that is that on the international scene, there is a strong movement pushed by the United Nations and many countries that are not as free as America, to reach global agreements growing out of the climate change scare.

The alleged purpose of those agreements is to bring greenhouse gas emissions down worldwide via binding agreements, but the actual impact and longer-term goal is ultimately to take control of the world's distribution and use of energy and resources away from individual countries that produce the energy, and place that control under an international body.

It involves a de facto surrender by the U.S. of our control over our own energy resources, to an international body. Liberal Democrats love this idea. It is your ultimate redistribution of wealth plan, on an international basis.

What's Agenda 21?

In 1992 the United Nations Conference on Environment and Development met in Rio De Janeiro and adopted a 300 page, 40-chapter policy docu- ment that has come to be known as Agenda 21. While the provisions are not law in America yet, many liberals in America are working in support of it already. The document is filled with policy recommendations that are de- signed to reshape global society around social equity as defined by them, and "sustainable development," again as defined by them, all under the overrid- ing standard that government must mold and manage society so that it con- forms to the goals of the Agenda 21, United Nations, global-control crowd.

Private property rights are not in the least sacred in the Agenda 21 world: property is to be controlled in accordance with government-managed land use. It calls for a massive expansion of government power over people, and a surrender of the notion of property rights that is sacred and sacrosanct under the United States Constitution and under our historic rights and freedoms.

Examples from Agenda 21. It calls for:

Recommendation A.1

(b) All countries should establish as a matter of urgency a national policy on human settlements, embodying the distribution of population… over then national territory.

(c)(v) Such policy should be devised to facilitate population redistribution to accord with the availability of resources.

Recommendation D.1

(a) Public ownership or effective control of land in the public interest is the single most important means of …. achieving a more equitable distribution of the benefits of development whilst assuring that environmental impacts are considered.

(b) Land is a scarce resource whose management should be subject to public surveillance or control in the interest of the nation.

(d) Governments must maintain full jurisdiction and exercise complete sovereignty over such land with a view to freely planning development of human settlements..

Ladies, I encourage you to do some reading on this subject too, and recognize its parallels to the statist style of thinking that's premised on the notion that government knows best and it must control you. Some of the provisions and recommendations in Agenda 21 are already in place in America, in accordance with President Bill Clinton's establishment in 1993 of the President's Council on Sustainable Development.

The climate alarmist mentality has in large part invaded and overtaken America's Democrat Party of today! If absolutely nothing else in this entire book persuaded you to vote conservative, this should! We Americans need elected officials in Washington D.C. who will represent America at the U.N. and in all international bodies, who understand and respect the unique place private property rights, limited government and personal freedom hold in our nation.

A Big Wiki Warning

I turn to online information sources regularly, and occasionally one of them is Wikipedia, one of the encyclopedias on the Internet. You likely know that "the universe," meaning literally anyone who goes online and fills in an entry, writes Wikipedia. In working on this book project I realized that the global warming alarmists have clearly co-opted the definitions for most environmentally oriented terms, events and organizations. Those definitions are therefore slanted and for the most part inaccurate. The entry for example about the Climate Gate emails is acerbically dismissive of the idea that those emails showed any bad conduct or suspicious behavior at all. Kind of symbolic of the way the Left treats the whole issue: they define and decide truth, and all other viewpoints, and real truth, shall be ignored or dismissed.

Now We Can Talk About the Environment, Energy Development, and Energy Independence

Ladies, my purpose in writing this book is to urge you to vote conservative, and because many of us are inspired in our voting by concern for environmental issues, it was important to take the time in this chapter to actually review the biggest environmental issue in the world, the climate change theory. Fear of impending climactic doom has been a false roadblock in the development of America's natural energy resources, and it is time for Americans to stand up!

★ I could summarize this last section of the chapter this way: American needs energy. American has abundant untapped natural resources.

★ Today's Democrats block energy development via law, regulation, red tape, and government interference at every turn, unless it is an alternative energy source they chose. Liberal guilt over America's abundance feeds this Democrat attitude.

★ Republicans support the responsible development of America's energy resources, the "all-of-the-above" approach to developing all available resources, and view abundance as the natural result of the free market and hard working people who are free to use their energies and passions to better themselves and their lives. This is reason enough alone for everyone to vote Republican!

Consider:

Given our country's desire for energy independence, wouldn't it be great if we had a huge supply of oil right here in America, under our own feet, that we could access and use to power our vehicles here? Think how wonderful it would be if we had a supply of oil that we could tap into, that would create thousands of jobs in exploration, extraction, processing, and refining, and that would give us energy and therefore gas price security, while we are developing the cars of the future that run on different forms of energy. Well, we do!

The Green River Formation—Massive Accessible Oil in America

Ladies, we have that oil right now, right here in America! For those who missed it, Anu K. Mittal, the Director of Natural Resources for the GAO (Government Accounting Office) testified before Congress in May of

2012 about just one area of oil discovery, called the Green River Formation, located mostly under federal land at the intersection of Colorado, Utah and Wyoming, that has "about as much recoverable oil as all the rest of the world's proven reserves, combined." (http://cnsnews.com/news/ article/ gao-recoverable-oil-colorado-utah-wyoming-about-equal-entire-world-s- proven-oil; accessed May 29, 2012)

Please let that fact sink in. This Green River Formation "an assemblage of over 1,000 feet of sedimentary rocks.... contains the world's largest deposits of oil shale." (Ibid.) Half of that field's 3 trillion barrels of oil is recoverable, and *that half we can extract is equal to the entire world's proven oil reserves.* As one writer put it, we are "swimming in oil."

But will we access it? Or will government block access to it via regulation, stalled permitting and licensing delay tactics, extensive and repetitive environmental analyses? That depends—on which party is in the majority in Washington.

Energy development in America is perpetually and relentlessly delayed when Democrats are in power, in part due to their desire to exert control over the amount of energy Americans can use. We have seen that as the Democrats blocked the Keystone Pipeline, as they engaged in delay tactics in allowing the resumption of offshore drilling. A small number of officials in government is deciding that Americans cannot have access to energy they need and want, because those Washington elites know better than the people whether or not we should be allowed to have access to our American resources.

Ladies, this is a freedom thing.

ANWR (Alaskan National Wildlife Refuge)

The Green River find is on top of the completely untapped resources in the Alaska National Wildlife Refuge, estimated to have a 95 percent chance of having 500 million barrels of oil. [http://www.anwr.org/Background/How-much-oil-is-in-ANWR.php] Extremist environmentalists and Democrat Party leaders have kept America from tapping into the ANWR oil, despite the very successful Alyeska Alaskan oil pipeline in place since 1977. (http://alyeska-pipe.com/pipelinefacts.html; accessed May 29, 2012)

Environmentalist advocacy groups of course had great interest/concern as the existing Alaska pipeline was being considered and then built, and it is very important that you, ladies, and others who are rightfully concerned about the environment, recognize what a magnificent success that pipeline has been, both as a supplier of oil, and as a "nonfactor" in terms of harming the environment.

A University of Michigan summary of the pipeline's impact concluded "The Trans-Alaskan Pipeline is well worth the environmental risks because of the minimal damage it does, and it is the most realistic, convenient, and sustainable way to transport oil out of Northern Alaska" and "the pipeline is one of the most economically efficient ways to transport oil and probably the most environmentally friendly method that exists today." (withhttp://sitemaker.umich.edu/section003_group001/ home; accessed May 29, 2012)

ANWR's potential is even greater than the current Alaskan Pipeline's, and the size and location make it even more amenable to successful oil extraction. And less than half of 1 percent of ANWR's total area is under consideration for drilling. (http://www.anwr.org/ANWR-Basics/Top-ten-reasons-to-support-ANWR-development.php)

What's Really Happening With Domestic Oil

I could write 10 more pages just about all of the oil we have available to us as a nation, right now, right here at home. We could talk about the Keystone Pipeline, as well as the oil Democrats in Congress have blocked Americans from extracting from the Continental Shelf, and also the oil we could be extracting via deep sea drilling in the Gulf Coast that was halted first by a moratorium, and then when a federal court lifted that moratorium, by apparent permit-issuing foot-dragging.

We have no oil shortage. We have a shortage of the willingness to put our American know-how and ingenuity to work to extract it. We are like an impoverished man begging on the street while standing next to a bank where he has a 10-million-dollar bank account. And make no mistake: Republicans support drilling and exploration and extraction, tapping into our resources, using the latest environmentally sound methods, and always working to improve our methods. They support drilling and extracting and getting that oil/energy into the marketplace.

So you have to ask yourself why Democrats have built such a barrier preventing Americans from going to work to develop our natural resources, which would put us on the road to energy independence and go a long way to reducing our unemployment numbers. I will suggest a few reasons, none of them sufficient to justify the Democrat obduracy on oil exploration:

1. *America Leftist leaders/Democrats are concerned about the possibility of oil spills.* Everyone cares about spills of course, but friends, if we are going to stop drilling, extracting, and building pipelines because maybe a spill will happen, we should stop letting airplanes fly because maybe one will crash. No one has more incentive to prevent spills, or more know-how about the best methods of extraction and drilling, than our world-class American oil companies. Fear of spills is just not a good enough reason to interfere with the American people's desire for reasonably priced, reli- ably available oil/gas, and with the oil companies' willingness and expertise that is ready to move forward. And our enemy competitor suppliers most certainly will keep on drilling, and charging us, and they could spill too.

2. *Leftists offer the circular argument that we shouldn't drill for oil because it will take too long to extract it.* "No help for

our short term problem, don't you see." An old Chinese proverb says: "The best time to plant a tree is 20 years ago. The second best time is now." Ladies, if we always decide not to drill because it'll take too long, we will leave our resources in the ground, unusable in our future. And we'll be saying the same thing 20 years from now, when we could be consuming the oil we started drilling for, today.

3. *The real opposition on the part of America's Leftist leaders is the underlying liberal sentiment of guilt and resentment about America's abundance.* Ladies, we need to turn that guilt mode on its head, and decide that we view our abundance with gratitude, and that we explore and develop our natural resources at the same time that we support every country's right and option to explore and develop theirs.

   For many, abundance is seen as evidence of God's grace. Encouraging growth in prosperity for everyone instead of unnecessarily imposing restrictions and limits on ourselves helps improve Americans' lives, creates jobs, and helps America to remain a beacon of freedom and opportunity to the world. We should export our qualities of ingenuity and hard work and encourage other nations to de- velop their resources. It is an "everybody wins" situation when we export inspiration, encouragement, a great example and confidence that other na- tions can achieve as we have. Just as the American economy is not a limited pie, neither is the world's economy. It grows as more people add their efforts and ingenuity and passion and hard work.

Ladies, we need to turn that guilt mode on its head, and decide that we view our abundance with gratitude, and that we explore and develop our natural resources at the same time that we support every country's right and option to explore and develop theirs. For many, abundance is seen as evidence of God's grace. Encouraging growth in prosperity for everyone instead of unnecessarily imposing restrictions and limits on ourselves helps improve Americans' lives, creates jobs, and helps America to remain a beacon of freedom and opportunity to the world. We should export our qualities of ingenuity and hard work and encourage other nations to develop their resources. It is an "everybody wins" situation when we export inspiration, encouragement, a great example and confidence that other nations can achieve as we have. Just as the American economy is not a limited pie, neither is the world's economy. It grows as more people add their efforts and ingenuity and passion and hard work.

EPA under Democrats as Major Political/Governmental Bully

I would be remiss in a chapter on energy and the environment , in the year 2012, in America, if I did not at least briefly discuss the attitude and actual conduct of the Environmental Protection Agency, the EPA, under this Democrat administration. I'll keep it brief.

One of the core themes of America's structure of government, which is set out in the Declaration of Independence, is the idea that government in America derives its "just powers from the consent of the governed." This was a big change from European governments of the Founders' era, which felt no such need to limit their powers.

Government under today's Democrat Party, especially within the last three years, has become more elitist, more arbitrary, and more anti-citizen, less concerned with doing the will of the people and more determined to impose their will on the people. The EPA is a great example of this.

Abusive fining conduct under Clean Water Act

The Environmental Protection Agency (EPA) is entrusted with the power of the federal government to enforce most of the environmental laws Congress passes. One of those laws is the CWA—the Clean Water

Act. *Read the Sacketts' saga box to learn just how abusively the EPA acts in enforcing this law.*

> The EPA's conduct in enforcing the Clean Water Act in 2011 and 2012 brought out reprehensible and arrogant behavior that speaks volumes about the EPA and the administration supporting that EPA.
>
> When the United States Supreme Court votes 9 to 0 against a federal agency, something has clearly gone awry.

One of the complaints commonly heard in the business community today is that the EPA has turned away from being a compliance agency, working to help businesses comply with the law, into a fining agency. An agency that exists to fine—to extract money from—as many businesses as it can, often arbitrarily.

And the numbers bear out that complaint. The EPA's total fines and penalty collections has been on a steady trajectory upward over the last three years, going from nearly $80 million in 2009, to over $106 million in 2010, to almost $120 million in 2011. (http://www.epa.gov/compliance/resources/reports/nets/nets-d4-finesandpenaltycollections.pdf; accessed on May 29, 2012)

Businesses Fined for Not Using a Required Product That Does Not Exist

Another truly amazing example of EPA's lack of reasonableness is the 2011 collection totaling $6.8 million in fines from companies that supply motor fuel, for failing to mix into their gasoline and diesel a special type of biofuel that does not exist. The biofuel, cellulose, is (naturally) designed to reduce greenhouse gases, and the EPA is quick to point out that the fines are lower than permissible under law. (How lucky for those innocent companies that were fined! It could have been a bigger fine!) The underlying problem is that Congress mandated the inclusion of this biofuel before the producers, the labs and factories, had the capacity to produce it. But the

EPA could have used discretion and not fined these companies, but that is just not how they operate today. (http://www.nytimes.com/2012/01/10/business/energyenvironment/companies-face-fines-for-not-using-un-available-biofuel.html; accessed May 29, 2012)

> This is another story you need to know about. Many of you may have heard about the EPA official who compared his agency's conduct toward oil and gas companies to the conduct of invading Roman armies.
>
> Al Armendariz, the EPA Region VI Administrator, told about his "general philosophy" being like the Romans who would "you know, conquer villages in the Mediterranean. They'd go in to a little Turkish town somewhere, they'd find the first five guys they saw and they'd crucify them. Then, you know, that town was really easy to manage for the next few years…. It's a deterrent factor." EPA (now former) official Armendariz spoke of the EPA conquering American companies as the Romans conquered the Turks, on video.
>
> (http://cnsnews.com/blog/craig-bannister/epa-officials-philosophy-oil-companies-crucify-them-just-romans-crucified; accessed May 29, 2012)

EPA Official Advocates "Crucifying" American Oil and Gas Companies

U.S Senator James Inhofe brought that video to the attention of the United States Senate, and Inhofe's office pointed out that shortly after these comments from 2010, the EPA began targeting natural gas producers in Pennsylvania, Texas and Wyoming, accusing them of causing water contamination through the use of hydraulic fracturing ("fracking"). Despite the EPA creating headlines and public concern, the charge that water contamination results from fracking has not been established with sound scientific evidence. (Ibid.)

What does all of this mean?

Ladies, every one of you reading this at least knows that this sounds like an EPA, a government agency, gone wild, and no longer treating Americans fairly or reasonably. I would suggest that it further reveals an at- titude of environmental absurdity, a near worship of the environment and disdain for people and their activities, which is at odds with the American system of laws, and the concept of governance based on the consent of the governed. As the great Mark Steyn wrote, "Where do you go to vote out the EPA?"

While both Parties enforce the Environmental Protection Act, it is only in these last three years of Democrat control that we have observed this near fanatical environmentalist style of governance that ignores reason and cavalierly brushes off the rational. It's an attitude of government against the people, not government representing the people.

And that attitude is coming right from the top of the Democrat Party, from America's Leftist Leaders. This is reason all by itself, ladies, to vote conservative for the foreseeable future, because none of us should be supporting a government that sees America this way.

The Sacketts' Saga

Meet Chantell and Mike Sackett, an American couple who bought some property in Idaho in 2005, and decided to build a small home on that property in 2007. They started by having workers spend three days "filling in" part of the property with dirt and rocks. Then EPA officials arrived at their property, asked to see their EPA permit (which they did not have), and stated that they believed the Sacketts' property was a "wetlands," a designation relevant to whether the EPA had authority over their land, under the "navigable waters" standard in the Clean Waters Act (CWA).

The EPA halted the Sackett's work on their own land, and several months later issued a Compliance Order which stated that the Sacketts' property is a wetlands within the meaning of the law, and that the Sacketts had discharged "fill material" into wetlands without a permit, which was considered to be a discharge of pollutants. As a result of their findings, the EPA created a "Restoration Work Plan" for the Sacketts' property describing what they had to do to clean up the problem. The Sacketts wanted to challenge the EPA's finding that their property was subject to the "navigable waters" standard under the CWA, so they asked for a hearing, but the EPA denied their request.

Then they went to federal cour t to ask for a ruling (declaratory and injunctive relief) that the EPA's order was arbitrary, but both the trial and appellate court refused to hear their case.

The EPA has the power to fine Americans a possible total of $75,000 per day (yes, per day!) in cases like this. The Sacketts' case revolved around the fact that they wished to have the EPA give them a hearing on the question of whether the compliance order was valid, without risking triggering the $75,000/day fine.

All legalese aside, the bottom-line question was whether the EPA could deny the Sacketts a hearing and force them to choose risking a $75,000 per day fine in order to have that hearing.

The EPA believed it was just and appropriate conduct for a federal agency to deprive American citizens of the right to build a home on their own property, and to put those citizens in an impossible financial bind where they would have to capitulate to the government without ever having a hearing.

This was the EPA's conduct that caused the U.S. Supreme Court to call the EPA's actions "high-handed" and "outrageous," something that most people would say "can't happen in the United States." The court ordered the EPA to give the Sacketts their hearing.

The Obama Administration completely backed the EPA, defending it in court all the way.

United States Supreme Court Case No 10-1062, Sackett vs. EPA, March 21, 2012. Ruling 9 to 0 against the EPA.

Back to the Question that Is the Title of this Chapter—Why Energy and Environmental Issues are, Today, Political Issues

The title of this chapter asks the question why energy and the environment are political issues, when logic might suggest that they are scientific issues. The answer is now hopefully clear, and this issue again offers an opportunity to articulate some significant differences between the philosophies of America's two political parties:

★ The historic American free-market conservative approach supports the freedom and the right of the people to prosper and work hard to produce abundance. In the energy arena, that translates into Republican support for all-of-the-above energy development, and supporting the free markets and the decisions of business leaders, the American people and industry to develop our available natural resources in an environmentally responsible manner, providing much-needed jobs for thousands of Americans, and energy to drive the cars we choose to drive. That's the Republican approach. Conservatives see the goodness and prosperity of America as the direct result of a nation founded on principles of freedom, personal responsibility, individual liberty, and hard work. The government's job is to protect that God-given individual freedom. Environmental regulation is designed to keep air and water clean, and accomplish other legitimate purposes, but is not to serve as a vehicle for a political agenda of controlling the people.

★   The Left wing approach supported by today's Democrat Party is just the opposite. It is to manage and control energy decisions from within the narrow confines of a small elite group in government, block the development of domestic fossil fuel energy, pick and choose for society which energy sources are to be rewarded with taxpayer support and which must be blocked either overtly or by delay in the issuance of permits and other mechanisms. The Left is not only willing but determined to redistribute wealth within America via the tax system, and to redistribute energy supplies around the world in accordance with Agenda 21 style thinking.. The global climate change scare gives the Left some "ammo" to use in their fight against ongoing progress: it is the excuse that Democrats offer for refusing to allow the development of the massive new oil finds in America, for their increasing regulation of the kinds of cars we can have, and how much energy we can develop and consume.

Did You Know?...Stories and Facts to Share Chapter Ten

There are four areas ripe for conversation for talkers armed with facts: energy availability, the EPA's conduct, the fuller story on the Global Warming/Climate Change theory, and the U.N./Agenda 21.

Ladies, the data and information on these subjects are not as susceptible to quick bullet discussion points, but they are vitally important subjects. I am offering just a short list of possible conversation points.

Energy:

Spread the word about the massive accessible oil in America in the Green River Formation, and in ANWR. Mention the Keystone Pipeline. Seriously, why vote for the Democrats who will persistently and eternally block access to needed energy? Let's stop complaining about reliance on foreign oil and start producing our own, and along the way create thousands of American jobs. Vote for the Party that will take action!

The EPA

Share the story of the Sacketts battle with the EPA, and start watching for news stories about the EPA's abusive/fining/punishing approach. Share the story of the EPA official who compared that agency with murderous invading armies killing random innocent citizens. The attitude of that agency is just so wrong, so off-base, so extreme, and it has become that way under the far Left leadership of today's Democrat Party.

The global warming (not) science

Climate change is one area where the Leftists in America are especially willing to speak up. They demand that everyone agree with them. And global warming is one area where political correctness has developed into extreme scornful, angry pressure and in fact vilification of any who dares to challenge or even slightly question the global warming gospel. Let people know about the Climategate emails, and ask them what could possibly motivate scientists, supposed pursuers and researchers of truth and facts, to manipulate and hide data, and intentionally mislead the public. Why is there so much pressure on scientists to agree with the global warming gospel, or be fired? Send your friends a few email links about the number of genuine scientists who disagree with the global warming/climate change alarmists: lots of people do not even realize there is a legitimate controversy.

Agenda 21:

This may be the scariest Left-wing agenda item of them all. The surrender of U.S. sovereignty to international bodies and organizations that want to decide who gets energy and how much, where and how, and in what type of communities people can live, is utterly unconscionable, unacceptably unpatriotic. Every American needs to arm himself and herself with information about this odious agenda and then start telling your friends! We cannot let the leftist elements in America win this battle---it truly will be the end of America as we know it.

The best course internationally, instead of reducing and parsing and limiting energy development, would be for America and other developed nations to share technology and know-how with developing nations so they can prosper and develop too!

Ladies, the environmental and energy issues present tremendous opportunities for honest conversation. Of course everyone supports good stewardship of the environment! You can help your friends see that good environmental stewardship does not require ending traditional energy development, or buying into false global warming alarmism, or surrendering the American lifestyle of freedom and abundance to satisfy an international body intent of taking control of energy and many other aspects of life in America!

I hope you feel ready to talk about it!

★ ★ Chapter Eleven ★ ★

The War Over "Julia" and All American Women

Can We Talk…About Women's Rights in America?

What "rights" do we want?

Are we seeking independence or helplessness?

"Julia" is a fictional character featured on Democrat President Barack Obama's 2012 campaign website in an ad directed specifically at women. The ad tells the story of how the fictional Julia's life between the ages of 3 to 67 is made better by programs that Democrats support. It is a literal template, an outline presentation, of the thinking behind today's Democrat Party.

The unmistakable purpose of the Julia political campaign ad is to encourage American women to vote Democrat because that Party will guarantee women a long list of free or reduced-cost special benefits.

How does treating women as so helpless and needy that we need cradle-to-grave government handouts square with women's hard-fought-for status as independent and self-reliant?

Let's talk about this.

Famous Suffragette Susan B. Anthony once said:

There is not the woman born who desires to eat the bread of dependence, no matter whether it be from the hand of father, husband, or brother; for any one who does so eat her bread places herself in the power of the person from whom she takes it.

Topics We'll Talk About in Chapter Eleven

Are the "Julia Benefits" About Women's Rights?

Remember the Fight for Women's Rights in America? From Ending Slavery, to Winning the Right to Vote, to Demanding Equal Rights in the Workplace. What Were We Fighting For?

What Does the Term "Women's Rights" Mean Today? What Should It Mean?

Julia Benefits—Is it Fair to Stop There?

Women's Rights Today—The Fight for Equal Pay

"Julia, Meet the Laws of Economics"

The Politics of Ideas Versus the Politics of Group Benefits

Should Intelligent, Responsible, Compassionate American Women Vote for Julia and Her Democrat Political Creators?

Did You Know?...Stories and Facts to Share

Are the "Julia Benefits" About Women's Rights?

Many believe that the 2012 election in America will be determined by the women's vote. And probably the election outcomes for the long-term future will be too. So how are the parties selling themselves? Campaign themes, slogans and ads tell us so much.

The Julia ad features a list of government benefits, some older and some new, that are taxpayer funded "free" government programs including: a tax credit for people who pay no taxes (funded by the 2009 stimulus bill), free government grants to pay for college, insurance "special deals" (a healthcare reform bill provision), the right to sue an employer at any time free of the customary restriction of a statute of limitations, free birth control and preventive care that the government requires insurance companies provide without charge, further free health screenings mandated by the healthcare reform bill, Medicare coverage including preventive care and prescription drugs, and Social Security that "allows her to volunteer at a community garden." (No mention of the impending insolvency of those federal programs.) (http://www.barackobama.com/life-of-julia; accessed May 8, 2012)

Time constraints and the fear of boring you preclude me from reviewing in detail each of the benefits Julia is being promised, and the laws underlying those benefits. Instead, let's talk a moment about the idea of rights, and then about just a few of the benefits mentioned in this political ad. (For a quick but helpful summary of the idea of what "rights" are, go back to Chapter Two, "Protecting America Is Women's Work and It Is Never Done.")

"Rights" Created by the New HHS Mandate for Women's Services

In August 2011 the U.S. Department of Health and Human Services (HHS), issued new guidelines under the Affordable Care Act (the bill that accomplished the national takeover of America's healthcare system), requiring insurance companies to cover an extensive list of healthcare procedures for women at no charge to women. (Kind of like if the federal government required a grocery store to give away free food, or someone who made his living painting houses, to paint houses for free.) Several of the "Julia" benefits relate to these new federal mandates to insurance companies to provide free care.

FN=Before this 2011 HHS action, that federal agency had issued, in the summer of 2010, new rules under the healthcare reform bill requiring all new private health plans to cover a whole series of preventative services such as blood pressure checks, and childhood immunizations. But this was a society-wide benefit, meaning not limited to any one group. End Footnote.

Specifically, HHS issued a comprehensive list of healthcare services for women, including items such as breast-feeding support and supplies, contraception including abortion-inducing drugs, screening for gestational diabetes, HIV screening and counseling, well-woman visits, and more, which the government required that insurance companies provide without charging the woman receiving these services any co-payment, co-insurance or deductible. (http://www.hhs.gov/news/press/2011pres/08/20110801b.html; accessed May 8, 2012)

"Women's Rights!" and "Reproductive Freedom!" are two of the Democrat slogans used to explain or justify the new HHS mandate requiring insurers to cover certain healthcare for women at no charge to women. I've discussed the economics of this mandate below. Here let's just talk about what we can honestly call "women's rights."

Is Having Government Coerce Insurance Companies to Provide Free Benefits to Women Legitimately a "Women's Right"?

The HHS Mandate that insurers give away services for free to women, is not at all a "women's issue" or a "reproductive freedom" issue. It is an issue of forcing an insurer to give away their services for free.

Women are free to use contraception, but just not to make someone else pay for it. Kind of like you are free to shop at the grocery store, but not to demand that the government require the grocer to give you food for free.

No one is trying to regulate private behavior, but plenty of people do not want government to mandate that an insurer must give away contraception (and other healthcare) for free. Plenty of people worry about the *next* thing government could coerce, if they do this.

"Real" Reproductive Rights

Here are genuine examples of things that, if the government should ever try to do them, would be, without question, a violation of "reproductive freedom," or "women's rights": if the government made contraception illegal, or forcibly limited the number of children a family or woman can have, or required women to have a certain number of children, or failed to provide legal protection or recourse to women who are victims of rape or incest or spousal abuse. And to be clear, no one on either side of the aisle in America's government is trying to do any of those things.

The difference between these types of hypothetical threats that would be genuine threats to women's reproductive freedom if they ever became law, and the HHS mandates? These "real" threats would all involve trampling on a woman's personal and private freedom to conduct her private life and make childbearing decisions. They are personal decisions women get to make. Exercising these genuine rights does not necessarily require any private company, taxpayer or other individual, to pay for the woman's exercise of these rights.

Remember the Fight for Women's Rights in America? From Ending Slavery, to Winning the Right to Vote, to Demanding Equal Rights in the Workplace.

What Were We Fighting For?

In the American history of the struggle for women's rights, we were struggling for independence, to end our helpless position in society of being utterly dependent on men, whether it was our fathers, or our husbands. We were fighting for the right to be treated fairly in the workplace and to prove that we could use our talents, energy, passion, and intelligence to be successful in the world. We wanted to prove ourselves able to be independent and successful, to be brilliant doctors, lawyers, architects, authors and a thousand other choices.

> *How does that earnest striving for independence fit in with the "women need Julia's free benefits or else they will never make it" Democrat Party political philosophy?*

Harriet Tubman, Abolitionist and Suffragette Leader

Harriet Tubman's role as a runaway slave in America is legendary. After escaping from slavery herself, she bravely made 13 missions to rescue other slaves. Ultimately, she helped more than 70 escape using the famous Underground Railroad which was a series of safe houses and other hiding places slaves could use on their journeys from slavery in the South, to freedom in the North. She is credited with helping more than 70 slaves escape.

Her life would have been heroic if that were all that she did, but there is so much more! Harriet Tubman became a cook and nurse working for the Union Army (the North, antislavery side of the Civil War), and later became an armed scout and spy for the Union Army. She led a raid in South Carolina that resulted in the freeing of around 700 slaves.

Did you know that Harriet Tubman was also a Suffragette? Yes, she aligned herself with famous Suffragette Susan B. Anthony, and advocated for the right of women to vote. And speaking of women winning the right to vote, I want to share briefly just a few stories about that battle many Americans do not know.

Winning the Right to Vote

The Nineteenth Amendment to the United States Constitution, passed in 1920, gave American women the long-awaited right to vote. Many American women, called Suffragettes, fought long and hard for the right to vote.

Did you know that when Suffragettes picketed outside Democrat President Woodrow Wilson's White House carrying signs demanding the right to vote, they were jailed? And that some 33 female protestors were severely beaten in jail, including one Lucy Burns whose hands were chained to the cell bars? This all happened on the famous Night of Terror on November 15, 1917.

What were the suffragettes demanding?

Of course they were demanding the right to vote, but more broadly, they were demanding equality. They wanted to be equal with men in their political and electoral freedoms, and free from having to be dependent on men.

They wanted to *not* be dependent on the men in their lives. And they certainly did not protest and suffer to win the right to become dependent on the government!

What Does the Term "Women's Rights" Mean Today? What Should It Mean?

After winning the battle over slavery, and the right to vote, women continued the battle for equal rights. Women pursued the right to participate in higher education, and the right to equal access in every imaginable field of professional endeavor. We demanded unbiased access to the working world, and the result of those efforts was and is that America has a strong system of federal and state laws and regulations that make discrimination based on sex (and race, religion, national origin) illegal.

As a former litigation attorney working in the area of employment discrimination, I both understand and respect those laws, and the strength of the protection they afford women to challenge sex discrimination in the workplace. The laws cannot of course prevent discrimination; they just give women the vehicle to fight it.

We Fought for Equality in the Workplace—So We Could Be Financially Independent!

Too many women over the decades and centuries learned firsthand the devastating impact of being financially dependent on a husband who later deserts her or passes away, leaving his widow both without sufficient funds to survive, and until the advent of laws protecting women's rights to equal access to the job market, unable to find adequate employment.

All of these efforts were targeted at helping women achieve legal equality and therefore the ability to be independent. The "Julia benefits" are headed in the completely opposite direction---they are geared toward treating women as though we are not capable of independence and self-sufficiency, and of making our own way in the world legitimately.

> *The Democrats' Julia campaign ad is screaming at women,*
> *"You are helpless without government! There is no way you could possibly take*
> *care of yourself without government assistance!"*

Aren't these promises of free health service and special "cradle-to-grave" government handouts a step backwards for equality and for women's independence?

★ For women to view these handouts as "women's rights" is like admitting we really are weak and cannot make it on our own.

★ For Democrats to think that the way to lure women over to their political side is to make special package deals to give free things to women is demeaning and insulting to women. They clearly don't think we can handle independence!

Julia Benefits—Is it Fair to Stop There?

Two other unintended, or perhaps intended, consequences of the "Julie package deal" are that

1. Once government programs take hold and people become accustomed to artificially set pricing or just plain "free" things, it is almost impossible for government to "take back," those programs, because people become dependent on them, and

2. Inevitably, other groups will follow with similar demands.

Why Would We Fight to Become More Dependent?

Keep in mind when you hear liberals claiming that they have a right to free birth control, free medical exams, they are demanding the right to become dependent on government. "Free" today becomes "dependent on handouts" tomorrow.

The government mandate to insurers to provide all of these services for free may be novel now, but over time it will become the norm. This is true of all government-sponsored or funded programs. Look at the growth in dependency in food stamps and other government assistance programs; dependency creation is nearly unavoidable when products or services that cost something to produce or provide, are given away for free.

The "Unfairness" of Offering Only Some Free Benefits to One Group

The 2011 HHS mandate requires insurance companies to provide even more kinds of healthcare for free than was required under the 2010 mandate, and this new list of free benefits is targeted exclusively at women. It could just as easily have been applied to other equally important medical services and groups in our society.

For example, news reports abound about America's growing obesity problem. Some claim there is almost an obesity "epidemic." If women's breastfeeding support is such a critical service that HHS mandates it be provided for free by insurers, don't obesity services warrant equal treatment? And what about the emotional agony, potential for isolation and permanent physical and emotional scarring that can flow from severe teenage acne? Surely that group of Americans is equally worthy of getting free care? Also, what about those diseases that fall exclusively on one particular ethnic or racial group? With no rhyme or reason for those unusual cases, and the utter blamelessness of those patients, a compelling case can be made that they are especially deserving of free care. None of these sufferers, or people in need of healthcare services, is more worthy than others.

Women's Rights Today—The Fight for Equal Pay

What's the Truth About Equal Pay Between Men and Women?

It is hard to have a discussion that means anything without accurate facts.

One area where the lack of accurate facts makes discussion impossible is the question of whether women are paid less then men for the same jobs

> *The Democrat controlled HHS chose in 2011 to provide just one group— women—a long list of healthcare items which insurers must offer for free. There is no logic to their decision from a purely, well, logical, point of view. But their decision does make perfect sense from a crassly politically calculating point of view. Why not offer half of the population free stuff? Votes and support will follow, they no doubt reasoned.*

in America. Politicians repeat so often that "men earn more than women who are doing the same job," that people treat that false accusation as unquestioned truth. (Yes, I said false accusation.)

Taking the time to find truth is harder than flinging inflammatory falsehoods. But truth matters. And the truth is that women are not paid less than men, for the same work. Read the box below about Dr. Warren Farrell's research and book, *Why Men Earn More*.

Here is one example of the kind of data that liberals use to create voter outrage, and then to justify more new laws and regulations.

★   The U.S. Labor Department's (DOL) Bureau of Labor Statistics (BLS) reported at the end of 2011 that the median full-time working woman made only 81.6 percent of the wages of the median full-time working man. Liberals of course instantly pounced on this as proof of a "wage gap" between men and women.

★   But the report is not comparing people in similar jobs; it just takes the average female full-time worker and the average male full-time worker, and points out that the average man gets paid more. But paid for doing what job?

★   For those kinds of statistics to mean anything, the report would have to compare men and women in similar jobs, requiring the same or similar education, skills, and knowledge. Surgeons earn more than data entry workers, naturally.

★   For many reasons, men on average choose to work in jobs than are higher paying than the jobs women choose. And women tend to choose jobs with fewer hours and greater flexibility so they can have precious and valued time with children. Hardly rocket science, and hardly discriminatory. Also, the DOL 2011 Time Use Survey revealed that men spend 5 percent more time at work every day, on average, than women.

★ So, in short, those BLS numbers could be called BS numbers, in terms of their usefulness in telling us whether there is real pay discrimination, meaning a real inequity in pay for equal work.

Taking the time to understand this data helps us avoid being lured into anger-fomenting political hype. Democrats regularly resort to the "men earn more money than women" slogan because it tends to enrage uninformed women, who then jump on board with whatever latest legislation the Democrats propose.

Recognizing yet that old Democrat CVVR (Crisis, Villain, Victim, Rescuer) modus operandi? In this case they create the crisis of supposed pay inequality with faulty data to support the conclusion, point to the business community as the villain, and you, women, as the victims, and then swoop in as Rescuer.

What's the Law About Equal Pay for Men and Women?

Listening to some politicians today, you might think that no one ever thought of passing a law about a woman's right to equal pay for equal work until last week sometime. But the truth?

★ In 1963, Congress passed the Equal Pay Act that prohibits sex-based discrimination between men and women with the same employer who perform jobs that require "substantially equal skill, effort and responsibility" under "similar working conditions."

★ In 1964, Congress passed the Title VII Civil Rights Act that prohibits discrimination in employment decisions based on sex (and race, color, religion or natural origin).

Why Men Earn More (the book)

Dr. Warren Farrell wrote an enlightening book called *Why Men Earn More*, which offers an in-depth study of the fact that men earn more than women in America. Again, the fact that men earn more does not necessarily mean that discrimination is occurring: facts such as the comparative kinds of jobs and hours worked must be aligned to offer any meaningful conclusions. The challenge is to find similarly situated men and women, in genuinely comparable jobs, and then comparing pay.

Dr. Farrell's findings challenge many of the prevailing liberal mantras. In short, he found that in comparisons of actually similarly situated men and women with roughly equal backgrounds, women earned more than men. For example, "women professors who had never married and never published earned 145 percent of the income of their counterpart male colleagues." Dr. Warren Farrell, *Why Men Earn More, AMACOM, 2005, page xxii.*

Also, comparing educated men and women working full time, "The men earn only 85 percent of what the women earn." (Ibid, p. xxii.)

I share this data not to claim that everything is perfect in this world, but to point out that differences in career choices people make impact incomes. I also want to encourage women to think smarter than the Democrats believe that we can: don't get sucked in by false alarm-creating, anger-inducing mantras. No law can make every employer behave perfectly, and the consequence to the economy of more "helpful" laws and regulations is to further burden employers and business, which hurts job creation and the economy.

Read below about the laws that already exist.

★ In 2009, the Lilly Ledbetter Fair Pay act was signed into law, and that Act re-set the rules about the Statute of Limitations in Equal Pay Act cases.

★ Now liberals have proposed the "Paycheck Fairness" Act (they do come up with some great names!) that would make it easier for lawyers to make more money suing businesses over claims of Equal Pay Act violations. The PFA also includes the renewal of a previously failed government program of collecting information from employers about compensation practices, which generates more time and money businesses must dedicate to nonproductive, government compliance work.

★ And you know that the information gathering government does today, will lead to the wage discrimination crisis they discover tomorrow, followed by more regulations, more control, less freedom. Just say no!

"Julia, Meet the Laws of Economics"

As we talked about in Chapter Three, businesses don't just give away stuff for free. If and when government requires them to do that, that mandate will have the same effect as if they are required to pay more in taxes. They will raise their prices on other things, like insurance premiums, lay people off, or do something else to make up for the lost revenue.

Nothing is ever really free.

The Economics of "Free"

More precisely, any good or service that can be sold in the marketplace, the free market, has some value to the business selling it. If the business is required to give away what they are trying to sell, they will adjust their budget in some other way to make up for it.

Somehow, someone or some group always pays for stuff other people got for "free." In this case, whether it is the hard-working single mom who now pays higher premiums, or the person who loses her job because the company can no longer afford to employ her, someone else is paying.

So when women say they have the "right" to free contraception, they are really saying they have the right to force other Americans (the person paying premiums, the person who loses her job), to pay for it.

Slogan-Slinging Political Manipulation About "Rights"

American women have not, historically, been agitating for the right of "free, paid for by society or insurance or by somebody else besides

Lilly Ledbetter Liability If you think that the Lilly Ledbetter Law, that "redefined" the statute of limitations in Equal Pay Act cases made life "fairer" for women, let's talk for just a moment.

Statutes of limitation protect you, and everyone. Say for example that in a moment of slight inattentiveness driving you very softly rear end the car in front of you. Minimal bumper damage, no one seems injured, but the other driver mentions at the scene while the police report is being taken, "my neck hurts a little bit." So you naturally go home wondering if that other driver will sue you.

How long you have to wonder is decided by your state's law on the statute of limitations for negligence. Statutes of limitation set up a time period during which the other driver must file suit if she is going to, or lose her right to sue. (In most states, for negligence claims, it is one or two years.) The law marks the day that the statute of limitations "starts running," which in this case would be the date of the accident. Not only does the statute of limitations protect you from worrying forever, but also it protects you and the entire system from having to try cases when memories have become faint, evidence could be missing, and witnesses have moved away or died.

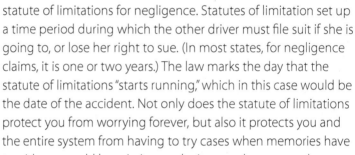

The Lilly Ledbetter law re-sets the statute of limitations—starts it running again for Equal Pay Act cases—every time an employee receives a paycheck that she claims was based on an earlier wage or salary decision that she now views as discriminatory. Remember too that Equal Pay Act claims are not limited to cases where two people are in identical jobs, but rather the standard is whether a woman is receiving less pay than a man in jobs with "substantially equal skill, effort and responsibility," under "similar working conditions."

So if 20 years ago a supervisor set the level of pay for two different jobs, one held by a man and the other by a woman, at different levels based on her assessment of their relative difficulty, every time the woman receives a paycheck that is less than the man's, the stature of limitations starts running again. Half the battle in any EPA litigation is going to be about comparing two different jobs under the law's standard. Now envision that case when the supervisor who made that decision has retired and moved away, the two jobs are not identical, and the plaintiff never told anyone she thought her pay was unfair.

I took the time to point all of this out for several reasons. First, more and more women are business owners who are going to be potentially subject to EPA claims, even though they try to be fair. *Why should women necessarily be more sympathetic to the female plaintiff rather than to the female business owner?* Second, why do we agree that women are so helpless that we need "special rules for us" laws? Third, you now know some of the policy details that made reasonable people think twice about signing onto the Ledbetter Law. But note how the media and America's Leftist Leaders criticized the American Right for not jumping on board instantly to support a law that has great potential for creating expensive litigation and unfair results. That last point is key: It's very important to start to recognize this behavior pattern by America's Leftists, so you don't get swept up in it.

---

me" contraception. We did rightfully demand the right to vote, and the right to participate in the workforce on equal footing with men. But I'm going to guess that even an exhaustive review of all of the writings of great American women leaders will not uncover a long-standing campaign to demand that society or government find some way to provide all women free contraception.

But the "reproductive freedom" and "women's rights" slogans have managed to stir at least some portion of young women into thinking that free contraception is their right. This is a stellar example of the power of slogans to confuse and in fact obliterate logic and thoughtful contemplation by otherwise intelligent women.

Today's Democrat Party leaders are world-class masters of this type of manipulation; it was the Democrats' political agitation on this subject that planted and watered the seed of righteous indignation about and fervent demand for the previously unknown women's right to free contraception (and lots of other free stuff, too).

Whose "War on Women"?

One goal of the Democrats' strategy of creating rights where none previously existed was to give them a platform to launch their claim that Republicans are engaged in a "War on Women." When Republicans with typical logic and fact-based reasoning opposed the "free women's healthcare" HHS mandate, on economic and free-market grounds, the Democrats took that ball and ran with it, arguing that unless Republicans would support free contraception and all other women's healthcare mandates, they were "against" women.

This is a prime example of the Political Manipulation Tactic Number 3, from Chapter Two, the Impossible Choices method, which in this case was demanding that Republicans either agree with Democrats on free healthcare, or else they will be accused of being engaged in a war on women.

Ladies, we have to be smarter than the Democrats think we are. We have to see through these tactics and refuse to be manipulated by them. If there is any war on women ongoing, the full-fledged Democrat campaign to make women more and more dependent on government, and to entice women to support Democrats so their elected officials will increase "free" services and make women more dependent, is a vicious and insidious war on women, and on our long-fought-for status of independence and equality.

The Politics of Ideas Versus the Politics of Free Group Benefits

You may be thinking by now that this is quite a bit of talk about one little Democrat campaign ad. But this isn't really just about the Julia ad. It is about helping make clear an important distinction between the approach to America by today's Democrat Party and today's Republican Party. (As noted numerous times, not every elected official in either party has always completely aligned his or her votes with party principles. But the party leaders do set the tone and the ideology, and when they are in the majority, they get their way.)

Ideas Versus Freebies

Democrats have evolved into the party of Free Group-Based Benefits, meaning mandating free stuff to be supplied by businesses or taxpayers, offered to entice certain groups to support their party, and which by definition and probably by design, cultivate dependence on government. And cultivate future Democrat voters.

The build up to announcing the latest new rights and benefits is always the creation of a "crisis," which you will note as you observe politics more and more is a word commonly used by Democrats, normally involving women or some other group (middle-class taxpayers, you) as a victims, and them (the Democrats) as your protectors against the villains. There is more in Chapter Two about the difference between rights, and things that are necessary, but are not rights.

Republicans have remained the Party of Ideas such as free markets, limited government, personal responsibility, and using market forces to bring about prosperity and independence. They embrace the same rules for everyone, are opposed to group-specific benefits, all of which signals actual belief in the equality of women, and respect for the ability of women to function independently. Just what women wanted!

"Selling" the Politics of Free Group Benefits—So Much Easier Than Selling Free Market Economic Realities

One way that Democrat Party leaders "sold" their package deal of free contraception and other women's medical services was by saying that they are "standing with women." After all, who could be against standing with women? The emotional appeal of that concept seems to block rational assessment by some people of the question of who bears the cost, and of the long-term harm to women that comes from increasing dependence on government.

If Democrats called it the *"make working people pay higher premiums and other people lose jobs so women can have free contraception and become helplessly dependent on government"* plan, they would likely not have been so successful in "selling" it.

Much of this discussion parallels ideas we talked about in Chapter Three about collectivism vs. free markets, so I'll not repeat all of those points in detail here. But a few quick items are worth noting.

The benefits Julia's ad is selling grow out of the collectivist mentality that has engulfed today's Democrat Party. Collectivism does not sell in America, and acknowledging honestly that free healthcare is never free and that working families will have to pay for it one way or the other, would have made healthcare reform unpopular. So the Democrats relied on their frequently used "pitch this emotionally and avoid talking facts" strategy.

It's easier to "sell" free stuff than to stand with the tried and true American free market principles that the Republicans embrace. But those free market principles are the ONLY reason America has the world-class health care system that we have. And those who support collectivism and socialized medicine are systematically dismantling that best system on earth.

Should Intelligent, Responsible, Compassionate American Women Vote for Julia and Her Democrat Political Creators?

The Julia Democrat political campaign ad is a lure to view women as helpless and weak, an invitation to join the ranks of victims and dependents, and a choice between two paths.

Ladies, quite simply, I believe American women are smarter, more responsible, and more compassionate than the Democrats think you are. The overriding message of the Julia ad, and more broadly the Democrat Party message, is that women need government assistance to take on the most basic responsibilities of life. In utter rejection of the victories of the women's movement that brought us to equality in the workplace, to strength and independence, today's Democrat Party is urging on women a return to weakness, dependence, and helplessness.

The dismal state of the American economy, and the unprecedented numbers of Americans receiving government assistance, including the one in seven who are now recipients of food stamps under SNAP, are the result in great part of the V&V (Vilify and Victimize) Democrat Party tactic. That tactic—Vilify (any normal challenge in life is attributed to some big bad person or group or industry which becomes their latest Villain) and Victimize (and you and some group are made to appear to be victims of this villain in this latest crisis)—which results in an increasing number of Americans looking to the government to be their Victor over all challenges.

Let's reject the Democrats' invitation to join the ranks of the victims! We are better than that!

Finally, let's be wise enough to see the bigger picture. Today's Democrat Party has embraced and accepted the collectivist mindset that is utterly contrary to the American mindset of free markets, free people, individual liberty and personal responsibility. No collectivism-based economy has ever thrived, prospered or created a nation as abundant, free, and prosperous as the United States. That's just a fact. Collectivism has failed because its core ideas are utterly contrary to basic human nature, the nature that drives men and women to be free, self-reliant, independent, and successful.

Did You Know?...Stories and Facts to Share Chapter Eleven

Ladies, there are just a few basics here that I hope you can share in your daily conversations. You will be bucking the trend of popular thought on these, but take heart, because you are right!

First, contrary to popular belief, women are not paid less than men who are doing the same jobs. That is a myth the America Left happily perpetuates because it allows them to act as the valiant fighter for women. Urge folks to read the book Why Men Earn More, or even just to Google the question. Yes, men do earn more than women in general, but that is due to the choices women make in the kind of careers and the kinds of hours and the schedules they prefer. When men's and women's salaries are compared when they are performing truly similar work and have the same relative skills and experiences, women earn more than men in many categories.

Second, many women just assume other women will latch onto the "Republicans' war on women" and assume that most women agree with the liberal views. Here are some basic points to share:

★ It is insulting that Democrats stoop to try to get the women's votes by offering us "free" stuff. We know better—there is no such thing as free and we don't think that others in society should suffer to pay for our "free" stuff.

★ Building dependence on government is never a good thing—but that's what the Democrats are trying to do.

★ It is more respectful of women to assume that given a level playing field we can succeed in the workplace, than to keep on thinking up new and redundant laws.

★ Third—we reject your false and silly slogans. "Reproductive rights" do not include free birth control!

Ladies, have fun talking!

★ ★ Chapter Twelve ★ ★

So How Do We Talk About All Of This?

Entire books have been written on conversational techniques, but I'll focus here on two subjects of prime importance when talking about politics:

★ Using questions to create dialogue and exchange vs. statements designed to instantly persuade or convince.

★ Engaging the issues the way liberals do—from an emotional basis and with personal stories vs. using facts, data, and information.

Using Questions to Create Dialogue and Exchange Versus Statements Designed to Instantly Persuade or Convince

Some Basic Ideas

I want to share with you some tips and techniques that can help you engage in conversations about politics, through the use of questions and establishing a dialogue rather than arguing with the other person. It is important to me to be clear that these are not techniques to trick people or contort their thinking, but rather they are genuine conversation methods designed to enhance communication and clarity.

I am especially advocating talking about political issues when you are confronted by those "opinion flingers" who volunteer, normally in groups, some liberal position with which you disagree. Your life does not have to become a walking political conversation, but you can and should feel empowered to at least "hold your own" in responding to these people. Making clear that intelligent women disagree with the liberal mindset is helpful for society overall and for the national political conversation. For too long, political correctness has emboldened liberals and silenced conservatives in normal, day-to-day conversations, especially among women.

You just cannot talk everywhere

One of the reasons our parents taught us not to discuss politics in social contexts is obviously because those conversations sometimes develop into unpleasant disagreements, or in the worst cases, outright and loud arguments. Many a family barbeque have been disrupted by political "discussions" gone awry. So one basic point is that you need to be the judge of the situation and decide that in some contexts, you may need to just politely remain silent, or say " why don't we just agree to disagree?" or "maybe we could have lunch together next week and talk about that some more – we probably agree on lots of things but I'd love to understand more about your thinking on that."

Some people

We probably all have a short list of friends, relatives and acquaintances with whom we just simply do not discuss politics. You will have to be the judge of whether in your life and on your list, there are some who are just best left safely on the "no talking about politics" list. But I will offer in this chapter some ideas and examples of techniques and approaches that may allow you to talk with those with whom you do not agree, about the subjects on which you disagree, without anger.

Credit Where Credit Is Due

I must give credit and tribute to my good friend Linda Olden-Smith, mediator extraordinaire and author of *Playing the "Resolution" Card: Mediating Disputes with the Thought Resolution Protocol.* Some ideas I will share in this chapter are derived from my own experience trying to talk about politics, but this chapter would not be possible without Linda's ideas and brilliance. Linda has trained at least 300 mediators so they are qualified to mediate court-annexed cases in Texas. She gives a talk aptly named "Engage without Rage," and is also the founder of the American People Today organization (www.SupportTheAmericanPeopleToday.com). Linda has walked the walk of sharing ideas with those who disagree with her, and actually emerged unscathed and sometimes with a new friend.

The emotional versus logical thinker

One of the primary differences between conservative and liberal voters (and this is a generalization) is that conservatives reason with facts and figures while liberals "reason" with emotional, personal information. One way to have a meaningful conversation, if you are a Republican, is to stress the human side, the real life side of the policy issues. In the next section I will offer examples of how to make the same points you want to make, in a way that the more emotional, liberal mindset can "hear" them. This is not at all manipulation: It is finding a communication wavelength with people who think differently than you do.

Political conversational basics:

★ *Change can take time, and people are invested in their views.* Most people are seriously invested in their political views. So when you, the rational and informed conservative, point out to your liberal friends the most compelling reasons for your views, you may think that anyone, upon hearing your flawless logic, will surely agree. But that rarely happens, because liberals are emotionally invested in their views.

Instead of thinking that the goal of every political conversation is to win over the other person to your view on the spot, make your goal to plant some seeds of ideas, so the other person realizes that you do have genuine and valid reasons for your views that are not just the stereotypical "Republicans don't care about (whatever)," and be willing to be content with sharing ideas and planting seeds. Read on to see what I mean.

★ *Impersonalize the subject of the disagreement.* If someone says, "I'm so glad that Congress passed the free cell phones for the unemployed law," it could be tempting to respond with "how could you possibly say that—that is the worst idea I ever heard!" Now the conversation is set up as you against the cell phone celebrator.

Try to speak of the idea under discussion—in this case free cell phones for the unemployed—as an impersonal idea, rather than speaking of an opinion that the other guy holds which disagrees with your opinion. Talk about concepts in the abstract or impersonally, rather than people who think X and not Y. It keeps the whole discussion impersonal. So you could respond to the cell phone celebrator "what is the theory or principle behind the idea of free cell phones for the unemployed...who would be paying for those cell phones...how would government monitor or control the expenses associated with the use of those phones...how would government maintain control of them once the unemployed person finds a job... how could this free service be misused or abused. Do you see any risks or downsides to the cell phone handout law.... Are there other means to accomplish the goals of that law?"

★ *Horse to water*. We all know the old saying, "You can lead a horse to water but you can't make him drink." The same is true of the liberal thinker who may be led to the water's edge of conservatism. She may find the logic of conservatism appealing, but she has been a good liberal for years and this is scary new territory. So long as she knows that you are there to offer her water (conservative ideas) and that you won't make her drink out of it in front of her friends who hang out at the liberal watering hole, she knows enough for now. She can come to the conservative watering hole any time she wants, and when she comes on her own, she will be more comfortable and just might jump right in.

★ *People like to think they came around to their views via their own thinking and growth, not because someone else foisted new ideas on them.* This follows on the watering hole idea, but it is also at a deeper level very true. You can lecture someone till you run out of words, but a change of heart is made on the inside, and people need to mull over ideas before they can really connect with and embrace them. So once you've planted a seed or two of good conservative ideas, let your friends think on their own about them. Unlike in sales when you must close the deal as soon as possible, recognize for true transitioning of ideas, pushing to close the deal just doesn't work: People need to arrive at clarity and certainty on their own.

★ *Seed planting*. The friend I mentioned above who gives the Engage without Rage talk uses a great analogy about how sharing political ideas with those you disagree with is like a farmer planting seeds. When the farmer plants seeds, he first tills the soil, softens and prepares it, then he plants the

seed, covers it up again, waters, and walks away. He periodically comes back to check on it, pulls weeds as needed, and
waits for the seed to naturally grow. We plant conservative
ideas in soil (thought) that has been prepared by our genuine and nonconfrontational questions, we water it and expect the natural truth and rightness of conservative ideas to
take hold naturally and grow. The farmer doesn't yell at the
seed, doesn't demand instant growth, and doesn't stomp off
angrily when he doesn't see the seed growing right away.
He knows that the seed will naturally grow given all of the
right preparation and occasional nourishing. Take heart:
conservative ideas are right and good. America's entire
unprecedented history of strength, prosperity, abundance
and freedom are all based on conservative ideas. They are
centuries old, time-tested and true.

A Sample Conversation
The Welfare reform discussion

I'll start with a real conversation I was part of with an older family
friend. The 1996 welfare reform proposal was under consideration at that
time, and this older friend asked, at a family barbeque at my parent's home,
what I thought of the welfare reform idea. I responded something like "I
think it's a good idea," to which he replied (in front of a group of people),
"that's because you've become successful—you've lost your compassion."

My only (lame) response at that time was, "I have not!"

Here's how I would respond to that today:

Friend: "You support welfare reform because you've lost your compassion."

Me: "Let me ask you, because I want to be sure I understand what you
are saying…just want to be sure I heard you correctly. Are you saying that
you think that the fact that I support welfare reform legislation means that
I do not have compassion for the needy? Am I understanding your statement correctly?"

Ladies, I am talking about asking in a genuine, nonconfrontational, "just asking for clarification," tone. Taking offense does not help.

And take the time, if the person says, "No—that's not what I said," to let them restate their view, and then you restate it, again, as a question, as close to verbatim as possible. The point is to be sure that you are both talking about the same opinion that this person has expressed. Sometimes even restating it will cause the person, upon hearing his own thought, to change his or her mind or at least to refine the point.

Friend: Yes! Obviously that is what I said!

Me: What is the principle or idea that you base your assertion upon? I mean, what's the principle behind your statement that if I support welfare reform that I have lost my compassion?"

Friend: You don't want to help the poor; you're not willing to support helping the needy. You obviously don't care!

Me: Thanks for clarifying your view. May I share my thoughts on that subject with you?

Ladies—asking if you can share your thoughts is vital.

The "liberal accuser"– our family friend – had been traveling a one-way mental path—spewing from his worldview at me—not really trying to travel a two-way mental road where he was trying to listen to anything I had to say. Asking "may I share some of my thoughts with you" and then actually waiting for an answer, changes the mental path to a two-way street. If he agrees, he is now listening.

If the friend says (which almost everyone does), "Yes," you can go on with the conversation as set out below.

If he says "No, I don't want to hear your thoughts," I have another dialogue you can try—set out below under "If your friend says NO—you cannot share your thoughts, I don't want to hear your ideas."

Assuming for now that the friend has agreed to your sharing your thoughts.

Friend: Sure—go ahead.

Me: Well, first (*and this is in a completely nondefensive tone*), I do want to share with you that I do donate money to charities regularly, in fact to my church and to a program that helps kids who are burn victims. And I actually volunteer every week at a community center in a children's program. I think that private charity is a really good thing. Do you think that private charity is important too?

(Ask in the most nonconfrontational, nonaccusatory, "not triumphant for having made a good point," way. Wait for an answer and then move on.)

Friend: Whatever...sure, yes, but that's beside the point. We are talking about the federal government and their welfare programs.

Me: Yes. You know, one concern I have about some of the government assistance programs is that I am not comfortable that all of those billions of dollars of tax money are handled efficiently...I think there is likely quite a bit of waste and duplication, and maybe even some fraud. What is your thought about that?

Friend: Of course it's not perfect but it does help people.

Me: Well, I think we both agree we want to help people.

One other thought I have about the federal government's assistance programs is that I feel it is more principled for me to make decisions about how the money I earn is used to help people. I don't feel so sure that the government always makes good decisions—or really should be making the decisions—about taking the money I have earned and giving it to other people. It seems to me to be more principled to let individuals who work to earn money decide where to donate it and whom they wish to help.

(You don't have to invite the Friend to agree with you on every point, but you can—and you should also leave them time to chime in if they want. The goal is not to out-talk or over-talk them.)

Friend: But there are so many needy—and welfare reform would cut them off!

Me: Is it your assertion that some people should be eligible for welfare benefits for an entire lifetime? Of course we always care for those mentally or physically unable to work, so we are talking about able-bodied people who are capable of working.

What is the idea or principle behind the proposal that some Americans should be eligible or entitled to receive government assistance for their whole lives? (You could wait for an answer here.)

Or

I feel concerned that having a large class of Americans who can live their lives without ever working and who never find that joy and sense of self-worth that comes from achievement is not kind or fair even to them—it robs them of their potential in life. And society is also deprived of all of the good that those people would have brought to the table in terms of ideas or products. Do you have a thought on that?

Or

I think that it is not good for American society for people who work hard to earn money, to have that money taken away by the government by force of the tax system, just for the purpose of giving it to other Americans. What is the principle or ideal that supports that concept?

Or

I am concerned that if politicians keep promising one group of citizens free things like food stamps and free housing and free medical care and other things of value that others have to pay for through their hard work and taxes, that we may be creating a situation that is not healthy for society or for our government. I think the principle of self-sufficiency and the goal of having a society where everyone can participate in the economy and is free to pursue their dreams and ambitions would be undermined if we perpetuate a system of long term government assistance.

Friend: But the poor need our help and the rich should help them.

Me: What is the standard or principle that we can turn to as a resource for deciding that government does a better or more efficient or fairer job of helping the poor? Or for determining how much of people's hard-earned income should be taken away for purposes like this?

Ladies, I could go on and on. If the tone has remained conversational and respectful, you may actually get some answer or statement of principle back from your friend.

A big part of what you are doing is isolating or refining the points each of you is standing for. When that is your goal, you do not feel the need to "fling the zinger" to prove that you were right all along, even if you are winning on a point.

You may get to some point where you can agree that you two, in this conversation, have either narrowed your areas of disagreement or at least more clearly defined them. You can at some point close off with "I am so glad we had this conversation and that we better understand each other's thinking."

If you feel that you have put them on the spot, and you are "cornering" them, back off. People who feel cornered into acquiescing to your view may feel angry or resentful, and that doesn't help actually bring them around.

But the most important thing you have done is to plant the seed of reason. Virtually no liberal will instantly see the wisdom of conservative thought, but conversations like these help dig the furrows where the seedlings of political thought can be planted. Time and contemplation and reason will do the rest, for many.

"If your friend says NO—you cannot share your thoughts, I don't want to hear your ideas."

Me: Oh, I am sorry to hear that. Is there a more convenient time when we could talk about this? I would be happy to set another time.

Friend: No, not really.

Me: Well, if you're not comfortable talking here (say you are talking at work), we could go to lunch one day and talk about the welfare reform proposal.

Friend: No, I really do not want to hear your thoughts at all.

Me: Okay, but I am disappointed that we couldn't have a mutual exchange of ideas, after your comment that you think I have lost my compassion because I support the welfare reform bill. One thing I love about

America is that we are free to express our ideas. But if you don't want to, that's okay.

Ladies, one goal of this particular exchange, even if you don't get to share your ideas, is to at least make clear that you are willing to do that. You may find that your friend comes back later to ask you about the topic you were discussing, and if not, she at least knows that you have some serious and thoughtful points to make.

Argument Using Emotion and Personal Stories Versus Using Facts

You have likely noticed that liberals, or Democrats, are swayed by emotion, while Republicans tend to be swayed by facts and data. The other central message of this chapter is that when we are talking with Americans who are liberal or left leaning, consider presenting the conservative view from the personal perspective, defending the virtues of conservative values and policies because they bring better results for people's lives.

Recently I have come to realize that all of the facts and figures and data on the planet will not persuade the liberal mindset of anything.

So we conservatives, when discussing ideas with liberals, need to change the way we argue about issues, away from facts and figures. We need to speak in real-life human terms about issues our country faces. Conservative ideas can be explained and defended by their positive impact on people's lives, just as well as they can be by setting out logical arguments, facts, and data. Here are just a few examples.

Hollywood In-depth Political Theory

Twenty years ago or so, a Hollywood actress and singer was interviewed on a late night talk show. This lady is a very famous liberal, and a great singer and decent actress. She was asked (paraphrasing) "Why do you so strongly support the Democrat Party?" She paused for a long moment, stared off in to space as though deeply and thoughtfully contemplating and then said, " You know, I think it's because I care about…people." The audience oooo'd and aaah'd and then finally burst into a proud, liberal round of applause.

It was pure Hollywood: vapidly shallow yet uttered with an air of melo-dramatic profundity. And the (liberal) audience ate it right up.

 This is a great example of how liberals win "arguments" with no facts. HOW do the Democrat Party's policies translate into "helping people?" She never said. Didn't offer a shred of rational thought.

The Democrat Party supports unions' rights to force individu-als against their will to join and pay dues to unions—how does that constitute "caring about people?"

The Democrat Party supports blocking access to and the de-velopment of the largest find of oil in all of U.S. history, which would provide jobs for tens of thousands of unemployed Americans, vastly decrease our dependence on foreign oil and keep gas prices down for American consum-ers—how does that constitute "caring about people?"

The Democrat Party supports unending and ever-growing government assistance programs that have trapped millions in helpless dependence—how does that constitute "caring about people?"

I could go on and on, but you get the point.

Defending Free Markets and Capitalism— From the Human Perspective

Defenders of the Democrat Party's current trend toward western Euro-pean-style socialism—marked by extensive governmental regulation of the private sector and the use of the tax system to redistribute wealth by greatly expanding social programs --- view turning to that socialistic approach as "kind" and "helpful" to people.

But free markets and the freedom and opportunity they offer for ev-eryone are the "fairest" and "kindest" approach of all---truly far better in terms of impact and outcome on the daily lives of citizens, than socialism.

One could ask, for example:

★ Most doctors borrow hundreds of thousands of dollars and work horrendously long hours to complete their medical school, internship and residency, all for the purpose of becoming a physician so they can help heal the wounds and ills of their fellow Americans. How can we justify the new socialized medicine law that vastly limits what doctors can conceivably earn? If we allow government control instead of free markets to determine what doctors earn, fewer people will become doctors, and people will wait longer to get needed care. Fewer doctors means more pain and illness.

★ How is it fair for one child who works hard in high school and college and graduates with honors, and becomes a successful professional, to have to pay high taxes to fund social programs so that the child who grew up next door to him but who dropped out of high school, failed to pursue any career or vocation, and has become a long-term resident in the line for government assistance, can live off of those tax dollars? Rewarding hard work with economic success is basic fairness. And rewarding the lifestyle of no-effort and nonachievement is both unfair and downright cruel to the person who is never inspired or motivated to learn to care for himself.

Speaking About the impact of Social Spending on Families and Children

Rather than critiquing massive social spending from the sheer cost perspective and the unsustainability of the fiscal path those social spending programs are on, we can equally honestly and accurately discuss the harshly detrimental impact they have had on children and families.

★ Before the Great Society social spending started, the unwed birth rate in America was 5.3 percent (in 1960), and by 2009, it was 41 percent. Quite simply, the existence of government substituting itself for, and taking over the responsibilities historically reserved for the father/parent figure, directly led to the decline in intact family units.

★ Children who are born into single parent households are seven times more likely to suffer poverty than children born into two-parent families. Kids of single parents suffer slower development, far lower academic/educational achievement, and an increased propensity toward delinquency and substance abuse. More than 80 percent of long-term child poverty occurs in single parent homes.

★ To put it bluntly, liberal social programs cause children pain, and stunt their health, growth and potential for achievement. If you want the best for kids, stop funding the programs that lead to children suffering the disadvantages of growing up in single parent households.
(The 2012 Index of Dependence on Government, Heritage Center for Data Analysis, February 8, 2012. Page 15. (http://www.heritage.org/research/reports/2012/02/2012-index-of-dependence-on-government; accessed May 14, 2012)

Ladies, you will grow in your comfort level speaking up on political issues as you grow in knowledge on issues, and in your confidence in the rightness of these views. You might want to practice engaging in political conversation, via role-playing, with your conservative friends, using some of the tips in this chapter. These practice sessions can be fun, and you can help each other learn to resist the temptation to get drawn into unpleasant arguments.

Then feel free to take on the next liberal opinion-flinger who volunteers that she is go grateful that government is giving away free iPads to homeless people (which they are not doing, yet). There is no guarantee that each conversation will flow perfectly, but conservative messages need to be heard in this incredibly PC-saturated political environment. And you have a right to speak!

★ ★ Chapter Thirteen ★ ★

Conclusion
Which Future Do You Want
for America?

Can We Talk…About What Future You Want for America?

Many commentators today ask whether America is "in decline." Others reflect on whether America was ever, or is today, "exceptional." Ladies, it is up to America's voters to determine her future. There is no power on earth capable of taking away America's exceptionalism or of bringing America into decline, except the failure by voters to defend the ideals on which she was founded.

Let's talk about it…

> *"Freedom is never more than one generation away from extinction. We didn't pass it to our children in the bloodstream. It must be fought for, protected, and handed on for them to do the same, or one day we will spend our sunset years telling our children and our children's children what it was once like in the United States where men were free."*
> —President Ronald Reagan, 40th President of the United States

Where We Are

Ladies, every single challenge America faces—every problem—is completely solvable. I wrote this book to talk with you, to invite women to consider voting for conservative solutions to America's challenges. What is needed is the strength and willingness of American women voters (and men!) to stand up for America in the voting booth and in our daily conversations.

In this era of American history, voting conservative nearly always means voting Republican. Among the main points I tried to make clear in as many ways as possible is that today's Democrat Party has veered very far left, completely off the "American track" envisioned by the Founders of a society based on rights from our Creator to life, liberty, and the pursuit of happiness, a limited government, strong and vibrant free market economy, personal responsibility and individual liberty. It was America's firm hold on those founding values that made her the world leader in freedom, prosperity, and hope over the last 200 plus years.

We would be crazy to abandon those values.

America—Exceptional or in Decline?

America will never be in "decline," unless we abandon what made this nation exceptional to start with.

Too many Americans ask whether America is in decline, and speak of decline as if it were something unavoidable like a meteor headed toward earth, so that all we can do is stand and watch, hoping for the best. But America will only decline if we surrender what made her exceptional.

"American exceptionalism" assigns a unique and unprecedented place to the United States as the leading global proponent and exemplar of liberty, freedom and equality around the world. But what "American exceptionalism" really boils down to is the recognition that our country's Judeo-Christian foundation is unique in human history; that it deserves to be cherished and honored; that we as a country do best when we let those foundational principles and ideas direct us; that if we're really honest and objective, America as founded has been a magnificent force for good in the world.

Republicans tend to embrace the concept of American exceptionalism, and the underlying notion that it is America's grounding in Judeo-Christian values that led to that exceptionalism. Democrats are more likely to denounce the notion that there was anything unique or extraordinary in the founding of this nation, and attempt to diminish the importance of or even deny the existence of those Judeo-Christian principles in our founding.

Exceptionalism, rightly understood, is not the belief that Americans are better than people of other nations. It is not a "God likes us best" belief. It is a belief that because we got our founding values right, we experienced the blessings of Divine Providence, but that those same founding values, and the benefits flowing from them, are available to any nation now and always.

Essential "American-ness"

Ladies, every generation in the past and in the future faces its own set of unique issues, its own challenges. And politicians make speeches and offer solutions, and voters chose leaders. We know the issues of 2012, but soon that year will sound ancient, and our grandchildren will be assessing the issues America will be facing in 2050. It's so important not just to make good policy choices in every era, but also to make good "big picture, what is America all about" choices.

Leaving aside party labels as much as possible (and it is difficult to do that because our American governance is based on our two-party system), most Americans want solutions that keep intact those incredibly precious founding ideals: equality of opportunity, personal responsibility and individual liberty, the rule of law, government whose purpose is to protect people's God-given rights, freedom and free markets, limited government that confines its powers to those outlined in the Constitution, and the right to life and liberty, and to pursue our own path to happiness. These values transcend all of the issues we face as a nation.

We can recognize the choices that honor and preserve the uniqueness of America, the "American-ness" we are all morally impelled to defend, and those that do not honor that American-ness.

American solutions are those that:

Honor the *individual* living in freedom as unique, intrinsically valuable, purposeful, and capable of great goodness, generosity, nobility and sincerity.

★ Appeal to the *individual's* ability to use his inherent resourcefulness, intelligence, generosity, talents, and determination to address most problems.

★ Accept as a foundational premise that equality and justice derive from adherence to the teachings of the Judeo-Christian tradition.

★ Doubt and distrust the idea that a designated group of people residing in Washington DC ("the government") is necessarily wiser and better suited to resolve problems than are individuals living in freedom and inspired to protect and advance America's culture and wellbeing.

★ Incline toward greater freedom, opportunity and ordered liberty.

The *un-American* solutions are ones that:

★ Appeal to *groups* divided up based on race, ethnicity, religion, gender, perceived class, income, socio-economic level, and on and on and on.

★ Assign helplessness and victimhood to accompany every unpleasant human event or condition, offering no way out and no way forward other than a promise by people (elected elitists) to marshal other people's money to fix it.

★ Assure that "equality" and "justice" can be achieved only if all authority and law is transferred away from the Creator and into the hands of the superior ones (called 'the government')—who will then tell us our "rights."

★ Presume that all problems can only be solved through the creation and expansion of government assistance, projects, programs, and services.

★ Incline toward less freedom for all in exchange for vague promises of greater safety or security.

I won't hold back on sharing with you how strongly and in fact urgently I feel about how the Democrat Party has drifted away from the America we all love. But I will remind you that I used to vote Democrat, and I know that lots of wonderful American women have voted Democrat historically. I want to convince you that the Democrats of today are out of touch with what made America great, and I think it is our job as voters to bring America home again.

Let's Prove Alexis de Tocqueville Wrong

"A democracy cannot exist as a permanent form of government. It can only exist until the voters discover that they can vote themselves largesse from the public treasury.

From that moment on, the majority always votes for the candidates promising the most benefits from the public treasury with the result that a democracy always collapses over loose fiscal policy, always followed by a dictatorship.

The average age of the world's greatest civilizations has been 200 years."

—Alexis de Tocqueville, French Historian and Political Scientist

---

Ladies, I don't know what the issues will be in 2022, and it will be up to my great-great grandchildren to deal the issues of 2112. But the American and un-American concepts described above will hold just as true and be just as effective in guiding voting decisions then, as they are now.

We've talked. Now it is time for you to talk to your family and friends, and to *act* in the voting booth to defend America's greatness for the coming generations!

About the Author

Debora Georgatos never planned to be an author. She loves her life's journey so far—from being a New Yorker to a Californian to a D.C. resident to becoming a Texan, and from an employment litigation attorney in California, to wife and stay-at-home mother of three, and volunteer in her kids' schools and in community organizations. She'd always been a passionate student of American history, an intuitively feisty defender of equality for women and all people in American society, and a generally outspoken leader in various organizations she supports. Like many American women (and men), she had been enjoying the benefits of liberty and life in America, but also taking them for granted.

Within the last several years she observed that not all American political leaders are presenting views within the guardrails of basic American, Constitution-based ideals. She saw America in political turmoil not *just* over particular ideas or policies, but also over what kind of future America will have. The battle is between those who support our traditional freedom and individual liberty on the one side, and those working to create a large and powerful central government that destroys that freedom, on the other. Debbie sees that "other" side as far too close to the famously described

"...government big enough to give you everything you need, is a government big enough to take away everything that you have...."

Debbie concluded that she always wanted to be able to say that when the goodness and greatness of America was so clearly under assault, she stood up, and spoke up, for our nation. She began by working in political campaigns, and as an activist in women's political organizations. She also began writing for blogs. She then felt impelled to pour her passion into writing this book—designed to inspire other women to get engaged in the battle to protect America's future.

Index